ESSENTIALS OF NEGOTIATION

Roy J. Lewicki

David M. Saunders

John W. Minton

IRWIN

Chicago • Bogotá • Boston • Buenos Aires • Caracas
London • Madrid • Mexico City • Sydney • Toronto

Irwin Book Team

Publisher: *Rob Zwettler*
Sponsoring editor: *John E. Biernat*
Editorial assistant: *Kimberly Kanakes*
Marketing manager: *Michael Campbell*
Project supervisor: *Jim Labeots*
Production supervisor: *Pat Frederickson*
Designer: *Matthew Baldwin*
Director, Prepress Purchasing: *Kimberly Meriwether David*
Compositor: *Electronic Publishing Services, Inc.*
Typeface: *10/12 Times Roman*
Printer: *R. R. Donnelley & Sons Company*

Times Mirror
Higher Education Group

Library of Congress Cataloging-in-Publication Data

Lewicki, Roy J.
   Essentials of Negotiation / Roy J. Lewicki, David M. Saunders,
John W. Minton.
     p. cm.
   Rev. ed. of: Negotiation (2nd ed.), c 1994.
   Includes index.
   ISBN 0-256-24168-6
   1. Negotiation in business.   2. Negotiation.   I. Saunders, David
M.   II. Minton, John W., 1946-   .   III. Negotiation (1994)
IV. Title.
HD58.6.L49   1997
658.4—dc20   96–9325

Printed in the United States of America
1 2 3 4 5 6 7 8 9 0 DO 3 2 1 0 9 8 7

P R E F A C E

Welcome to *Essentials of Negotiation*. This book represents our response to many faculty who wanted a briefer version of *Negotiation*. The objective of this book is to provide some of the core concepts of the *Negotiation* text in a more succinct version. Many faculty wanted such a book to use in short courses, executive education programs, or as an accompaniment to other text for an academic course on negotiation, labor relations, conflict management, and the like. With this objective in mind, we reviewed the *Negotiation* text and decided to make the following modifications for the *Essentials* volume:

- We have eliminated two chapters from the *Negotiation* text— "Persuasion" and "Individual Differences"—because these topics are less likely to be addressed in short courses.
- We have combined the first two chapters—"Introduction" and the chapter on "Interdependence."
- We divided other chapters into smaller chucks and we created a short chapter on "Social Context, Groups, and Power" and a separate chapter on "Negotiation in Groups."
- Every chapter has been edited to remove extraneous materials, long examples, and so forth. We often substituted bullet points for longer descriptions and examples. Finally, all references are now represented as End Notes, making the text easier to read and more suitable for nonacademic audiences.

In preparing this volume, we have benefited greatly from several students and faculty who have read and used the books in their previous versions. Many of you have offered ideas, suggestions, criticism, and help over the years—all of which has contributed to making this a better book. We specifically want to thank the anonymous faculty who have reviewed this volume for Richard D. Irwin, and those of you who have suggested ways to make this book more marketable and user-friendly. Thanks to all of you!

Finally, we are very saddened by the untimely death during the past year of two very good friends and colleagues. Both were "essentials" themselves in the field of negotiation and in the creation of earlier versions of this text. Professor Joseph Litterer, Professor Emeritus of the University of Massachusetts, worked with Roy to develop the first edition of this text in 1985. Joe was a wonderful co-author and inspiration, and we are indebted to him for the creativity and vision that provided the intellectual foundation for this volume. Professor Jeffrey Rubin, of Tufts University and the Harvard Negotiation Program, was a major leader and pioneer in negotiation research and teaching. The field of negotiation has been shaped tremendously by Jeff's boundless energy, commitment, creativity and skills, and his intellectual legacy will pervade this discipline for years to come. Thanks, Joe and Jeff, for the intellectual and personal gifts you have made to us as authors, and to the field of negotiation.

RJL
DMS
JWM

BRIEF CONTENTS

C O N T E N T S

3   Strategy and Tactics of Integrative Negotiation   63

10 Third-Party Interventions   199

11 Ethics in Negotiation   214

1 THE NATURE OF NEGOTIATION

Negotiating is a basic, generic human activity—a process that is often used in labor–management relations, in business deals like mergers and sales, in international affairs, and in our everyday activities. The negotiations that occur between two businesses for a large joint venture, between a merchant and a customer, or between two friends or spouses can satisfy the needs of both parties and improve their welfare and satisfaction. The negotiations that take place to free hostages, to keep peace between nations, or to end a labor strike dramatize the need for bargaining and its capabilities as a dispute management process. Yet negotiation is not a process reserved for the skilled diplomat, the top salesperson, or the ardent advocate for organized labor; it is something that *everyone* does, almost daily. Although the stakes are not usually as dramatic as peace accords or large corporate mergers, everyone negotiates—sometimes on major things like a job, at other times on relatively minor issues such as who will wash the dishes. The structure and processes of negotiation are fundamentally the same at the personal level as they are at the diplomatic and corporate levels.

Because everyone negotiates about numerous things in many different situations, knowledge and skill in negotiating are essential to anyone who works with and through other people to accomplish objectives. We may fail to negotiate sometimes, perhaps because we do not recognize that we are in a bargaining situation. However, by choosing options other than negotiation, we may not handle our problems as well as we might like to. Also, we may recognize the need for bargaining, but do poorly at the process because we misunderstand it and do not know the methods for negotiating. This book teaches our readers (*a*) how to recognize situations that call for bargaining, (*b*) what the process of bargaining involves, and (*c*) how to analyze, plan, and implement successful negotiations.

In most conversations, the words *bargaining* and *negotiation* mean the same thing, but sometimes they are used as if they mean different things. For example, *bargaining* is more like the competitive haggling over price that happens during a yard sale or flea market, whereas *negotiation* is the more formal, civilized process that occurs when parties are trying to find a mutually acceptable solution to a complex conflict. In this book, we tend to use the terms bargaining and negotiation interchangeably. However, in Chapters 2 and 3 when we describe the differences between two very different forms of negotiation, we will call one *bargaining* and the other *negotiation* to make the comparisons between the two clearer.

To better understand what this book is about, and the breadth and scope of negotiation in our professional and personal lives, we ask you to consider a hypothetical, but not unrealistic, situation. The case below describes a "typical" day in the life of Joe and Sue Carter, two people who are involved in several negotiations throughout the day.

Joe and Sue Carter

The day started early, as usual. Over breakfast, Sue Carter raised the question of where they would go for their summer vacation. She wanted to sign up for a tour of the Far East being sponsored by her college's alumni association. However, two weeks on a guided tour with a lot of other people was not what Joe had in mind. He needed to get away from people, crowds, and schedules, and he wanted to charter a sailboat and cruise the New England coast. In addition, they were still not sure whether the kids would go with them. Both kids really wanted to go to camp, and Joe and Sue couldn't afford both summer camp and a vacation for the four of them. They had not argued (yet), but it was clear that they had a real problem here. Some of their friends handled problems like this by taking separate vacations. With both of them working full time, though, one thing Joe and Sue did agree on was that they would take their vacation together.

As Joe drove to work, he thought about the vacation problem. What bothered Joe most was that there seemed to be no good way to manage the conflict productively. With some conflicts, they could compromise, but given what each wanted this time, compromise didn't seem possible. At other times they would flip a coin. That might work for choosing a restaurant, but it seemed an unwise procedure to solve this problem because spending that much money and that big a block of time on the basis of a coin flip was pretty risky. In addition, flipping a coin might be more likely to make one of them feel like a loser and the other feel guilty than to help either one feel really satisfied.

Walking through the parking lot, Joe met his company's purchasing manager, Ed Laine. Joe was the head of the engineering design group for MicroWatt, a manufacturer of small electric motors. Ed reminded Joe that they had to settle a problem created by the engineers in Joe's department: the engineers were contacting vendors directly rather than going through MicroWatt's purchasing department. Joe knew that purchasing wanted all vendor contacts to go through them. But he also knew that his engineers badly needed technical information for design purposes, and waiting for the information to come through purchasing slowed things considerably. Ed Laine was aware of Joe's views about this problem, and Joe thought the two of them could probably find some way to resolve this if they really sat down to work on it. Joe and Ed were also both aware that higher management expected them (and all other managers) to settle differences among themselves; if this problem "got upstairs" to senior management, it would make both of them look bad.

Shortly after returning to his desk, Joe received a telephone call from an automobile salesman with whom he had been talking about a new car. The salesman asked how Sue felt about the car and whether she wanted to drive it. Joe wasn't quite sure that Sue would go along with his choice; Joe had picked out a luxury import, and he expected Sue would say that it cost too much money. Joe was pleased with the latest offer the salesman had made. But he thought he might still get a few more concessions out of him, so he introduced Sue's concerns to put more pressure on the salesman to lower the price.

Immediately after Joe hung up the phone, it rang again and it was Sue. She was calling to vent her frustration to Joe over some of the procedures at the local bank where she worked as a senior loan officer. Sue was frustrated working for an old "family-run" bank which was not very computerized, was heavily bureaucratic, and was very slow to respond to customer needs. The competition would approve loans within three hours while it took Sue a week to get a loan approved! Although the bank staff was very public-oriented and polite to their customers, they were losing clients to large state and multinational banks who were entering the city and providing more efficient services. It seemed that every week Sue was losing more and more of her clients to the larger banks, and whenever she tried to discuss this with the senior management of the bank, she was met with resistance and a lecture on loyalty.

Most of Joe's afternoon was taken up by the annual budget meeting. Joe hated these meetings. The people from the finance department came in and arbitrarily cut everyone's figures by 30 percent, and then all the managers had to argue endlessly to try to get some of their new-project money reinstated. Joe had learned to work with a lot of people, some of whom he did not like very much, but these people from finance were the most arrogant and arbitrary number crunchers imaginable. He could not understand why the top brass did not see how much harm these people were doing to the engineering group's research and development efforts. Joe considered himself a reasonable guy, but he recognized that the way these people acted made him feel like he didn't want to give them an inch. He was prepared to draw the line and fight it out as long as it took.

In the evening, Sue and Joe attended a meeting of the town Conservation Commission, which, among other things, was charged with protecting the town's streams, wetlands, and nature preserves. Sue is a member of the Conservation Commission, and Sue and Joe both strongly believe in sound environmental protection and management. This evening's case involved a request by a real estate development firm to drain a swampy area and move a small creek to build a new regional shopping mall. All projections showed that the new shopping mall would attract a significant number of jobs and revenue to the area and considerably fatten the town's treasury. The new mall was badly needed to replace several others that had closed, which had put a sizable number of people out of work and reduced the town's tax revenues. But the plan might also do irreparable damage to the wetlands and the wildlife in that area. The initial plan proposed by the development firm had some serious problems, and the commission had asked Sue to see if an acceptable solution could be developed. Eventually a site plan had been worked out that would have considerably more benefits than drawbacks. But now Sue was having difficulties with some members of the commission who were ardent conservationists and argued against *any* change in the wetlands on that lot. In addition, word about the application had leaked out, and even some members of the town council had decided to join the conservationists in the fight.

Characteristics of a Negotiation or Bargaining Situation

The Joe and Sue Carter story highlights the variety of situations that can be handled by negotiation. Any of us might encounter one or more of these situations over the course of a few days or weeks. We identify them as *negotiation situations* because they have the same fundamental characteristics as peace negotiations between countries at war, business negotiations between two corporations, or a hostage crisis involving police and a radical political group. Many characteristics are common to all negotiation situations.[1]

1. There are two or more parties—two or more individuals, groups, or organizations. Although we can "negotiate" with ourselves—as when we debate whether we are going to spend the afternoon studying, playing tennis, or going to the football game—we will discuss negotiation as an *interpersonal* or *intergroup* process. In the case, Joe negotiates with his wife, the purchasing manager, and the auto salesman, and Sue negotiates with her husband, with senior management at the bank, and with the Conservation Commission, among others.

2. There is a conflict of interest between two or more parties; that is, what one wants is not necessarily what the other one wants, and the parties must search for a way to resolve the conflict. Joe and Sue negotiate over vacations, budgets, automobiles, and company procedures.

3. The parties negotiate because they think they can use some form of influence to get a better deal instead of simply taking what the other side will voluntarily give them or let them have. Negotiation is a largely voluntary process. It is a strategy pursued by choice; seldom are we required to negotiate.

4. The parties, at least for the moment, prefer to search for agreement rather than fight openly, have one side capitulate, permanently break off contact, or take their dispute to a higher authority to resolve it. Negotiation occurs when there is

no fixed or established set of rules, procedures, or system for resolving the conflict, or when the parties prefer to work outside of the system to invent their own solution to the conflict. If we keep a rented videotape too long, the store will charge us a fee, but we might be able to negotiate that fee if we have a good excuse as to why the tape is being returned late. Similarly, attorneys negotiate or plea-bargain for their clients because they would rather be assured of a negotiated settlement than take their chances with a judge and jury in the courtroom. In the case, Joe pursues negotiation as opposed to letting his wife decide on the vacation, accepting a fixed price for the car, or accepting the budget cut without question. Sue attempts to negotiate to change the bank's procedures rather than accepting the status quo, and she works to influence the outcome of the shopping mall plan rather than letting others decide how to resolve the problem or watching it go to court.

5. When we negotiate, we expect give and take. We expect that both sides will modify or give in somewhat on their opening statements, requests, or demands. Although the parties may not give in initially and may argue strenuously for what they want and push the other side for concessions, usually both sides must modify their positions and move toward the other. As we will discuss, however, truly creative negotiations may not require compromise because the parties can invent a solution that meets the objectives of all sides.

6. Successful negotiation involves the management of the *intangibles* as well as the resolution of the *tangibles* (e.g., the price and terms of agreement). By intangible factors, we are referring to the deeper psychological motivations that may directly or indirectly influence the parties during the negotiation. Some examples of intangibles include: (*a*) the need to look good to the people you represent, (*b*) the desire to book more business than any other salesperson in your office, and (*c*) the fear of setting precedent in the negotiations. Intangible factors can have an enormous influence on negotiation processes and outcomes and need to be managed proactively during negotiations. For example, Joe may not want to make Ed Laine angry about the purchasing problem because he needs Ed's support in the upcoming budget negotiations, but Joe also doesn't want to lose face with his engineers, who expect him to back them up.

Interdependence

In negotiation, both parties need each other. A buyer cannot buy unless someone else sells and vice versa; each is dependent upon the other. This situation of mutual dependency is called *interdependence*. Interdependent relations are complex and have their own special challenge. They are more complex than situations in which we are independent of another person or in which we are dependent on another. When we are independent of another person, we can, if we choose, have a relatively detached, indifferent, and uninvolved outlook. When we are dependent on another, we have to accept and accommodate the demands of another. For example, if an employee is totally dependent on an employer for a job, he or she will have to do the job as instructed or quit. When we are interdependent, however, we have an opportunity to influence the other party, and many options are open to us. Managing those options can be difficult, however, because of the complexity of the interdependent relationship.

Interdependent relationships are characterized by interlocking goals—both parties need each other to accomplish their goals. For instance, in a business project management team, no single person could complete a complex project alone within the time limit required by the organization. Each person needs to rely upon the other project team members for the group to accomplish its goals. In that sense, the goals of the project team members are interdependent. Note that having interdependent goals does not mean that everyone wants exactly the same thing. Different project team members may want different things, but for the group to achieve its goals, they must work together. This mix of personal and group goals is typical of interdependent situations. Another example of interdependence is two people playing a competitive game of squash. Each person wants to win the game, so their goals are in conflict (only one person can win). On the other hand, each wants to play the game, so their goals converge (one cannot play squash alone). This mix of convergent and conflicting goals characterizes many interdependent relationships.

Interdependent goals are an important aspect of negotiation. The structure of the interdependence between different negotiating parties determines the range of possible outcomes of the negotiation and suggests the appropriate strategies and tactics that the negotiators should use. For instance, if the interdependence is a "win–lose" situation—that is, the more that one party gains, the more the other party loses—then the negotiation will focus on how to divide a fixed amount of outcomes. An example of this type of negotiation is determining the price of a major appliance or capital purchase (these "distributive" bargaining situations are discussed in detail in Chapter 2). Another type of interdependence occurs in a "win–win" situation—that is, solutions exist so that both parties can do well in the negotiation. An example of this type of negotiation is determining the relationship between two companies in a joint venture (these "integrative" negotiation situations are discussed in detail in Chapter 3). The type of interdependence between the negotiating parties will determine both the range of possible negotiation solutions and the type of strategies the negotiators should use.

The interdependence of people's goals is the basis for much social interaction. By examining the way goals are interdependent, we can estimate what type of behavior is most likely to emerge. When the goals of two or more people are interconnected so that only one can achieve the goal—such as winning a gold medal in a race and therefore making the others losers of the race—we have a competitive situation, also known as a zero-sum, or distributive, situation, in which "individuals are so linked together that there is a negative correlation between their goal attainments."[2] To the degree that one person achieves his or her goal, the other's goal

---

FIGURE 1.1

Standards for Evaluating Relationship Outcomes

Definitions

Anticipated Outcome: What we expect to receive from this relationship.

Comparison Level: The standard against which a person evaluates a relationship—what we could receive from other relationships.

Comparison Level for Alternatives (CLalt): The lowest level of outcome that would be accepted from this relationship before changing to another relationship.

Example

Laura has been employed by an organization for six months and is making $31,000 per year. The average salary of Laura's college classmates who were accepting new jobs was $30,000. Recently, the organization where Laura works was downsized and Laura's job was eliminated. Her boss offered her another job in the organization at $28,000. Laura realizes that most other companies are not currently hiring because it is not the end of the school year, and she believes that it would be difficult to find a new job for more than $25,000.

Anticipated Outcome: The salary for the new job in the organization is $28,000.

Comparison Level: The average starting salary of Laura's classmates is $30,000.

Comparison Level for Alternatives (CLalt): The perceived salary of a readily available alternative job is $25,000.

---

attainment is blocked. In contrast, when parties' goals are linked so one person's goal achievement helps others to achieve their goals, we have a mutual-gains situation, also known as a non-zero-sum or integrative situation, where there is a positive correlation between the goal attainment of both parties. The nature of the interdependence will have a major impact on the nature of the relationship, the way negotiations are conducted, and the outcomes of a negotiation.[3]

Characteristics of Interpersonal Relationships

To better understand interdependence, we will use the analytical concepts developed by Thibaut and Kelley.[4] In a relationship, we usually have some idea of what kinds of outcomes to expect, and we can assess the desirability of these outcomes against some standard (see Figure 1.1). If we are buying a house, there is a limit above which we will not (or cannot) pay; if we are accepting a job, there is a limit in salary below which we will not work. These points beyond which we will not go act as a standard of comparison for an offered price. In a broader context, we can assess an entire negotiating relationship: how we feel about negotiation in general, how we feel about negotiating with this person, and what we feel to be an acceptable price or resistance point. Thibaut and Kelley call this standard the Comparison Level (CL); it is the standard against which a person "evaluates the attractiveness of a relationship or how satisfactory it is."[5] A relationship or anticipated outcome (O) that is above the CL is desirable; one below the CL is unattractive or unsatisfactory. The greater the distance between O and CL, the greater the attractiveness or unattractiveness of the relationship. For example, if Sue Carter was seeking a new job with another bank and her minimally acceptable salary is $40,000 per year, this becomes her comparison level for jobs. Anticipated salaries above $40,000 will be viewed as more attractive, whereas salaries below $40,000 will be viewed as unattractive and will probably be rejected.

When a relationship is unattractive, we may think of leaving, but whether we do depends upon our options. We may not like our current job, but if we are relatively unskilled, we may find it difficult to get another job. If we have many skills, however, we may know of several jobs to which we can easily move. Another standard by which we judge outcomes, then, is the lowest level of outcomes (experienced or anticipated) a person will accept in light of the alternatives available. This is called the Comparison Level for Alternatives (CLalt). People leave relationships when outcomes fall below this CLalt. It is assumed that the more a person's actual outcome exceeds the CLalt, the more dependent upon the relationship she is. Thus, for example, let us assume that Sue took a new job at $42,000 per year. Six months later her boss announced that because of major cutbacks in the bank, her job had been eliminated; she could accept another job in the organization at $36,000 or she would have to be laid off. Although $36,000 is considerably below the $40,000 limit Sue had set six months earlier, the prospects of being unemployed and seeking a new job (the CLalt) may appear to be much worse than the $36,000 job. The more dependent Sue is on the job, the more she will stay with a salary that is below the CL but above the CLalt.

This mode of analysis permits us to draw a distinction between attractiveness and satisfaction on one hand and dependency on the other. A person can dislike a relationship and stay, or like a relationship and leave. In clarifying our own situation and understanding the situation of the other party, these distinctions are important. In negotiation, the other party may dislike dealing with us, but since we have "the best deal in town," he or she will continue to negotiate with us. Alternately, the other party may like us, but nonetheless break off negotiations because of more attractive possibilities elsewhere.

Fisher, Ury, and Patton, in their popular book *Getting to Yes,* stress the importance of understanding the nature of your interdependence with the other party.[6] They suggest that knowing and developing alternatives to reaching an agreement with the other party in a negotiation is an important source of power in negotiation. They write: "Whether you should or should not agree on something in a negotiation depends entirely upon the attractiveness to you of the best available alternative."[7] They call this concept BATNA (an acronym for *B*est *A*lternative *T*o a *N*egotiated *A*greement) and suggest that negotiators need to understand both parties' BATNAs when they negotiate.

Interdependence is a critical aspect of a BATNA. Someone with a low CLalt also has a low BATNA, and the other party has more bargaining power. Returning to Sue Carter's job search, we note that if few jobs are available for $40,000 (and unemployment is high), then Sue will be more likely to accept the reduced salary instead of the layoff, compared to the situation where many jobs are available at other banks for $40,000 or more. If Sue has a high CLalt, such as returning to school, changing careers, or finding many jobs available at $40,000, then she also has a high BATNA, and the likelihood that she will accept the reduced salary is much lower.

CLalt and BATNA are very similar concepts, but they not are identical. A BATNA is one type of CLalt used to evaluate the worth of a negotiation outcome by comparing it to the best outcome that could be gained by negotiating with another party; CLalt considers all of the other possible outcomes available to the negotiator, not just the best one. CLalt is a broader concept that is not limited to evaluating the outcome of a negotiation; it may be used to make comparisons about the value of anything.

Mutual Adjustment

Interdependent relationships—those in which people are mutually dependent—are complex. Both parties know that they can influence the other's outcomes and that their outcomes can, in turn, be influenced by the other.[8] Let us explore Sue Carter's job situation in more detail. Rather than accepting a layoff or reduced pay, Sue would like to have a job that is available in a large multinational bank in her town. Her prospective manager for that position, Bob, perceives Sue as a desirable employee for the position. They are now attempting to establish Sue's salary. The job description announced the salary as "competitive." Sue has identified a salary below which she will not work ($40,000) but suspects she may be able to get considerably more. The bank has a reputation for running "hard and lean," and she suspects that means they will pay no more than necessary. For this reason, Sue has decided *not* to state her minimally acceptable salary because she suspects it would be accepted quickly. Moreover, she knows that it would be difficult to raise the level if it should turn out that $40,000 was considerably below what Bob would pay. Sue has thought of stating her ideal salary ($45,000), but suspects that Bob will view her as either presumptuous or rude for asking that much. If this happened, then the interview would probably end with Bob viewing her negatively and making it harder for her to get the best possible salary.

Let's take a closer look at what is happening here. Sue is making her decision based on how she *anticipates* Bob will react to her actions. Sue recognizes that her actions will affect Bob. Sue also recognizes that the way Bob acts towards her in the future will be influenced by the way her actions affect Bob now. As a result, Sue is assessing the *indirect* impact of her behavior on herself. Further, she also knows that Bob is alert to all this and will look upon any statement by Sue as reflecting a preliminary position on salary rather than a final one. To counter this expected view, Sue will probably try to find some way to state a number as close to her desired final salary as possible. For example, she could refer to salaries that she knows other people with similar qualifications have received in other banks. Sue is choosing among behavioral options with a thought not only to how they will affect Bob, but also to how they will then lead Bob to act towards Sue. Further, Sue knows that Bob believes she will act in this way and acts on the basis of this belief.

One may wonder if people really pay attention to all this complexity in their relationships with others. Certainly people don't do this most of the time, or we would all be frozen in inactivity while we tried to think through the possibilities. However, when people face complex, important, or novel situations, they are more likely to think in this way. Given that many negotiations are complex, important, and novel, the effective negotiator needs to understand that people will adjust and readjust what they say during negotiations based on what the other party does and is expected to do.

Behavior in an interdependent relationship, frequently, is calculated behavior—calculated on the premise that the more information one has about the other person, the better. There is the possibility, however, that too much knowledge only confuses.[9] For example, suppose Sue knows the average salary ranges for clerical, supervisory, and managerial positions for local, national, and multinational banks in her county, state, and country. Does all this help Sue determine her actions or only confuse things? In fact, given all these complexities, Sue may not have reached a decision about what salary she should be paid, other than a minimum figure below which she will not go. This is the classic bargaining situation. Both parties have their outer limits for an acceptable settlement (how high or low they are willing to go), but within that range, neither has determined what the exact number will be or should be. It is a solution to be worked toward. The parties have to exchange information and make an effort at influencing each other and at problem solving. They must work toward a solution that takes into account each person's requirements and, hopefully, that optimizes the outcomes for both.[10]

Problem solving is essentially a process of specifying the elements of a desired outcome, examining the components available to produce the outcome, and searching for a way to fit them together. A person can approach problem solving in negotiation from her own perspective and attempt to solve the problem by considering only the components that affect her own desired outcome. For instance, Sue could decide what was best for her and ignore Bob's needs. When approaching the situation as a joint problem-solving effort, however, the outcomes desired by the other party must be taken into account. For instance, Bob may be constrained by company rules that limit how far he can go in the salary negotiation, but he may be able to be very flexible in negotiating other aspects of the employment relationship such as benefits or vacation. One difficulty is that opposing parties may not be open about their desired outcomes, or they may not be clear in their own minds about what they actually want. Hence, a necessary step in all negotiation is *to clarify and share information about what both parties really want as outcomes.*

As negotiations evolve, some knowledge of the combined set of desired outcomes becomes known (be they stated as bargaining positions or needs). If the suggested outcomes don't immediately fit, negotiation continues as a series of proposals. These proposals usually suggest alterations in the other party's position, and perhaps contain alterations in the proposer's own position. When one party accepts an alteration in its position, a concession has been made.[11] Concessions restrict the range of options within which a solution or agreement will be reached; when a party makes a concession, the bargaining range is *confined closer* to one side's or both sides' limits or resistance point. For instance, Sue would like to get a starting salary of $45,000, but scales her request down to $40,000, thereby eliminating all possible salary options above $40,000. People may recognize that concessions are necessary for a settlement, but they will obviously be reluctant to make all or most of them. For Sue to make further concessions below $40,000, she probably will want to see some willingness on the part of the bank to increase its offer or add other attractive benefits to its salary package.

Making and interpreting concessions is no easy task, especially when there is little trust between negotiators. Two of the dilemmas that all negotiators face, identified by Harold Kelley, help explain why this is the case.[12] The first dilemma, the *dilemma of honesty*, concerns how much of the truth to tell the other party (the ethical considerations of these dilemmas are discussed in Chapter 8). Telling the other party everything about your situation may give that person the opportunity to take advantage of you. However, not telling the other person anything about your needs, wants, and desires may lead to a stalemate. Just how much of the truth should you tell the other party? If Sue told Bob that she would work for as little as $35,000 but would like to start at $40,000, it is quite possible that Bob would hire her for $35,000 and allocate the extra money, that he might have paid to her, elsewhere in the budget. We are not suggesting that Bob should do this; rather, because the long-term relationship is important in this situation, Bob should ensure that both parties' needs are met (see Chapter 3 for an expanded discussion of this point). If, on the other hand, Sue did not tell Bob any information about her salary aspirations, then Bob would have a much more difficult time knowing how to satisfy those needs.

The second dilemma that every negotiator faces, the *dilemma of trust,* concerns how much to believe what the other party tells you. If you believe everything the other party says, then he or she could take advantage of you. However, if you believe nothing the other party says, then you will have a great deal of difficulty in reaching an agreement. Exactly how much to believe of what the other party tells you depends on many factors, including the reputation of the other party, how he treated you in the past, the present circumstances, and so on. If Bob told Sue that $38,000 was the maximum he was allowed to pay her for the job, without seeking approval "from above," should Sue believe him or not? As you can see, sharing and clarifying information may not be as easy as expected!

The search for an optimal solution through the processes of giving information and making concessions is greatly aided by trust and a belief that you're being treated honestly and fairly. Two efforts in negotiation help to create this trust and belief—one is based on perceptions of outcomes, and the other on perceptions of the process. The former attempts to change a party's estimation of the perceived importance or value of something. If Bob convinces Sue that a lower salary for the job is relatively unimportant given the high promotion potential associated with the new job, then Sue can feel more comfortable making a concession on this point. In contrast, efforts based on the negotiating process help convey images of equity, fairness, and reciprocity in proposals and concessions. When one party makes several proposals that are rejected by the other party and the other party makes no alternate proposal, the first party often feels improperly treated and may break off negotiations. A party that makes a concession will feel much more comfortable and be more trusting if the other party responds with a concession. In fact, the belief that concessions will occur in negotiations appears to be almost universal. During training seminars, we have asked negotiators from more than 50 countries if they expect give-and-take to occur during negotiations in their culture; all have said they do. This pattern of give-and-take is not just a characteristic of negotiation; it is also essential to joint problem solving in most interdependent relationships.[13] Satisfaction with a negotiation is as much determined by the process through which an agreement is reached as with the actual outcome obtained. To eliminate or even deliberately attempt to reduce this give-and-take, as some labor–management negotiating strategies have attempted, is to short-circuit the process, eliminating both the basis for trust and any possibility of joint decision making.[14] Even if the strategy results in maximizing joint outcomes, the other party will dislike the process by which these outcomes are reached. But following a fair process will contribute to feelings of satisfaction and success for both parties.

Interdependence and Perceptions

We have been treating interdependence as a more or less objective phenomenon. That is, the structure of the negotiation itself plays an important part in determining how two negotiating parties should interact. At times, the situation will be structured as win–lose: the more one party gains, the more the other party loses. People frequently perceive economic exchanges, such as the purchase of a new car or a commodity, as examples of this type of situation (appropriate strategies and tactics for these situations are discussed in Chapter 2). At other times, however, the situation may be structured as win–win: there are opportunities for both parties to gain. A classic example of this situation, attributed to Mary Parker

Follett, is the story of two sisters deciding how to divide an orange. Both sisters wanted the same orange, one sister for the peel and the other for the juice. Both demanded the whole orange, however, and neither considered asking for only the part of the orange she needed. The sisters can reach a win–win solution by each obtaining only that part of the orange she needs; the challenge when negotiating is to find that solution (appropriate strategies and tactics for these situations are discussed in Chapter 3).

Understanding the nature of the interdependence between parties in a negotiation is a critical negotiation skill. Unfortunately, negotiation situations do not present themselves with neat labels, typically, describing the nature of the interdependence between parties. Rather, negotiators make judgments about the nature of the interdependence in their negotiation situations, and negotiator *perceptions* about interdependence become as important as the actual structure of the interdependence.[15]

To examine how perception and structure are critically linked, let us return to Follett's example of the two sisters with the orange. Remember, the actual structure of the situation is that each sister needs only part of the orange (the juice or the peel), and each has stated that she wants the whole orange. The objective structure of the situation is that there is an opportunity for mutual gain. Assume for a moment that the sisters have negotiated frequently in the past and each is concerned about the other's needs and interests. A series of questions would allow them each to learn that they have different needs for the orange and that each could take only that part of the orange that she needs. Now assume a different situation. Perhaps the sisters have negotiated frequently in the past and perceive that most of their disagreements are win–lose situations. They would then approach this as a win–lose negotiation and use distributive strategies to divide the orange. Perhaps they would split the difference and each take half of the orange—and neither would have enough juice or peel to be satisfied. The use of distributive strategies would decrease the likelihood that they would identify that each needs only part of the orange. Or assume a third scenario: perhaps one of the sisters realizes that the other is unhappy and needs something to brighten her day. The first sister could simply give the orange to the other and allow her to use it as she wanted. A fourth scenario might be that one of the sisters could avoid the discussion by going out; the other sister would then have to decide how (whether) to divide the orange herself.

The point here is that people bring much baggage with them to a negotiation, including past history, personality characteristics, moods, habits, beliefs about how to negotiate, and the like. These factors will influence how people perceive an interdependent situation, and this perception will in turn have a strong effect on the subsequent negotiation.

Considerable research has been conducted on the role of perception and cognition in negotiation.[16] This research suggests that the way that people perceive interdependent situations has an important effect on how they will negotiate. Leigh Thompson and Reid Hastie suggest that negotiator perceptions and judgments can have important influences on judgments that negotiators make about (*a*) the other party, (*b*) themselves, (*c*) the utilities of both parties, (*d*) offers and counteroffers, (*e*) negotiation outcomes, and (*f*) the negotiation process.[17]

A classic treatise by Harold Kelley and Anthony Stahelski, carefully reviewing research on the prisoner's dilemma game, suggests that negotiator perceptions have a critical influence on how negotiators evaluate the situation and how they subsequently behave.[18] Kelley and Stahelski propose that there are two general types of negotiators: cooperators and competitors. Competitors enter negotiations expecting the other party to compete, and to compete with everyone. Cooperators will cooperate with other cooperators and compete with competitors. The consequences of these expectations are fascinating. Competitors believe that all negotiations are competitive, and that the world contains only competitors, because all the people they negotiate with compete (either they were natural competitors, or they were cooperators who have adapted and compete rather than being taken advantage of). Cooperators, however, understand that negotiations may be cooperative or competitive, and recognize that there are both cooperators and competitors in the world; they view the task while negotiating as identifying the predisposition of the other party. In addition, their experiences continue to reinforce their beliefs about others who are competitors and cooperators, thus making these beliefs highly resistant to change.

Another line of research has sought to identify systematic biases in negotiators' initial perceptions of the nature of the interdependence between the negotiating parties. Max Bazerman, Thomas Magliozzi, and Margaret Neale labeled one such systematic bias as the "mythical fixed-pie" in negotiation.[19] Bazerman and his colleagues suggest that most negotiators in mixed-motive situations (negotiations containing both cooperative and competitive elements) will assume that there is a fixed pie; that is, the more I get, the less you have. In a laboratory study of negotiation that investigated this hypothesis, Leigh Thompson and Reid Hastie found that more than twice as many negotiators (68 percent) assumed their upcoming negotiations were win–lose situations rather than win–win situations (32 percent).[20] Additionally, Thompson and Hastie found that the degree to which negotiators adjusted to the situation during the first five minutes of the negotiation had an important effect on the outcome of the negotiation. Negotiators who better adjusted their assessments of the structure of the negotiation early in the process earned higher profits than those negotiators who did not adjust until later.

Researchers continue to identify other systematic perceptual biases that make negotiators less than ideal decision makers.[21] However, it is no simple task to correct the biased perceptions that occur when negotiating. Most authors agree that *identifying* the systematic biases in negotiators' perceptions is an important first step. Whether the next step, reducing the effect of the biases, is best accomplished through the use of an unfreezing-change-refreezing model,[22] systematic consideration of the other party's position,[23] or other techniques remains an important unsolved issue.

Conflict

One potential consequence of interdependent relationships is *conflict.* Conflict can be due to the highly divergent needs of the two parties, a misunderstanding that occurs between two people, or as a result of an intangible factor. Conflict can occur when the two parties are working towards the same goal and generally want the same outcome, or when both parties want a very different settlement. Regardless of the cause of the conflict, negotiation can play an important role in resolving it. Because many opportunities for negotiation are a result of conflict, we present a broad overview of the key definitions, concepts, terms, and models in this area.

Definitions

There are numerous ways to define conflict. Traditionally, Webster defines conflict as a "fight, battle or struggle."[24] The definition of conflict has evolved to include events that are somewhat less physically violent and that encompass psychological terms, such as a "sharp disagreement or opposition, as of interests, ideas, etc." A third way to approach conflict is as "the perceived divergence of interest, or a belief that the parties' current aspirations cannot be achieved simultaneously."[25] Or, similarly, conflict is "the interaction of interdependent people who perceived incompatible goals and interference from each other in achieving those goals."[26]

Levels of Conflict

Conflict is ubiquitous—it exists everywhere. One way to classify conflicts is by *level,* and four levels of conflict are commonly identified:

1. Intrapersonal or Intrapsychic Conflict. At this level, conflict occurs within an individual. Sources of conflict can include ideas, thoughts, emotions, values, predispositions, or drives that are in conflict with each other. We want an ice cream cone badly but we know that ice cream is very fattening. We are angry at our boss but afraid to express that anger because the boss might fire us for being insubordinate. Depending upon the source and origin of the intrapsychic conflict, this domain, traditionally, is studied by various fields of psychology: cognitive psychologists, personality theorists, clinical psychologists, and psychiatrists. Although we will occasionally delve into the internal states of negotiators (e.g., Chapter 5, on cognitive traps that negotiators often set for themselves), this book generally doesn't address this area.

2. Interpersonal Conflict. A second major level of conflict, which we will call interpersonal conflict, is between individual people. Conflict that occurs between husbands and wives, bosses and subordinates, siblings, or roommates is all interpersonal conflict. Most of the negotiation theory in this book is addressed primarily toward the resolution of interpersonal conflict, although much of it can also be applied to the other levels specified below.

3. Intragroup Conflict. A third major level of conflict is within a small group—among team and committee members and within families, classes, fraternities and sororities, and work groups. At the intragroup level, we analyze conflict as it affects the ability of the group to resolve disputes and continue to achieve its goals effectively. We address some aspects of within-group negotiation in Chapter 8.

4. Intergroup Conflict. The final level of conflict is intergroup—between groups, union and management, warring nations, feuding families, or communities challenging governmental authorities. At this level, conflict is quite intricate because of the large number of people involved and the possible interactions between them. Conflict can occur within groups and between groups simultaneously. Negotiations at this level are also the most complex, and we will discuss the nature of intergroup negotiations throughout the book, particularly in Chapters 7 and 8.

Functions and Dysfunctions of Conflict

Most people's initial view of conflict is that it is primarily bad or dysfunctional. This notion has two aspects: first, that conflict is an indication that something is wrong or that a problem needs to be fixed; second, that conflict creates largely destructive consequences. Deutsch and others have elaborated on many of the elements that contribute to conflict's destructive image.[27]

1. Competitive Processes. Parties compete against each other because they believe that their goals are in opposition and that the two of them cannot both achieve their objectives. Frequently, however, goals are not actually in opposition, and the parties need not compete. In addition, competitive processes often have their own side effects so that the conflict that created the competition also leads to its further escalation.

2. Misperception and Bias. As conflict intensifies, perceptions become distorted. People tend to view things consistently with their own perspective on the conflict. Hence they tend to interpret people and events as either being on their side or on the other side. In addition, thinking tends to become stereotypical and biased—parties in conflict endorse people and events that support their position and reject outright those that they suspect oppose their position.

3. Emotionality. Conflicts tend to become emotionally charged as the parties become anxious, irritated, annoyed, angry, or frustrated. Emotions tend to dominate thinking, and the parties may become more emotional and irrational as the conflict escalates.

4. Decreased Communication. Communication declines. Parties stop communicating with those who disagree with them, and communicate more with those who agree. What communication does occur between disputing parties may be an attempt to defeat, demean, or debunk the other's view or to add additional weight to one's own prior arguments.

5. Blurred Issues. The central issues in the dispute become blurred and less well defined. Generalizations abound. New, unrelated issues are drawn in as the conflict becomes a vortex that attracts both related issues and innocent bystanders. The parties become less clear about how the dispute started, what it is really about, or what it will take to solve it.

6. Rigid Commitments. The parties become locked into positions. As they are challenged by the other side, parties become more committed to their points of view and less willing to back down from them for fear of losing face and looking foolish. Thinking processes become rigid, and the parties tend to see issues as very simple and either–or rather than as complex and multidimensional.

7. Magnified Differences; Minimized Similarities. As parties lock into commitments and issues become blurred, they tend to see each other—and each other's positions—as polar opposites when they may not be. All the factors that distinguish and separate them from each other become highlighted and emphasized, while any similarities and commonalities that they share become oversimplified and minimized. This perceptual distortion leads the parties to believe they are farther apart from each other than they really may be, and hence they work harder to win the conflict and work less hard at finding a common ground.

8. Escalation of the Conflict. As the above points suggest, each side becomes more entrenched in its own view, less tolerant and accepting of the other, more defensive and less communicative, and more emotional. The net result is that parties on each side attempt to win by increasing their commitment to their position, increasing the resources they are willing to put up to win, and increasing their tenacity in holding their ground under pressure. Each side believes that by adding a little more pressure (resources, commitment, enthusiasm, energy, etc.), it can make the other side capitulate and concede defeat. As most destructive conflicts tell us, nothing could be farther from the truth! However, escalation of the level of the conflict and commitment to winning can increase to very high levels, at which point the parties destroy their ability ever to deal with each other again or to resolve the dispute.

These are the processes that are commonly associated with conflict, but they are characteristic only of *destructive* conflict. In fact, as some authors have suggested, conflict can be productive.[28] In Figure 1.2, Dean Tjosvold outlines many of the more functional (productive) aspects of conflict.[29] In this model conflict is not simply destructive or productive, it is *both*. The objective is *not to eliminate conflict but to learn how to manage it* so the destructive elements are controlled while the more productive aspects are enjoyed. Negotiation is a strategy for productively managing conflict.

FIGURE 1.2

Functions and Benefits of Conflict

- Discussing conflict makes organizational members more aware and able to cope with problems. Knowing that others are frustrated and want change creates incentives to try to solve the underlying problem.

- Conflict promises organizational change and adaptation. Procedures, assignments, budget allocations, and other organizational practices are challenged. Conflict draws attention to those issues that may interfere with and frustrate employees.

- Conflict strengthens relationships and heightens morale. Employees realize that their relationships are strong enough to withstand the test of conflict; they need not avoid frustrations and problems. They can release their tensions through discussion and problem solving.

- Conflict promotes awareness of self and others. Through conflict, people learn what makes them angry, frustrated, and frightened and also what is important to them. Knowing what we are willing to fight for tells us a lot about ourselves. Knowing what makes our colleagues unhappy helps us to understand them.

- Conflict enhances personal development. Managers find out how their style affects their subordinates through conflict. Workers learn what technical and interpersonal skills they need to upgrade themselves.

- Conflict encourages psychological development. Persons become more accurate and realistic in their self-appraisals. Through conflict, persons take others' perspectives and become less egocentric. Conflict helps persons to believe that they are powerful and capable of controlling their own lives. They do not simply need to endure hostility and frustration but can act to improve their lives.

- Conflict can be stimulating and fun. Persons feel aroused, involved, and alive in conflict, and it can be a welcome break from an easygoing pace. It invites employees to take another look and to appreciate the intricacies of their relationships.

Source: Reprinted with the permission of Lexington Books, an imprint of Macmillan Publishing Company from *Working Together to Get Things Done: Managing for Organizational Productivity* by Dean Tjosvold. Copyright © 1986 by Lexington Books.

Factors That Make Conflict Difficult to Manage

Len Greenhalgh has suggested a number of factors that make conflicts more or less difficult to resolve.[30] Figure 1.3 presents the most important ones. Conflicts with more of the characteristics in the middle column will be much more difficult to resolve. Those that have more characteristics in the right column will be easier to resolve. Greenhalgh's lists offer useful criteria for analyzing a dispute and determining how easy it will be to resolve.

Conflict Management

Approaches by the Parties Themselves

One of the most popular areas of conflict management research and practice has been to define the different ways that conflict can be managed by the parties to it.

FIGURE 1.3

Conflict Diagnostic Model

| | *Viewpoint Continuum* | |
Dimension	*Difficult to Resolve*	*Easy to Resolve*
Issue in question	Matter of principle—values, ethics, or precedent a key part of the issue	Divisible issue—issue can be easily divided into small parts, pieces, units.
Size of stakes—magnitude of what can be won or lost	Large—big consequences	Small—little, insignificant consequences.
Interdependence of the parties—degree to which one's outcomes determine the other's outcomes	Zero-sum—what one wins, the other loses	Positive sum—both believe that **both** can do better than simply distributing current outcomes.
Continuity of interaction—will they be working together in the future?	Single transaction—no past or future	Long-term relationship—expected interaction in the future.
Structure of the parties—how cohesive, organized they are as a group	Disorganized—uncohesive, weak leadership	Organized—cohesive, strong leadership
Involvement of third parties—can others get involved to help resolve the dispute?	No neutral third party available	Trusted, powerful, prestigious third party available
Perceived progress of the conflict—balanced (equal gains and equal harm) or unbalanced (unequal gain, unequal harm)?	Unbalanced—one party feels more harm and will want revenge and retribution, whereas stronger party wants to maintain control	Balanced—both parties suffer equal harm and equal gain; both may be more willing to call it a draw

Adapted from "Managing Conflict: by L. Greenhalgh, *Sloan Management Review* (Summer 1986), pp. 45-51, by permission of the publisher. Copyright 1986 by the Sloan Management Review Association. All rights reserved.

A number of different approaches to managing conflict have been suggested, and inventories have been constructed to measure these different approaches.[31] Each of these approaches begins with fundamentally the same two-dimensional framework and then applies different labels and descriptions to its five key points. We will describe these different approaches using the descriptive framework proposed by Dean Pruitt and Jeffrey Rubin.

The two-dimensional framework is represented in Figure 1.4 as the *dual concerns model*. The model postulates that individuals in conflict have two types of *independent* concerns: a level of *concern for their own outcomes* (shown on the horizontal dimension of the table) and a level of *concern for the other's outcomes* (shown on the vertical dimension of the table). These concerns can be represented at any point from none (representing very low concern) to high (representing very high concern). The vertical dimension is often referred to as the cooperativeness dimension and the horizontal dimension as the assertiveness dimension. The stronger their concern for their own outcomes, the more likely people will be to pursue strategies located on the right side of the chart, whereas the weaker their concern for their own outcomes, the more likely they will be to pursue strategies located on the left side of the chart. Similarly, the stronger their concern for permitting, encouraging, or even helping the other party achieve their outcomes, the more likely people will be to pursue strategies located at the top of the chart. The weaker their concern for the other party's outcomes, the more likely they will be to pursue strategies located at the bottom of the chart.

Although we can theoretically identify an almost infinite number of points within the two-dimensional space based upon the level of concern for pursuing one's own and the other's outcomes, five major strategies for conflict management have been commonly identified at key locations in the dual concerns model:

Contending (also called *competing* or *dominating*) is the strategy in the lower right-hand corner. Actors pursuing the contending strategy, as its location in the space indicates, pursue their own outcomes strongly and show little concern for whether the other party obtains his desired outcomes. As Pruitt and Rubin state, "Parties who employ this strategy maintain their own aspirations and try to persuade the other party to yield."[32] Threats, punishment, intimidation, and unilateral action are consistent with a contending approach.

Yielding (also called *accommodating* or *obliging*) is the strategy in the upper-left-hand corner. Actors pursuing the yielding strategy, as its location in the space indicates, show little interest or concern in whether they attain their own outcomes, but are quite interested in whether the other party attains her outcomes. Yielding involves lowering one's own aspirations to "let the other win" and gain what she wants. Yielding may seem like a strange strategy to some, but it has its definite advantages in some disputes.

Inaction (also called *avoiding*) is the strategy in the lower-left-hand corner. Actors pursuing the inaction strategy, as its location in the space indicates, show little interest or concern in whether they attain their own outcomes, nor do they show much concern about whether the other party obtains his outcomes. Inaction

FIGURE 1.4

The Dual Concerns Model

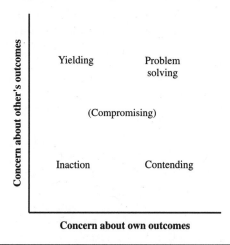

Concern about own outcomes

Adapted from D. Pruitt and J. Rubin, *Social Conflict: Escalation, Stalemate and Settlement* (New York: Random House, 1986). Used by permission of McGraw-Hill.

is often synonymous with withdrawal or passivity; the party prefers to retreat, be silent and still, or do nothing.

Problem solving (also called *collaborating* and *integrating*) is the strategy in the upper-right-hand corner. Actors pursuing the problem-solving strategy, as its location in the space indicates, show high concern for attaining their own outcomes *and* high concern for whether the other attains her outcomes. In problem solving, the two parties actively pursue approaches to maximize their joint outcome from the conflict, so that both sides win.

Compromising is a strategy located in the middle of the chart in Figure 1.4. As a conflict management strategy, it represents a moderate effort to pursue one's own outcomes and a moderate effort to help the other party achieve his outcomes. Pruitt and Rubin do *not* identify compromising as a viable strategy; they see it "as arising from one of two sources—either lazy problem solving involving a half-hearted attempt to satisfy the two parties' interests, or simple yielding by both parties." [33] However, because all the other scholars (see End Note 31) who use versions of this model believe that compromising represents a valid strategic approach to conflict, we have inserted it in Pruitt and Rubin's framework in Figure 1.4.

The dual concerns model and its variations have become some of the most ubiquitous and durable vehicles for approaching and understanding conflict management strategies. Several of the most common themes in this research are as follows:

1. Analysis of one's own style and preferences for particular strategies.
Many of the models have produced self-assessment instruments that indicate personal preferences for tactics associated with one strategy versus another, thereby determining whether one has a stronger or weaker preference for each manner of handling conflict. Differences in strength of preferences may be traced to direct experiences of success and failure in using a particular style, instruction as a child about which styles were more or less preferred, or simply beliefs about which style might be more or less likely to work in a particular situation.

2. Description of the likely level of conflict that will occur when individuals of similar or different conflict resolution styles interact with each other.
If two "contenders" come into conflict with each other, each wants to win, and one can predict an intense and passionate dispute. In contrast, if "yielders" and "contenders" come into conflict, the contenders will attain their objectives while the yielders should be happy that the contenders got what they wanted.

3. Articulation of the conditions under which each strategy is likely to be effective. As many researchers have pointed out, much of the writing on conflict—particularly the work in the 1960s and 1970s—had a strong normative value bias against conflict and toward cooperation.[34] Although the various models and instruments suggested at least five viable strategic approaches to conflict, the same works also suggested that cooperation, collaboration, or problem solving was the distinctly *preferred* approach. Thus, these writings preached the virtues of problem solving, advocated using it, and described how it could be pursued in almost any dispute. More recent authors in the field, although still strongly committed to problem solving, have also been more careful to stress that each conflict management strategy has its advantages and disadvantages, and is *more or less appropriate given the type of conflict* and situation in which the dispute occurs. Thus, conflict research has moved from a normative, prescriptive approach advocating problem solving at any cost toward a contingency approach advocating that the strategy selected should be based upon the objectives of the parties and the nature of their dispute. Although a full-fledged contingency approach to conflict management has yet to be fully articulated and supported by research (a task well beyond the scope of this introductory chapter), tables such as Figure 1.5 reflect efforts to delineate some of the conditions under which each strategy is appropriate or inappropriate.

Approaches by Other Parties

The dual concerns model and its five strategies reflect actions that the parties in conflict can take themselves in order to manage and resolve a dispute. However, conflicts can be resolved in other ways—either independent of the efforts of the parties themselves or by seeking outside assistance when the efforts of the parties break down. Two major mechanisms for resolving conflicts extend above and beyond the strategies of the parties themselves:

FIGURE 1.5

Styles of Handling Interpersonal Conflict and Situations Where They Are Appropriate or Inappropriate

Conflict Style	Situations Where Appropriate	Situations Where Inappropriate
Integrating	1. Issues are complex. 2. Synthesis of ideas is needed to come up with better solutions. 3. Commitment is needed for other parties for successful implementation. 4. Time is available for problem solving. 5. One party alone cannot solve the problem. 6. Resources possessed by different parties are needed to solve their common problems.	1. Task or problem is simple. 2. Immediate decision is required. 3. Other parties are unconcerned about outcome. 4. Other parties do not have problem-solving skills.
Obliging	1. You believe that you may be wrong. 2. Issue is more important to the other party. 3. You are willing to give up something in exchange for something from the other party in the future. 4. You are dealing from a position of weakness. 5. Preserving relationship is important.	1. Issue is important to you. 2. You believe that you are right. 3. The other party is wrong or unethical.
Dominating	1. Issue is trivial. 2. Speedy decision is needed. 3. Unpopular course of action is implemented. 4. Necessary to overcome assertive subordinates. 5. Unfavorable decision by the other party may be costly to you. 6. Subordinates lack expertise to make technical decisions. 7. Issue is important to you.	1. Issue is complex. 2. Issue is not important to you. 3. Both parties are equally powerful. 4. Decision does not have to be made quickly. 5. Subordinates possess high degree of competence.
Avoiding	1. Issue is trivial. 2. Potential dysfunctional effect of confronting the other party outweighs benefits of resolution. 3. Cooling-off period is needed.	1. Issue is important to you. 2. It is your responsibility to make decision. 3. Parties are unwilling to defer; issue must be resolved. 4. Prompt attention is needed.
Compromising	1. Goals of parties are mutually exclusive. 2. Parties are equally powerful. 3. Consensus cannot be reached. 4. Integrating or dominating style is not successful. 5. Temporary solution to a complex problem is needed.	1. One party is more powerful. 2. Problem is complex enough to need a problem-solving approach.

1. Third Parties. When the parties cannot resolve a dispute on their own, they may involve a third party. For example, two managers who disagree about a policy issue might ask their boss to help them determine the appropriate thing to do. Similarly, third parties may intervene independently when they believe a conflict is rapidly getting beyond the bounds of reasonable and likely settlement. For example, a parent who hears two children arguing in the family room over which TV program to watch might intervene quickly before the conflict escalates into physical confrontation.

Many different types of third parties and approaches are used to intervene in conflict. Third parties have always been popular in dealing with certain types of conflict (e.g., labor relations), and their popularity is increasing.[35] In Chapter 10, we will discuss numerous third-party styles and strategies in more detail.

2. Conflict Management Systems. As an alternative to involving an individual third party, conflicts are also handled by taking them to a system specifically set up to hear and resolve conflicts. The civil court system (the legal system) is the most common and visible system for handling conflict in our society. Parties who have almost any type of dispute with each other—property-line disputes between neighbors, marital disputes between husband and wife, patent-rights disputes between two companies—can hire any attorney (advocate and legal expert) and take their dispute through a system that will assure both a thorough, fair hearing and a resolution. Smaller and more manageable systems are also available in other contexts—sometimes because the parties want to manage conflict in a simpler way, at other times because the legal system has become so big, bureaucratic, and cumbersome that the parties no longer feel that fairness is possible. Labor contracts provide grievance systems by which possible violations of the contract or ambiguities in its interpretation can be heard and resolved. Organizations provide neutral third parties to listen to employee complaints and investigate charges of unfair treatment. Universities provide tribunals and judicial committees to review infractions of student codes of conduct. Many of these systems are actually third parties that have been institutionalized and legitimized into the organization's rules, policies, and procedures. Unlike the third parties we described above, who may invoke any number of procedures to resolve the dispute on the spot (dependent on the nature of the conflict, the parties, etc.), the third parties who operate in these systems are bound to follow the procedures set out by the system, and they cannot stray very far from those procedures without endangering their own legitimacy, credibility, reputation, and ability to resolve future disputes.[36]

Summary

In this section, we have presented a brief overview of the dynamics of conflict and its management—dynamics that underlie much of what we will have to say about the negotiation process. We defined conflict and pointed out that it exists at various

FIGURE 1.6

Schematic Overview of Chapters in This Book

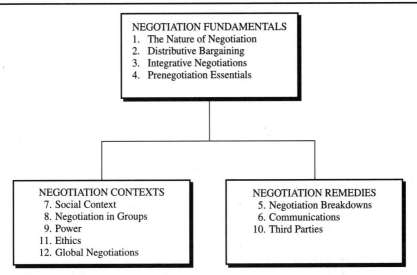

levels. We indicated that although many people tend to view conflict as primarily destructive, it also has many vital and productive aspects. It is important to manage conflict effectively to preserve its productive features while attempting to minimize its unproductive and destructive aspects. Finally, we examined the strategies most commonly identified for managing conflict: strategies that the parties can use themselves and strategies that the parties use by turning to others (third parties or conflict management systems) to resolve the dispute for them. As we will show, these strategies and approaches are fundamental to—and in some cases, even identical to—the strategies that parties use in negotiation.

Overview of Book

Each chapter in this book can be related to the introductory scenario about Joe and Sue Carter, which incorporates many of the critical elements addressed during negotiations. The book is organized into 12 chapters and can be viewed schematically in Figure 1.6. The first four chapters of the book examine negotiation fundamentals; three chapters present negotiation remedies, and five chapters explore important negotiation contexts. Researchers have defined several major strategies or approaches to negotiation, and negotiation strategies and tactics should be chosen to achieve one's needs in the situation. For example, in Joe and

Sue Carter's negotiations, Joe could choose one strategy to negotiate for the car: distributive, or win–lose, bargaining. Joe and Sue could use a different strategy for negotiating with each other over their vacation plans: integrative, or win–win, negotiation. We believe that effective negotiators should make a conscious choice about whether they are in a more distributive or integrative negotiation situation, and should actively prepare strategies and tactics that match this judgment. Of course, effective negotiators also have to be prepared to update that judgment as the negotiation unfolds, because information received during the negotiation may cause a change in the negotiator's perception of the structure of the negotiation situation.

Chapter 2 describes and evaluates the basic assumptions and strategies that characterize the competitive, win–lose, distributive bargaining process. In this chapter, we also review the tactics most commonly associated with distributive strategies and evaluate the consequences of using them.

Chapter 3 describes and evaluates the basic strategy and tactics common to cooperative, win–win, integrative bargaining. The process of integrative negotiation differs significantly different from that of distributive bargaining. Whereas distributive bargaining is usually characterized by mistrust, suspicion, and strategies designed to beat the opponent, integrative negotiation tends to be characterized by greater levels of trust and openness and by tactics designed to achieve the best possible solution for all parties involved. Integrative negotiation often resembles the process of problem solving; Chapter 3 reviews in detail the strategy and tactics necessary to perform this process successfully.

In Chapter 4, we step back from the two major negotiation approaches to explore more broadly the nature of strategy in negotiation and the key role that planning and preparation play in making a strategy work. This chapter first explores the broad nature and role of strategy as a process planning tool. We present a general model of strategic choice and identify the key factors that affect how a strategy is designed. We then move to the more specific elements of adequate and effective planning for negotiation. Planning and preparation are the most important steps in negotiation, yet these are the steps that many negotiators neglect or even completely ignore. Effective planning requires (a) a thorough understanding of the negotiation process so the negotiator has a general idea of what will happen and how things will evolve, (b) a clear formulation of goals and aspirations, (c) homework and research to put together the information and arguments to support and defend the desired goals, and (d) knowing the adversary, understanding the adversary's goals, and using that information to design a strategy to reach an effective resolution. The chapter also includes a series of diagnostic questions negotiators may use in planning for any negotiation.

Chapter 5 examines what negotiators can do when negotiation strategies and tactics do not work as intended. Most commonly, negotiations break down because the conflict dynamics get out of control or because poor communication interferes with the ability of the parties to reach an agreement. (Recall Joe's problem with purchasing and with Ed Laine, and Sue's problem with upper management.) This may occur in a number of ways: parties dig in to their positions and refuse to yield, communication becomes unproductive, the parties cannot find common ground or invent a solution to the problem, or anger and frustration drive out effective reasoning and listening. In Chapter 5, we describe how negotiators can help put derailed negotiations back on track—most of these are tactics the negotiators can use themselves to keep conflict from becoming more destructive. We also discuss the cognitive traps negotiators sometimes lay for themselves and ways in which negotiators can deal with difficult processes and opponents. Finally, we specifically address how to respond to opponents who use dirty tricks, act difficult, and are competitive when we wish to be cooperative.

In Chapter 6, we explore the dynamics of communication in negotiation. Negotiation is a communicative process involving the exchange of views, ideas and perspectives. In this chapter, we examine how the negotiation process moves through relatively predictable stages or phases of communication activities. We then explore a communication model of interpersonal exchange, emphasizing the mechanisms by which messages are encoded, sent, received, and decoded.

Chapter 7 examines the impact of the broader social context on the negotiation process. Joe and Sue Carter must deal with others who are not representing themselves, but instead are representing their department, organization, or political constituency. A lawyer advocates for a client; a salesperson makes a deal for the company that must be approved by senior management; a labor leader negotiates for the union rank and file. When parties represent the interests of others and are accountable to those others, a whole new dimension of complexity is added to negotiation. This chapter also explores the role played by audiences to negotiation (observers, third parties, and the media), and shows how they affect the behavior of the negotiators and fundamentally change the nature of negotiation dynamics.

Chapter 8 describes a different aspect of the social structure dynamic— negotiation in groups. Thus far, the book has described negotiations between two parties at a time. This chapter explores the special dynamics that occur when more than two interests are represented at the negotiation table, such as in a multiparty negotiation, task force or committee. Multiparty negotiations present special challenges; this chapter outlines those challenges and how to manage them effectively.

Chapter 9 deals with one of the most elusive concepts in negotiation—power. Power is elusive because, while it is possible to describe the different ways that negotiators gain and use power, it is difficult to describe exactly when or how these tactics should be used. The chapter defines the different sources of power that negotiators have—the tools they can potentially use to get what they want—and strategies and tactics of influence—how these tools are put to use to achieve their desired ends.

Chapter 10 discusses another way to get negotiations back on track by using other people—called third parties—to bring parties back together. We explore the different types of third-party strategies that can be used to resolve breakdowns in negotiation: arbitration, mediation and process facilitation. In the Joe and Sue Carter case, Sue is explicitly called on to help the Conservation Commission ''resolve'' the zoning issue.

Negotiation is a process in which each party engages in all manner of tactics to persuade the other. Sometimes these tactics lead negotiators over the line of appropriate and ethical behavior to unfair, inappropriate, unethical, or even illegal activities. They conceal information, bluff, or tell outright lies. They spy on the other to learn about his strategy. All these tactics fall within the category of unethical behavior. Chapter 11 indicates what types of conduct are generally viewed as unethical and describes what factors influence negotiators to use ethical or unethical tactics.

Finally, Chapter 12 discusses the role that international and cultural differences play in negotiation. In many ways, international and cultural factors operate much like the social structure dimensions we describe in Chapter 7; that is, they are a context that tempers, modifies, or even changes negotiation dynamics. Because this book is being written by three white, upper-middle-class North American authors, much of what we describe as typical and atypical is affected by the cultural biases we bring to negotiation. If the book were being written by three Asian Chinese or three Latin American Argentineans, our definitions of typical and atypical behavior might be quite different. Extensive research on international differences in negotiation has only begun to occur in the past 10 years. This research attempts to determine what factors are central to all negotiations regardless of culture and which factors and dimensions are strongly shaped by national and cultural style. We will present a current perspective on this emerging and evolving area of negotiation research.

End Notes

1. For further discussion see Rubin and Brown (1975) and Lewicki (1992).
2. Deutsch (1962, p. 276).
3. See Neslin and Greenhalgh (1983) and Raiffa (1982).
4. Thibaut and Kelley (1959).
5. Ibid., p. 21.
6. Fisher, Ury and Patton (1991).
7. Ibid., p. 105.
8. See Goffman (1969), Pruitt and Rubin (1986), and Raven and Rubin (1973).
9. See Beisecker, Walker, and Bart (1989) and Raven and Rubin (1973, p. 158).
10. See Fisher, Ury, and Patton (1991); Follett (1940); Nash (1950); Sebenius (1992); Sen (1970); and Walton and McKersie (1965).
11. Pruitt (1981).

12. Kelley (1966).

13. See Kimmel, Pruitt, Magenau, Konar-Goldband, and Carnevale (1980); Putnam and Jones (1982); and Weingart, Thompson, Bazerman, and Carroll (1990).

14. See Raiffa (1982) and Selekman, Fuller, Kennedy, and Baitsell (1964).

15. See Bazerman, Magliozzi, and Neale (1985); Neale and Bazerman (1985); Neale and Northcraft (1991); Pinkley (1992); and Thompson (1990).

16. See Bazerman and Neale (1992), Neale and Bazerman (1991, 1992b), and Thompson and Hastie (1990a, 1990b).

17. Thompson and Hastie (1990a).

18. Kelley and Stahelski (1970).

19. Bazerman, Magliozzi, and Neale (1985).

20. Thompson and Hastie, (1990a).

21. For excellent reviews of this literature, see Bazerman and Neale (1992) and Neale and Bazerman (1991).

22. Neale and Bazerman (1991).

23. Thompson and Loewenstein (1992).

24. Webster (1966).

25. All from Pruitt and Rubin (1986, p. 4).

26. Hocker and Wilmot, 1985.

27. See Deutsch (1973); also see Folger, Poole, and Stutman (1993) and Hocker and Wilmot (1985).

28. Coser (1956) and Deutsch (1973).

29. Tjosvold (1988).

30. Greenhalgh (1986).

31. See Pruitt and Rubin (1986), Filley (1975), Hall (1969), Rahim (1983a), Thomas (1992), and Thomas and Kilmann (1974).

32. Pruitt and Rubin (1986, p. 25).

33. Pruitt and Rubin (1986, p. 29).

34. For one summary see Lewicki, Weiss, and Lewin (1992).

35. See Elangovan (1995).

36. For reviews of approaches to dispute resolution systems, see Singer (1990) and Ury, Brett, and Goldberg (1988).

2 STRATEGY AND TACTICS OF DISTRIBUTIVE BARGAINING

Eighteen months ago, Larry decided to move closer to where he works. Following this decision to move, he put his house on the market and started to look for a new one. Fourteen months later, he had neither sold his house nor found another that he wanted to buy. He finally received the first offer to buy his house and, after a brief negotiation, settled on the selling price. Because he had not yet found a house to buy, he postponed closing the sale for six months to give himself additional time to look. The buyer, Barbara, was not happy to wait that long because of the inconvenience and the difficulty of getting a bank to guarantee an interest rate so far in advance. Larry adjusted the price so Barbara would accept this postponement, but it was clear that she would be much happier if the date could be moved closer.

There were relatively few houses on the market in the area where Larry wanted to live, and none of them was satisfactory. He jokingly said that unless something new came on the market, he would be sleeping in a tent in the town square when the leaves turned in the fall. Two months later a house came on the market that met his requirements. The seller, Monica, set the asking price at $145,000, which was $10,000 above what Larry hoped to pay but $5,000 below the most he would be willing to pay. Larry knew that the more he paid for the house, the less money he would have to make some very desirable alterations, buy draperies and some new furniture, and hire a moving company. There were attractive drapes already in Monica's house. She was moving to a new house; if she could not use the drapes in the new house, Larry might be able to purchase or include them with the house. The same might be true for several rugs, hall tables, and other items. Larry also learned that Monica's new home was supposed to be finished soon, about the time Larry was to close on the sale of his present house.

This illustration provides the basic elements of a distributive bargaining situation. It is also called *competitive,* or *win–lose,* bargaining. In a distributive bargaining situation, the goals of one party are usually in fundamental and direct conflict with the goals of the other party. Resources are fixed and limited, and each party wants to maximize his or her share of the resources. As a result, each party will use a set of strategies to maximize the share of the outcomes to be obtained. Most of these strategies and tactics guard information distribution carefully—information is given to the other party *only* when it provides a strategic advantage. However, it is highly desirable to *get* information from the other party in order to improve negotiation power. Distributive bargaining is basically a competition over who is going to get the most of a limited resource (often money). Whether or not one or both parties achieve their objectives will depend upon the strategy and tactics they employ.[1]

For many, the strategies and tactics of distributive bargaining are "what negotiation is all about." Images of smoke-filled rooms, packed with men (yes, they were usually all men) arguing and fighting for their points of view, come to mind. Many people are attracted to this view of negotiation and look forward to learning and sharpening their hard-bargaining skills; many others are repelled by this type of bargaining and would rather walk away than negotiate in this manner. They argue that this view of negotiation is old-fashioned, inappropriately macho, and destructive.

There are two reasons that *every* negotiator should be familiar with distributive bargaining. First, some interdependent situations that negotiators face *are* distributive in nature, and negotiators need to understand these situations to do well in them. Second, because many people use distributive bargaining strategies and tactics almost exclusively, it is necessary to understand how these strategies and tactics work if one wishes to counter their effects. We do not intend to glorify distributive bargaining techniques. Frequently they are counterproductive and costly to use. Often they cause negotiators to focus so much on the differences between negotiating parties that they ignore what the parties have in common. These negative effects notwithstanding, distributive bargaining strategies and tactics have their place, especially when a negotiator wants to maximize the value obtained in a single deal and when the relationship with the other party is not important. Also, some of the tactics discussed in this chapter will generate ethical concerns (the topic of ethics and negotiation is discussed in detail in Chapter 11). Do not assume that the other party shares your ethical values when negotiating. Although you may not believe that it is ethical to use some of the tactics discussed in this chapter, other negotiators may be quite comfortable using them. Alternatively, you may be comfortable using some tactics that make other negotiators quite uneasy. Some of the tactics discussed are commonly accepted as ethical behavior when bargaining distributively (e.g., portraying your BATNA as more positive than it really is), whereas other tactics are considered unacceptable (see the discussion of typical hardball tactics later in this chapter).

FIGURE 2.1

The Buyer's View of the House Negotiation

	Larry's target point		Monica's asking price	Larry's resistance point
$130,000	$135,000	$140,000	$145,000	$150,000

The Distributive Bargaining Situation

To understand how the distributive bargaining process works, return to our open-ing example of the new house purchase. Several prices were mentioned: (1) Monica's asking price, (2) the price Larry would like to pay for a new house, and (3) the price above which he would not pay to buy the house. These prices repre-sent key points in the analysis of any distributive bargaining situation. Larry's preferred price is the *target point,* the point at which a negotiator would like to conclude negotiations—his optimal goal. The price beyond which Larry will not go is the *resistance point,* a negotiator's bottom line—the most he will pay, the smallest amount she will settle for, and so on. Finally, the *asking price* is the ini-tial price set by the seller; Larry might decide to counter this price with his *initial offer*—the first number he will quote to the seller. Using the house purchase as an example, we can treat the range of possible prices as a continuum, and Figure 2.1 shows the various points along that dimension.

How does Larry decide on his initial offer? There are many ways to answer this question. Fundamentally, however, to make a good initial offer Larry must understand something about the process of negotiation. In Chapter 1, we stated that people expect give-and-take when they negotiate, and Larry needs to factor this into the way he sets his initial offer. If Larry opened the negotiation at his tar-get point ($135,000) and then had to make any concessions, with the first con-cession he would be moving *away* from his target point to a price closer to his resistance point. If he really wants to achieve his target, he should start at a price *lower* than his target point to create some room for making concessions. At the same time, the starting point cannot be too far from the target point. If Larry made the first offer too low, Monica might break off negotiations, believing him to be unreasonable or foolish. Although judgments about how to determine first offers can often be quite complex and can have a dramatic influence on the course of negotiation, let us stay with the simple case for the moment and assume that Larry decided to offer $133,000 as a "reasonable" first offer—less than his target point and well below his resistance point. In the meantime, remember that although this illustration concerns only price, *all* other issues or agenda items for the negotia-tion may also have a starting, target, and resistance point.

FIGURE 2.2

The Buyer's View of the House Negotiation (extended)

Monica's inferred resistance point	Larry's intial offer	Larry's target point	Monica's inferred target	Monica's asking price	Larry's resistance point
$130,000	$133,000	$135,000	$140,000	$145,000	$150,000

Both parties to a negotiation have starting, target, and resistance points. Starting points are usually in the opening statements each makes (i.e., the seller's listing price and the buyer's first offer). The target point is usually learned or inferred as negotiations get underway. People, typically, give up the margin between their starting points and target points as they make concessions. The resistance point, the point beyond which a person will not go or will break off negotiations, is not known to the other party and should be kept secret.[2] One party may not learn the other's resistance point even after the end of a successful negotiation. After an unsuccessful negotiation, when the other party breaks off talks, one party may infer that the other's resistance point is near the last offer the other was willing to consider before the negotiation ended.

Two parties' starting and resistance points are usually arranged in reverse order, with the resistance point being a high price for the buyer and a low price for the seller. Thus, continuing the illustration, Larry would have been willing to pay up to $150,000 for the house that Monica listed for $145,000. Larry can speculate that she may be willing to accept something less than $145,000 and probably would think $140,000 a desirable (target) figure. What Larry does not know (but would dearly like to) is the *lowest* figure that Monica would accept. Is it $140,000? $135,000? Let us assume it is $130,000. Monica, however, initially knows nothing about Larry's position but soon learns his starting point when he offers $133,000. Monica may suspect that Larry's target point is not too far away (we know it was $135,000) but she has no idea of his resistance point ($150,000). This information—what Larry knows or infers about Monica's positions—is represented in Figure 2.2.

The spread between the resistance points, called the *bargaining range, settlement range, or zone of potential agreement,* is particularly important. In this area the actual bargaining takes place, for anything outside these points will be summarily rejected by one of the negotiators. When the buyer's resistance point is above the seller's—he is minimally willing to pay more than she is minimally willing to sell for, as is true in the house example—there is a *positive bargaining range.* When the reverse is true—the seller's resistance point is above the buyer's, and the buyer won't pay more than the seller will minimally accept—there is a *negative bargaining range*. In the house example, if Monica would minimally accept $145,000 and Larry would maximally pay $140,000, then a negative bargaining range exists. Negotiations that begin with a negative bargaining range are likely to stalemate quickly. They can only be resolved if one or both parties are persuaded to change their resistance points, or if someone else forces a solution upon them that one or both parties dislike. However, because negotiators don't begin their deliberations by talking about their resistance points (they're talking about initial offers and demands instead), it is often hard to know whether a positive settlement range really exists until the negotiators get deep into the process. Both parties may realize that there was no overlap in their resistance points only after protracted negotiations have been exhausted; at that point, they will have to decide whether to end negotiations or reevaluate their resistance points, a process to be described in more detail later on.

The Role of Alternatives to a Negotiated Agreement

In addition to defining opening bids, target points, and resistance points, a fourth factor may enter the negotiations: the role played by an alternative outcome that can be obtained by completing a different deal with a different party (see Chapter 1). In some negotiations, the parties have only two fundamental choices: to reach a deal with the other party, or not to settle at all. In other negotiations, however, one or both parties may have the choice of completing an alternative deal. Thus, in the example of buying a house, there is probably more than one house for sale in the city where Larry wishes to buy. Similarly, if Monica waits long enough (or drops the price of the house far enough), she is sure to find another interested buyer. If Larry picks an alternative house to buy, talks to the owner of that house, and negotiates the best price that he can, that price represents his *alternative*. For the sake of argument, let us assume that Larry's alternative house costs $142,000, and Monica's alternative buyer will pay $134,000.

An alternative point can be identical to the resistance point, although the two do not necessarily have to be the same. If Larry's alternative is $142,000, then he should reject any price Monica asks above $142,000 because he could buy the second house above that amount. But Larry's alternative may not be all that desirable for reasons other than price—for example, he likes the neighborhood less, it is 10 minutes farther away from where he works, or he likes the way Monica decorated the house and wants to enjoy that when he moves in. In this situation, therefore, Larry may maintain his resistance point at $150,000; he is therefore willing to pay Monica up to $8,000 more than his alternative, simply to buy *her* house (see Figure 2.3).

Alternatives are important because they give the negotiator power to walk away from any negotiation when the emerging deal is not very good. The number of realistic alternatives we may have will vary considerably from negotiation to negotiation. In negotiations where we have many attractive alternatives, we can set our goals higher and make fewer concessions. In negotiations where we have

FIGURE 2.3

The Buyer's View of the House Negotiation (extended with alternatives)

Monica's inferred resistance point	Larry's initial offer	Monica's alternative buyer	Larry's target point	Monica's inferred target	Larry's alternative house	Monica's asking price	Larry's resistance point
$130,000	$133,000	$134,000	$135,000	$140,000	$142,000	$145,000	$150,000

no attractive alternative, such as when dealing with a sole-source supplier, we have much less bargaining power. Good distributive bargainers identify their realistic alternatives *before* beginning negotiations with the other party so that they can properly gauge how firm to be in the negotiation.[3]

Settlement Point

The fundamental process of distributive bargaining is to reach a settlement within a positive bargaining range. The objective of both parties is to obtain as much of the bargaining range as possible—that is, to get the settlement as close to the other party's resistance point as possible.

Both parties in distributive bargaining know that they might have to settle for less than what they would prefer, but they hope that the settlement point will be better than their own resistance point. In order for agreement to occur, both parties must believe that the settlement point, although perhaps less desirable than they would prefer, is still the best that they can get. It is important that each party believe the settlement point is the best she can get, and that both reach agreement and ensure support for the agreement after the negotiations. Parties who do not think they got the best agreement possible, or who believe that they lost, frequently try to get out of the agreement later or find other ways to recoup their losses. If Larry thinks he got the short end of the deal, he can make life miserable and expensive for Monica by making extraneous claims later on—claiming "hidden damages" to the house, or that fixtures that were supposed to come with the house were defective, and so on. Another factor that will affect satisfaction with the settlement point is whether the parties can get even in the future or whether they will ever see one another again. If Monica was moving out of the region, then Larry should ensure that he evaluates the current deal very carefully because he may be unable to contact her later for any adjustments.

Bargaining Mix

In the house purchase illustration, as in almost all negotiations, agreement is necessary on *several* issues: the price, the closing date of the sale, renovations to the house, and the price of items that could remain in the house (such as drapes and appliances). This package of issues for negotiation is the *bargaining mix*. Each item in the mix can have its own starting, target, and resistance points. Some items are of obvious importance to both parties; others are of importance to only one party. Negotiators need to know what is important to them and to the other party, and they need to make sure they take these priorities into account during the planning process (see Chapter 4 for a detailed discussion of planning).

For example, in the negotiation we are describing, a secondary issue important to both parties was the closing date of the sale—the date when the ownership of the house would actually be transferred. The date of sale was part of the bargaining mix. Larry learned when Monica's new house was going to be completed and anticipated that she would want to transfer ownership of the old house to him shortly after that point. Larry asked for a closing date very close to when Monica would probably want to close; thus, the deal looked very attractive to her. As it turned out, Larry's closing date on his own house—his own target point—was close to this date as well, thus making the deal attractive for both Larry and Monica. If Larry and Monica had wanted different selling dates, then the closing date would have been a more contentious issue in the bargaining mix.

Fundamental Strategies

The prime objective in distributive bargaining is to maximize the value of *this single deal*. In our example, the buyer has four fundamental strategies available:

1. To push for a settlement close to the seller's (as yet unknown) resistance point, thereby yielding for the buyer the largest part of the settlement range. The buyer may attempt to influence the seller's view of what settlements are possible by making extreme offers and small concessions.

2. To get the seller to change her resistance point by influencing the seller's beliefs about the value of the house. The buyer may try to convince her to reduce her resistance point (e.g., by telling her that the house is very overpriced) and thereby increase the bargaining range.

3. If a negative settlement range exists, to get the seller to reduce her resistance point in order to create a positive settlement range or to modify one's own resistance point to create that overlap. Thus, Monica could be persuaded to accept a lower price, or Larry could decide he has to pay more than he wanted to.

4. To get the other party to think that this settlement is the best that is possible—not that it is *all* she can get, or that she is *incapable* of getting more, or that the other side is *winning* by getting more. The distinction between a party's believing that an agreement is the *best possible* (and not the other interpretations) may appear subtle and semantic. However, in getting people to agree, it is important they *feel* as though they got the best possible deal. Ego satisfaction is often as important as achieving tangible objectives (recall the discussion of tangibles and intangibles in Chapter 1).

In all these strategies, the buyer is attempting to influence the seller's perceptions of what is possible through the exchange of information and persuasion. However, regardless of the general strategy taken, two tasks are important in all distributive bargaining situations: (1) discovering the other party's resistance point and (2) influencing the other party's resistance point.

Discovering the Other Party's Resistance Point

Information is the life force of negotiation. The more you can learn about the other party's outcome values, resistance point, feelings of confidence, motivation, and so on, the more capable you will be to strike a favorable agreement. At the same time, you do not want the other party to have some kinds of information about you. It is best to conceal your real resistance point, some of the outcome values, and confidential information about a weak strategic position or an emotional vulnerability. Alternatively, you *do* want the other party to have some information—some of it factual and correct, some of it contrived to lead the other party to believe things that are favorable to you. Because each side wants to get some information and to conceal other information, and because each side knows that the other also wants to conceal and get information, communication can become complex. Information is often conveyed in a code that evolves during negotiation. People answer questions with other questions or less-than-complete answers, yet for either side to influence the other's perceptions, they must establish some points effectively and convincingly.

Influencing the Other Party's Resistance Point

Central to planning the strategy and tactics for distributive bargaining is effectively locating the other party's resistance point and the relationship of that resistance point to your own. The resistance point is established by the value expected from a particular outcome, which in turn is the product of the worth and costs of an outcome. Larry sets a resistance point on the amount of money he would pay for a house based on the amount of money he can afford to pay (in total or in monthly mortgage payments), the estimated market value or worth of the house, and how other factors in his bargaining mix might be resolved (closing date, draperies, etc.). A resistance point will also be influenced by the cost an individual attaches to delay or difficulty in negotiation (an intangible) or to having the negotiations aborted. If Larry, who had set his resistance point at $150,000, were faced with the choice of paying $151,000 or living on the town square for a month, he might well reevaluate his resistance point. The following factors are important in attempting to influence the other person's resistance point: (1) the value the other attaches to a particular outcome, (2) the costs the other attaches to delay or difficulty in negotiations, and (3) the cost the other attaches to having the negotiations aborted.

A significant factor in shaping the other person's understanding of what is possible—and therefore the value the other places on particular outcomes—is the other's understanding of your own situation. Therefore, when influencing the other's viewpoint, you must *also deal with the other party's understanding* of your value for a particular outcome, the costs you attach to delay or difficulty in negotiation, and your cost of having the negotiations aborted.

To explain how these factors can affect the process of distributive bargaining, we will make four major propositions:[4]

1. The other party's resistance point will vary directly with her estimate of the cost of delay or aborting negotiations. If the other party sees that you need a settlement quickly and cannot defer it, she can seize this advantage and press for a better outcome. Therefore, expectations will rise and she will set a more demanding resistance point. The more you can convince the other that your costs of delay or aborting negotiations are *low* (we are in no hurry and can "wait forever"), the more modest will be the other's resistance point.

2. The other's resistance point will vary inversely with his cost of delay or aborting. The more a person needs a settlement, the more modest he will be in setting a resistance point. Therefore, the more you can do to convince the other party that delay or aborting negotiations will be costly, the more likely the other is to establish a modest resistance point. In contrast, the more attractive the other party's alternatives—and the better the other's BATNA (Best Alternative To a Negotiated Agreement)—the more that person can "hang tough" with a high resistance point. If negotiations are unsuccessful, the other party can move to an attractive alternative. In the earlier example, both Larry and Monica have satisfactory alternatives.

3. A resistance point will vary directly with the value the other party attaches to that outcome. Therefore, the resistance point may become more modest as the person reduces the value for that outcome. If you can convince the other party that a present negotiating position will not have the desired outcome or that the present position is not as attractive because other positions are even more attractive, then she will adjust her resistance point.

4. The other's resistance point varies inversely with the perceived value the first party attaches to an outcome. Knowing that a position is important to the other party, you will expect the other to resist giving up on that issue; thus, there should be less possibility of a favorable settlement in that area. As a result, expectations will be lowered to a more modest resistance point. Hence, the more you can convince the other that you value a particular outcome outside the other's bargaining range, the more pressure you put on the other party to set a more modest resistance point.

Tactical Tasks

From the above assessment of the fundamental strategies of distributive bargaining, four important tactical tasks emerge for a negotiator in a distributive bargaining situation: (1) assess the other party's outcome values and the costs of terminating negotiations, (2) manage the other party's impression of one's own outcome values, (3) modify the other party's perception of her own outcome values, and (4) manipulate the actual costs of delaying or aborting negotiations. Each of these tasks is now discussed in more detail.

Assess Outcome Values and the Costs of Termination

An important first step for a negotiator is to get information about the other party's outcome values and resistance point. The negotiator can pursue two general routes: getting more information indirectly about the background factors behind an issue (indirect assessment) or getting information directly from the other party about his outcome values and resistance points (direct assessment).

1. Indirect Assessment. The process by which an individual sets a resistance point may be based on many factors. How do we decide, for example, how much rent or mortgage payment we can afford each month? Or how do we decide what a house is really worth? There are lots of ways to go about doing this. *Indirect* assessment is aimed at determining what information an individual probably used to set her target and resistance points and how she interpreted this information. For example, in labor negotiations, management may infer whether or not a union is willing to strike by how hard the union bargains or by the size of its strike fund. Management decides whether or not the company can afford a strike based on size of inventories, market conditions for the company's product, and the percentage of workers who are members of the union. In a real estate negotiation, how long a piece of property has been on the market, how many other potential buyers actually exist, how soon a buyer needs the property for business or living, and the financial health of the seller will be important factors. An automobile buyer might view the number of new cars in inventory on the dealer's lot, refer to newspaper articles on automobile sales, read about the car's popularity in consumer buying guides, or consult reference guides to find out what a dealer pays for the car wholesale.

You can use a variety of information sources to assess the other party's resistance point. Making direct observations, consulting readily available documents and publications, or talking to experts are some ways to do so. It is important to note, however, that these are *indirect* indicators. How one person interprets this data could be very different from how another person does. A large inventory of automobiles may make a dealer willing to reduce the price of a car. However, the dealer may expect the market to change soon, may have just started a big promotional campaign that the buyer does not know about, or may see no real need to reduce prices, and instead intends to wait for a market upturn. Thus, indirect measures provide valuable information that *may* reflect a reality that the other person will eventually have to face. It is important to remember, however, that the same piece of information may mean different things to different people and hence may not tell us exactly what we think it does.

2. Direct Assessment. In bargaining, one does not usually expect accurate and precise information about outcome values, resistance points, and expectations from the other party. Sometimes, however, the other party *will* give accurate information. When pushed to the absolute limit and when they require a quick settlement, the other party may explain the facts quite clearly. If management believes a wage settlement above a certain point would drive the company out of business, they may choose to state that absolute limit very clearly and go to considerable lengths to explain how it was determined. Similarly, a house buyer may tell the seller his absolutely maximum price and support it with an explanation of income and other expenses. In these instances, of course, the party revealing the information believes that the settlement being proposed is within the settlement range—and that the other party will accept the offered information as true, rather than seeing it as a bargaining ploy. An industrial salesperson may tell the purchaser about product quality and service, alternative customers who want to buy the product, and the time required to manufacture special orders.

However, most of the time the other party is not so forthcoming, and the methods of getting direct information may become more complex. In international diplomacy, various means are used to gather information. Sources are cultivated, messages are intercepted, and codes broken. In labor negotiations, companies have been known to recruit informers or to bug the union's meeting rooms, and unions have had their members collect papers from executives' wastebaskets or bug telephones. In real estate negotiations, sellers have entertained prospective buyers with abundant alcoholic beverages in the hope that tongues will be loosened and information revealed. Other approaches involve provoking the other party into an angry outburst or putting negotiators under pressure to cause them to make a slip and reveal valuable information. One party may simulate exasperation and angrily storm out of negotiations in the hope that the other, in an effort to avoid a deadlock, will reveal what is really wanted.

Manage the Other Party's Impressions

Because each side attempts to get information about the other party through direct and indirect sources, an important tactical task may be to *prevent* the other from getting accurate information about your position, while simultaneously guiding the other party to form a "preferred impression" of it. Your tasks, then, are to screen actual information about positions and to represent them as you would *like* the other to believe them.

1. Screening Activities. Generally speaking, screening activities are more important at the beginning of negotiation, and representation is useful later on. This sequence gives more time to concentrate on gathering information from the other party, which will be useful in evaluating your own resistance point, and on determining the best way to feed information to the other party about your own position. The simplest way to screen a position is to say and do as little as possible. Silence is golden when answering questions; words should be invested in asking them instead. This selective reticence reduces the likelihood of making verbal slips or presenting any clues that the other side could use to draw conclusions. A look of disappointment or boredom, fidgeting and restlessness, or probing with interest all can give clues about the importance of the points under discussion.

Concealment is the most general screening activity. Another approach, possible when group negotiations are carried on through a representative, is "calculated incompetence." Here, the negotiating agent is not given all the needed information, making it impossible for information to be leaked. Instead, the negotiator is sent with the task of simply gathering facts and bringing them back to the group. This strategy can make negotiations more complex and tedious, and it often causes the other party to protest vigorously at the negotiator's inability to divulge important data or to make agreements. Lawyers, real estate agents, and investigators are frequently used by others to perform this role. Representatives may also be limited (or limit themselves) in their authority to make decisions. For example, a man buying a car may claim that he must consult his wife before making a final decision.

When negotiation is carried out by a team—as is common in diplomacy, labor–management relations, and many business negotiations—channeling all communication through a team spokesperson reduces inadvertent revelation of information. In addition to reducing the number of people who can actively reveal information, this allows other members of the negotiating team to observe and listen carefully to what the other party is saying so they can detect clues and pieces of information about the other party's position. Still another approach to screening activities is to present a great many items for negotiation, only a few of which are truly important to the presenter. In this way, the other party has to gather so much information about so many different items that it becomes difficult to detect which items are really important. This tactic is frequently called the snow job or kitchen sink—it raises so many demands that the negotiator's real priorities are disguised.[5]

2. Direct Action to Alter Impressions. Negotiators can take many actions to present facts that will either directly enhance their position or make their position appear stronger to the other party. One of the most obvious methods is *selective presentation,* in which negotiators reveal *only* the facts necessary to support their case. Selective presentation can also be used to lead the other party to form the desired impression of your resistance point or to open up new possibilities for agreement that are more favorable to the presenter than those that currently exist. Another approach is to explain or interpret known facts in order to present a logical argument that shows the costs or risks to oneself if the other party's proposals were implemented. An alternative is to say, "If you were in my shoes, here is the way these facts would look in light of the proposal you have presented." These arguments are most convincing when the facts used have been acquired from a neutral source because then they will not be seen as biased by a party's preferred outcome. However, even with facts that you provide, these interpretations can be helpful in managing the impression the other has of your preferences and priorities. It is not necessary for the other to agree that this is the way things would look if he or she were in your position. Nor must the other agree that the facts lead only to the conclusion you have presented. As long as the other party understands how you see things, her or his thinking is likely to be influenced.

The *emotional* reaction one displays to facts, proposals, and possible outcomes and conclusions provides the other party with information about what one considers important. Disappointment or enthusiasm usually suggests that an issue is important, whereas boredom or indifference suggests it is trivial or unimportant. A loud, angry outburst or an eager response suggests that the topic is very important and may give it a prominence that will shape what is discussed. Clearly, how-ever, emotional reactions can be real or feigned. The length of time and amount of detail used in presenting a point or position can also convey importance. Carefully checking through the details that the other side has presented about an item, or insisting on clarification and verification, all convey the impression of importance. Casually accepting the other party's arguments as true conveys the impression of lack of interest in the topic being discussed.

Taking direct action to alter another's impression raises a number of hazards. It is one thing to select certain facts to present and to emphasize or de-emphasize their importance accurately, but it is a different matter to lie and fabricate. The former is expected and understood in distributive bargaining; the latter, even in hardball negotiations, is resented and often angrily attacked if discovered. Between the two extremes, however, what is said and done as skillful puffery by one may be perceived as dishonest distortion by the other (the ethical considerations are explored in detail in Chapter 11). Other problems can arise when trivial items are introduced as distractions or when minor issues are magnified in importance. The purpose is to conceal the truly important and to direct the other's attention away from the significant, but there is a danger: the other person may become aware of this maneuver and, with great fanfare, concede on the minor points, thereby gaining the right to demand equally generous concessions on the central points. Thus, the other party can defeat the maneuverer at his own game.

Modify the Other Party's Perceptions

You can alter the other's impressions of his own objectives by making the outcomes appear less attractive or by making the cost of obtaining them appear higher. You may also try to make demands and positions appear more attractive or less unattractive to the other party.

There are several approaches to modifying the other party's perceptions. One approach is to interpret the outcomes of the other party's proposal. You can explain logically how undesirable it would be if the other party's outcome were realized. This could mean pointing out something that had been overlooked. For example, in union–management negotiations, management could point out that a union request for a six-hour work day, on the one hand, would not increase the number of employees because it would not be worthwhile to hire people for two hours a day to make up the hours taken from the standard eight-hour day. On the other hand, if the company were to keep production at the present level, it would be necessary to use the present employees on overtime, thereby increasing the total labor cost and, subsequently, the price of the product. This rise in cost would reduce demand for the product and, ultimately, the number of hours worked or the number of workers.

Another approach to modifying the other's perceptions is by concealing information. An industrial seller might not reveal to a purchaser that certain technological changes are going to significantly reduce the cost of producing the products. A seller of real estate might not tell a prospective buyer that in three years a proposed highway will isolate the for-sale property from attractive portions of the city. Concealment strategies may enter into the same ethical hazards mentioned earlier (also see Chapter 11).

Manipulate the Actual Costs of Delay or Termination

As noted previously, negotiators have deadlines. A contract will expire. Agreement has to be reached before a large meeting occurs. Someone has to catch a plane. Therefore, extending negotiations beyond a deadline can be costly, particularly to the person who has the deadline, because that person has to either extend the deadline or go home empty-handed. At the same time, research and practical experience suggest that a large majority of agreements in distributive bargaining are reached when the deadline is near.[6] Manipulating a deadline or failing to agree by a particular deadline can be a powerful tool in the hands of the person who does not face deadline pressure. In some ways the ultimate weapon in negotiation is to threaten to terminate negotiations, denying both parties the possibility of a settlement. This pressure will usually be felt more acutely by one side than by the other, and thus it presents a potent weapon. There are three ways to manipulate the costs of delay in negotiation: (1) plan disruptive action, (2) ally with outsiders, and (3) manipulate the scheduling of negotiations:

1. Disruptive Action. One way to encourage agreement is to increase the costs of *not* reaching a negotiated agreement. In one instance, a group of unionized food service workers negotiating with a restaurant rounded up supporters, had them enter the restaurant just prior to lunch, and had each person order a cup of coffee and drink it leisurely. When regular customers came to lunch, they found every seat occupied.[7] In another case, people dissatisfied with automobiles they had purchased painted their cars with large, bright yellow lemons and signs bearing the dealer's name, and then drove the cars around town in an effort to embarrass the dealer into making a settlement. Public picketing of a business, boycotting, and locking negotiators in a room until they reach agreement are all forms of disruptive action that increase the costs to negotiators for not settling and hence bring them back to the bargaining table. Such tactics can work, but they may also produce anger and escalate the conflict.

2. Ally with Outsiders. Another way to increase the costs of delay or terminating negotiations is to involve in the process other parties who can somehow influence the outcome. In many business transactions, a private party may profess that if negotiations with a merchant are unsuccessful, he or she will go to the Better Business Bureau and protest the merchant's actions. Individuals protesting the practices and policies of businesses or government agencies form task forces, political action groups, and protest organizations in order to bring greater collective pressure on the target. For example, professional schools in universities often enhance their negotiation with higher management on budget matters by citing required compliance with external accreditation standards in order to substantiate their budget requests.

3. Scheduling of Negotiations. The negotiation scheduling process can often put one party at a considerable disadvantage. Businesspeople going overseas to negotiate with customers or suppliers often find negotiations are scheduled to begin immediately after their arrival, when they are still suffering from the fatigue of travel and jet lag. Alternatively, delay tactics can be used to squeeze negotiations into the last remaining minutes of their visit in order to extract concessions from the visiting party.[8] Automobile dealers will probably negotiate differently with the customer a half hour before quitting time on Friday night than at the beginning of the work day. Industrial buyers have a much more difficult negotiation when they have a short "lead time" because their plants may have to sit idle if they cannot secure a new contract for raw materials in time.

The opportunities to increase or alter the timing of negotiation vary widely from field to field. In some industries it is possible to stockpile raw materials at relatively low cost or to buy them in large bulk lots; in other industries, however, it is essential that materials arrive at regular intervals because they have a brief shelf life (as many manufacturing firms move to just-in-time inventory procedures, this becomes increasingly true). Thus, the opportunity to vary the scheduling of negotiations differs across industries. There are far fewer opportunities for an individual to create costly delays when negotiating a home purchase than when negotiating a huge bulk order of raw materials. Nonetheless, the tactics of increasing these costs by manipulating deadlines and time pressures are possible options, both to enhance your own position and to protect yourself from the other party's actions.

Positions Taken during Negotiation

Effective distributive bargainers need to understand the process of taking a position during bargaining (the opening offer or opening stance) and the role of making concessions during the negotiation process.[9] At the beginning of negotiations, each party takes a position. These positions may then change in response to information from the other party or in response to the other party's behavior. Typically, the other party's position will also change during bargaining. Changes in position are usually accompanied by new information concerning the other's intentions, the value of outcomes, and likely places for settlement. Negotiation is iterative. It provides an opportunity for both sides to communicate information about their positions that may lead to opportunities to change them.

Opening Offer

When negotiations begin, the negotiator is faced with a perplexing problem. What should the opening offer be? Will the offer be seen as too high by the other party and contemptuously rejected? An offer seen as modest by the other party could perhaps have been higher, either to leave more room to maneuver or to achieve a higher eventual settlement. Should the opening offer be somewhat closer to the resistance point, suggesting a more cooperative stance? These questions become less perplexing as the negotiator learns more about the other party's personality, limits, and planned strategy. However, although knowledge about the other party helps negotiators set their opening offers, it does not tell them exactly what to do next. The fundamental question is whether the opening offer should be more extreme or modest. Studies indicate that negotiators who make more extreme opening offers get higher settlements than do those who make low or modest opening offers.[10] There are at least two reasons that an extreme opening offer is advantageous.[11] First, it gives more room for movement in negotiation and therefore allows more time to learn about the other party's priorities in order to influence them. Second, an extreme opening offer acts as a "metamessage" and may create, in the other party's mind, the impression that (1) there is a long way to go before a reasonable settlement is achieved, and (2) more concessions than originally intended may have to be made to bridge the difference between the two opening positions.[12] The disadvantages of an extreme opening offer are these: (1) it may be summarily rejected by the other party, and (2) it communicates an attitude of toughness that may be destructive to long-term relationships. Negotiators who make extreme opening offers should also have viable alternatives and BATNAs that they can employ if the opposing negotiator refuses to deal with them; the higher these extreme offers, the more likely the offer will be summarily rejected by the other side.

Opening Stance

A second decision to be made at the outset of negotiation is the stance or attitude to adopt. Will you be competitive—fighting to get the best on every point? Or will you be moderate—willing to make concessions and compromises? Some negotiators take a belligerent stand, attacking the positions, offers, and even the character of the other party. In response, the other party may mirror the initial stance, meeting belligerence with belligerence. Even if a belligerent stance is not directly countered, the other party is unlikely to respond with a reasonable stance. Some negotiators adopt a position of moderation and understanding, seeming to say, "Let's be reasonable people who can solve this problem to our mutual satisfaction." Even if the attitude is not mirrored, the other's response is most likely to be constrained by this opening stance.

To communicate the most effective message, a negotiator should try to send a consistent message through both attitude and opening offer. A reasonable bargaining position is usually coupled with a friendly attitude, and an extreme bargaining position is usually coupled with a tougher, more competitive attitude. When the messages sent by position and attitude conflict, the other party will find them confusing to interpret and answer.

Initial Concessions

An opening offer is usually met with a counteroffer, and these two offers define the initial bargaining range. Sometimes the other party will not counteroffer but will simply state that the first offer (or set of demands) is unacceptable and ask the opener to come back with "a more reasonable set of proposals." In any event, after the first round of offers, the next question is, What movement or concession is to be made? You can choose to make none, hold firm, and insist on the original position, or you can make some concessions. Note that it is *not* an option to escalate one's opening offer—that is, to set an offer *higher* than the first. This would be uniformly met with disapproval from the other party. If concessions are to be made, the next question is, How large should they be? It is important to note that the first concession conveys a message, frequently a symbolic one, to the other party about how you will proceed.

Opening offers, opening stances, and initial concessions are elements at the beginning of negotiations that parties can use to communicate how they intend to negotiate. An extreme original offer, a determined opening stance, a very small opening concession, or any combination signal a position of firmness; a more moderate opening offer, a reasonable and cooperative opening stance, and a more generous initial concession communicate a basic stance of flexibility. By taking a firm position, you attempt to capture most of the bargaining range for yourself in order to maximize the final outcome or to preserve maximum maneuvering room for later in the negotiations. Firmness also creates a climate in which the other side may decide concessions are so meager that it is worthwhile to capitulate and settle quickly rather than to drag things out. Hence, firmness may be a way to shorten negotiations. There is also a possibility, however, that firmness will be reciprocated by the other party. One or both parties may become either intransigent or disgusted, and withdraw completely.

There are several reasons for adopting a flexible position. First, by taking different stances along the way, you can learn from the other party's responses about his or her outcome values and perceived possibilities. You may want to establish a cooperative rather than a combative relationship, hoping to get a better agreement. In addition, flexibility keeps the negotiations going; the more flexible you seem, the more the other party will believe that a settlement is possible.

Role of Concessions

Concessions are central to negotiation. Without them, in fact, negotiations would not exist. If one side is not prepared to make concessions, either the other must capitulate or negotiations will deadlock.

People enter negotiations expecting concessions. A good distributive bargainer will not begin negotiations with the other party with an opening offer too close to the resistance point but, rather, will ensure that there is enough room in the bargaining range to make some concessions. The other party usually resents a take-it-or-leave-it approach; an offer that may have been accepted had it emerged as a result of concession making may be rejected when it is thrown on the table and presented as a fait accompli. This approach, called Boulwarism, has been illustrated many times in labor relations. In the past, management leaders have often "objectively" analyzed what they could afford to give in their upcoming contract talks and have made their *initial* offer at the point they intended for their *final* offer (i.e., they set the same opening offer, target point, and resistance point). They then insisted there were no concessions to be made because the initial offer was "fair and reasonable" based on their own analysis. Unions bitterly fought these positions and continued to resent management years after the companies abandoned this bargaining strategy.[13]

There is ample data that parties feel better about a settlement when negotiations involved a progression of concessions.[14] Rubin and Brown suggest that "a bargainer wants to believe he is capable of shaping the other's behavior, of causing the other to choose as he himself does."[15] When you make concessions, you communicate that you will make adjustments to the other party.

Because concession making indicates an acknowledgment of the other party and a movement toward the other's position, it implies a recognition of that position and its legitimacy. The intangible factors of status and position are as much at stake as the tangible issues themselves. Concession making also exposes the concession maker to some risk. If the other party does not reciprocate, the concession maker may appear to be weaker by having given up something and received nothing in return. Thus, not reciprocating a concession sends a powerful message about firmness and leaves the concession maker with a feeling of damaged esteem or diminished reputation.

A reciprocated concession cannot be haphazard. If the giver has made a major concession on a significant point, it is expected that the return offer will be on the same item or one of similar weight and somewhat comparable magnitude. To make an additional concession when none has been given (or when what was given was inadequate) can imply weakness and can squander valuable maneuvering room. When receiving an inadequate concession, a negotiator may explicitly state what is expected before offering further concessions: "That is not sufficient; you will have to go up X before I consider offering any further concessions."

To encourage further concessions from the other side, negotiators sometimes link their concessions to a prior concession made by the other. They may say, "Since you have reduced your demand on X, I am willing to concede on Y." More powerful concession making may be wrapped in a package, sometimes described as logrolling. For example, "If you will give A and B, I will give C and D." Packaging concessions also leads to better outcomes for a negotiator than making concessions singly on individual issues.[16] This tactic is discussed in more detail in the next chapter.

Pattern of Concession Making

The pattern of concessions a negotiator makes contains valuable information, but it is not always easy to interpret. When successive concessions get smaller, the most obvious message is that the concession maker's position is getting firmer and that the resistance point is being reached. This generalization needs to be tempered, however, by pointing out that a small concession late in negotiations may also indicate that there is little room left to move. When the opening offer is extreme, the negotiator has considerable room available for packaging new offers, which makes it relatively easy to give fairly substantial concessions. When the negotiation has moved closer to a negotiator's hoped-for settlement point, giving a concession the same size as the initial one may take a negotiator past her resistance point. Suppose a negotiator makes a first offer $100 below the other's target price; an initial concession of $10 would reduce the maneuvering room by 10 percent. When negotiations get to within $10 of the other's target price, a concession of $1 gives up 10 percent of the remaining maneuvering room. A negotiator cannot communicate such mechanical ratios in giving or interpreting concessions, but this example illustrates how the receiver might construe the meaning of concession size, depending on where it occurs in the negotiating sequence.

The pattern of concession making is also important. Consider the pattern of concessions made by two negotiators, Sandra and Linda, in Figure 2.4. Assume they are discussing the unit price of a shipment of computer parts, and each is dealing with a different client. Linda makes three concessions, each worth $4 per unit, for a total of $12. In contrast, Sandra makes four concessions, worth $4, $3, $2, and $1 per unit, for a total of $10. Both Linda and Sandra tell their counterparts that they have conceded "about all that they can." Sandra is more likely to be believed when she makes this assertion because she has signaled through the *pattern* of her concession making that there is not much left to concede. When Linda claims to have little left to concede, her counterpart is less likely to believe her because the pattern of Linda's concessions (three concessions worth the same amount) suggests that there is plenty left to concede, even though Linda has actually conceded more than Sandra in this example.[17] Note that we have not emphasized the words spoken by Linda and Sandra. *Behaviors* are interpreted by the other party when we negotiate; it is important to signal to the other party with both our behavior and our words that the concessions are almost over.

In multi-issue negotiations, skilled negotiators will also try out different forms of a potential settlement that are worth about the same to them. They recognize, however, that not all issues are worth the same amount to both parties. For example, a negotiator in a purchasing agreement may be interested solely in the total revenue of a package and not care whether it is paid in full without interest within one month or over six months with a financing fee at current interest rates. The time of the payment may be critical if the other party has a cash-flow problem, and the other party may be willing to pay the financing fee for the right to spread the payments over a longer period of time. In fact, different combinations

FIGURE 2.4

Pattern of Concession Making for Two Negotiators

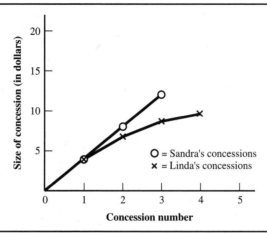

O = Sandra's concessions
✕ = Linda's concessions

of principal, interest'rate, and payback period may have the same value for one party but a quite different value for the other. After trying out different proposals that are worth about the same to them, skilled distributive negotiators will frequently save a final small concession for near the end of the negotiation to "sweeten" the deal.

Final Offer

Eventually a negotiator wants to convey the message that there is no further room for movement—that the present offer is final. A negotiator will probably make such statements as these: "This is all I can do," or "This is as far as I can go." Sometimes, however, it is clear that no simple statement will suffice; an alternative is to use concessions to convey the point. A negotiator might simply let the absence of any further concessions convey the message in spite of urging from the other party. The other party may not recognize at first that the last offer was the final one and might volunteer a further concession to get the other to respond. Finding that no further concession results, the other party may feel betrayed and perceive that the pattern of concession–counterconcession was violated. The resulting bitterness may further complicate negotiations.

One way negotiators may convey the message that "this is the last offer" is by making the last concession substantial. This conveys the message that you are throwing in the remainder of the negotiating range. The final offer has to be large enough to be dramatic, yet not so large that it creates the suspicion that the negotiator has been holding back and that there is more to be had on other issues in the bargaining mix.[18] This final concession may be personalized to the other party ("I went to my boss and got a special deal just for you") and signals that this is the last concession the negotiator will make.

Commitment

A key concept in creating a bargaining position is that of commitment. One definition of commitment is "taking of a bargaining position with some explicit or implicit pledge regarding the future course of action."[19] An example would be a sports agent who, during negotiation, says to a professional sports team, "If we do not get the salary we want, my player will sit out next year." Such an act identifies a position the negotiator insists on achieving and the threat of some future action if that position is not reached. The purpose of a commitment is to remove ambiguity about the actor's intended course of action. By making a commitment, a negotiator signals the intention to take this course of action, make this decision, and pursue this objective—it says, "If you pursue your goals as well, we are likely to come into direct conflict, and either one of us will win or neither of us will achieve our goals." Commitments also reduce the other party's options. They are designed to constrain the other party's choices to a reduced portfolio of options.

A commitment is often interpreted by the other as a threat—if the other doesn't comply or give in, some set of negative consequences will occur. Some commitments can be threats, but others are statements of intended action that leave the responsibility for avoiding mutual disaster in the hands of the other party. A nation that publicly states it is going to invade another country and that war can only be averted if no other nation tries to stop the action is taking a bold and dramatic commitment position. Commitments can also involve future promises such as the following: "If we get this salary increase, we'll agree to have all other points arbitrated as you request."

Because of their nature, commitments are statements that usually require a follow-through in action. A negotiator who threatens consequences (e.g., the player will sit out next year), fails to get what he wanted with the threat, and then does not enact the consequences (e.g., the player reports to training camp) is hardly going to be believed in the future. In addition, a person will suffer a loss of self-esteem after not following through on a publicly made commitment. Hence, once a negotiator makes a commitment, there is strong motivation to hold to it. Because the other party most likely will understand this, a commitment, once believed, will often have a powerful effect on what the other party believes to be possible.[20]

Tactical Considerations in Using Commitments

Like many tools, commitments are two-edged. They may be used to gain the advantages illustrated above, but they may also inextricably fix a negotiator to a particular position or point. Commitments exchange flexibility for certainty of action, but they create difficulties if you want to move to a new position. For example, suppose that after committing yourself to a course of action, additional information indicates that a different position is desirable. Later information shows an earlier estimate of the other party's resistance point to be inaccurate and that there is actually a negative negotiating range. It may be desirable, or even necessary, to shift positions after making a commitment. For these reasons, when you make commitments you should also make contingency plans that allow you to get out of them if necessary. The contingency plans must be secret for the original commitment to be effective. For example, the player's agent might have planned to retire shortly after the expected completion of negotiations. By advancing retirement, the agent can thereby cancel the commitment and leave a new negotiator unencumbered. A purchaser of a house may be able to back away from a commitment to buy by discovering the hitherto unnoticed "cracks in the plaster" in the living room or being unable to obtain financing from the bank.

Commitment may be a useful tool, but it is also advantageous to keep the other party from becoming committed. Further, if the other party should take a committed position, it is to your advantage to keep open ways for the other party to get out of the commitment. We now examine these tactical issues in more detail.

Establishing a Commitment

Given that strong, passionate statements—some of which are pure bluff—are made during negotiation, how does a negotiator establish that a statement is to be understood as a commitment?

A commitment statement has three properties: a high degree of *finality*, a high degree of *specificity*, and a clear statement of *consequences*.[21] A buyer could say "We are going to get a volume discount, or there will be trouble." This statement is far less powerful than the same negotiator saying "We must have a 10 percent volume discount in the next contract, or we will sign with an alternative supplier next month." This latter statement communicates *finality*, how and when the volume discount must be granted; *specificity*, how much of a volume discount is expected; and a clear statement of *consequences*, exactly what will happen if the discount is not given. It is far stronger than the previous statement and much more difficult to get released from. Several ways to create a commitment are discussed below.

1. Public Pronouncement. A commitment statement increases in potency when more people know about it. The sports agent's statement about sitting out the season, if given at the bargaining table, will have a differing impact than one made during a television interview. Some parties in negotiations have called press conferences or placed ads in newspapers or other publications stating what they want and what will or will not happen if they don't get their demands. In each of these situations, the larger the audience, the less likely the commitment will be changed. The effect of the broader social context on negotiations is discussed further in Chapter 7.

2. Linking with an Outside Base. Another way to strengthen a commitment is to link up with an ally. Employees who are dissatisfied with management can form a committee to express these concerns. Industry associations may coalesce to set standards for a product. A variation of this process is to create conditions that make it more difficult for the negotiator creating the commitment to move from her position. For example, by encouraging dedicated colonists to settle on the West Bank near Jerusalem, the Israeli government made it more difficult to concede this land to Jordan, a point they initially wanted to reinforce.

3. Increase the Prominence of Demands. Many things can be done to increase the prominence of commitment statements. If most offers and concessions have been made orally, then writing out a commitment statement may draw attention to it. If prior statements have been written, then using a different size typeface or a different color paper will draw attention to them. Repetition is one of the most powerful ways of making a statement prominent. Using multiple means to convey a commitment hammers a point home. For example, tell the other party of a commitment; then hand him a written statement; then read the statement to him.

4. Reinforce the Threat or Promise. When making a threat, there is the danger of going too far—stating a point so strongly that you look weak or foolish rather than threatening. Statements like "If I don't get this point, I'll see that you don't stay in business another day!" are more likely to be greeted with annoyance and dismissal than to evoke concern and compliance. Long, detailed statements— ones that are highly exaggerated—undermine credibility. In contrast, simple, direct statements of demands, conditions, and consequences are most effective.

Several things can be done to reinforce the implicit or explicit threat in a commitment. One is to review similar circumstances and what the consequences were; another is to make obvious preparations to carry out the threat. Facing the prospect of a strike, companies build up their inventories and move cots and food into their factories; unions build strike funds and give advice to their members on how to get by with less income should there be a strike. Another route is to create and fulfill minor threats in advance, thereby increasing credibility that major threats will be fulfilled. For example, a negotiator could say that "if the progress of these negotiations does not speed up, I am going to take a five-day weekend," and then do just that.

Preventing the Other Party from Committing Prematurely

All the advantages of a committed position work against a negotiator when the other party becomes committed. Therefore, a general strategy is to try to keep the other from becoming committed. People often take committed positions when they become angry or feel pushed to the limit; these commitments are often unplanned and can work to the disadvantage of both parties. Consequently, negotiators should pay careful attention to the other party's level of irritation, anger, and impatience.

Good, sound, deliberate commitments take time to establish, for the reasons already discussed. One way to prevent the other party from establishing a committed position is to deny him or her the opportunity to take this time. In a real estate deal with an option about to run out, a negotiator may use up the time by being unavailable or requiring extensive checking of deeds and boundaries, thereby denying time to the other party to make a case. Another approach to keep the other negotiator from taking a committed position is to ignore or downplay the threat by not acknowledging the other's commitment, or even by making a joke about it. A negotiator might lightheartedly say "You don't really mean that" or "I know you can't be serious about really going through with that" or simply move negotiations along as though the commitment statement had not been heard or understood. If the negotiator can pretend that the other party's statement was not heard or was not understood to be significant, the statement can be ignored at a later point without incurring the consequences that would have occurred had it been taken seriously. Although the other side can still carry out the threat, the belief that it must be carried out (that control of the situation has been given up) may be reduced.

There are times when it is to a negotiator's advantage for the other party to become committed. When the other party takes a position on an issue relatively early in a negotiation, it may be very much to a negotiator's advantage to pin down that position so it will not be changed as the negotiation on other issues progresses. A negotiator may handle this situation in two ways: by pointing out the significance of a commitment when it is made, or by taking notes and keeping track of the other's statements when it is to the negotiator's advantage to do so. An employee might be very upset about the way a particular problem was handled but may say that she will never get upset enough about it to resign. The manager might focus on this point when the statement is made or refer to it later when the employee is even more upset. Both actions are designed to keep the employee on the job in spite of her anger.

Finding Ways to Abandon a Committed Position

Most of the time, a negotiator wants to get the other party out of a committed position, and many times that party may also want to get out of the committed position. How can this be done? One method has already been noted: when establishing a commitment, a negotiator should also plan a private way out. One way is by wording the commitment so that the conditions by which it applied have changed. Sometimes information provided by the other party during negotiations can permit a negotiator to say this: "Given what I've learned from you during this discussion, I see I am going to have to rethink my earlier position." The same could be done for the other party. A negotiator, wanting to make it possible for the other to move from a committed position and yet not lose credibility, might say "Given what I've told you about the facts of the situation [or given this new information], maybe I can help you see that your earlier position no longer holds." Needless to say, the last thing a negotiator wants to do is to embarrass the other party or make judgmental statements about the shift in position; rather, the other party should be given every opportunity to retreat with dignity (see our discussion on face-saving in Chapter 7).

A second way to abandon a commitment is to let the matter die silently. After a lapse of time, a negotiator can make a new proposal in the area of the commitment without mentioning the earlier one. A variation on this process is to make a tentative step in a direction previously excluded by the other's commitment. If the other party, in response to either of these moves, indicates through silence or verbal comment a willingness to let things move in that direction, progress should be pursued.

A third route to take is to restate the commitment in more general terms. The party that wants to move will make a new proposal, changing some of the details to be more in line with her needs, while ostensibly still living with the "general principles" of the earlier wording. For example, the purchasing agent who demanded a 10 percent volume discount may rephrase this statement later to say she needs a significant volume discount. The other party can then explore what level this discount could be.

Last, if the other party backs off from a committed position, it is important to help him minimize any possible damage. One strategy to use in this instance is to attribute the other party's movement to some noble cause. Diplomats can withdraw from a committed position because of their "deep concern for peace and humankind." A party can back off from a point during a real estate transaction to "support the economic well-being of the community." Managers can leave a committed position "for the good of the company."

A committed position is a powerful tool in negotiation; it is also a rigid tool. As such, it must be used with care, and as with any other tool, we must be as alert to ways of denying it to the other party as we are to ways we can use it for ourselves. Unfortunately, far more commitments are made as a result of anger and the desire to stop making concessions than as a result of tactical planning that is clearly thought out. In either case, the essential property of a committed position is to arrange the consequences of an action so that some point is no longer an item of discussion or it can only be negotiated at grave risk to one or both parties. The events or consequences are now inevitable unless stopped at serious risk to one or both sides. The committed position has to be believable, and what has to be believed is that nothing can be done to change the conditions—if X happens, Y is inevitable. Convincing the other party that fate is sealed on the matter at hand is demanding and requires preparation, time, and skill. Consequently, getting out of a committed position is not easy, but it is made simpler by planning a secret means of escape at the time the commitment is being established. Many of the steps a negotiator can use to get out of a commitment can also be used to help the other party get out of a committed position or, even better, to keep the other from establishing one in the first place.

Typical Hardball Tactics

Many popular books of negotiation emphasize the thrill of using hardball negotiation tactics to beat the other party.[22] Such tactics are designed to pressure targeted parties to do things they would not otherwise do, and their use usually disguises the user's adherence to a decidedly distributive bargaining approach. It is not clear how often these tactics work, but they work best against poorly prepared negotiators. They also *can* backfire. Many people find these tactics offensive and are motivated for revenge when they are used against them. Many negotiators consider these tactics out-of-bounds for any negotiation situation. We do not recommend the use of any of the following techniques. In fact, it has been our experience that these tactics do more harm than good in negotiations. They are much more difficult to enact than they are to read about, and each tactic involves risk for the person using it, including harm to reputation, losing the deal, negative publicity, and dealing with the other party's revenge. But it is important that negotiators understand hardball tactics and how they work so they can recognize and understand them if they are the targeted recipients.

We will now discuss some of the more frequently described hardball tactics and their weaknesses. After we describe the tactics we will discuss the various options that negotiators have for dealing with others who use such tactics against them.

Good Guy/Bad Guy

This tactic is named after a police interrogation technique where two officers (one kind, the other tough) take turns questioning a suspect, and can frequently be seen in episodes of popular television series such as *Law and Order* and *NYPD Blue.* The use of this tactic in negotiations typically goes as follows: The first negotiator ("bad guy") presents a tough opening position, punctuated with threats, obnoxious behavior, and intransigence. The negotiator then leaves the room to make an important telephone call or to "cool off"—frequently at a partner's suggestion. While out of the room, the other negotiator ("good guy") tries to reach a quick agreement before the bad guy returns and makes life difficult for both negotiators. A more subtle form of this tactic is to assign the bad guy the role of speaking only when the negotiations are headed in a direction that the team does not want; as long as things are going well, the good guy does the talking.

There are many weaknesses to using this tactic. It is relatively transparent and can be countered by the other party's willingness to discuss the tactic openly and describe what the negotiators are doing. It is also much harder to enact than it is to describe; typically, it alienates the targeted party, and frequently more energy is directed towards making the tactic work smoothly than towards accomplishing the negotiation goals.

Highball/Lowball

The negotiator using this tactic starts with a ridiculously high (or low) opening offer. The theory is that such an offer will cause the other party to reevaluate his or her own opening offer and move closer to the resistance point. The real danger with this strategy is that the other party will halt negotiations because they think negotiating is a waste of time. Even if the targeted person continues to negotiate after receiving a highball (lowball) offer, however, it takes a skilled negotiator to be able to justify the high opening offer and to finesse the negotiation back to a point where the other side will be willing to make a major concession toward the outrageous bid.

Bogey

Negotiators using this tactic pretend that an issue of little or no importance to them is quite important. Later in the negotiation this issue can then be traded for major concessions on issues that are actually important to the negotiator. This technique is most effective when the negotiator can identify an issue that is quite important to the other side but of little value to the negotiator. For example, a seller may have a product in the warehouse ready for delivery. When negotiating with a purchasing agent, however, the seller may ask for large concessions to process a "rush order" for the client. The seller can reduce the size of the concession demanded for the rush order in exchange for concessions on other issues, such as the price or the size of the order. Again, this is a difficult tactic to enact. Typically, the other party will take you seriously when you are trying to make a case for the issue that you want to bogey, and this can lead to a very awkward situation where both negotiators may be arguing against their true wishes (the other party is asking for large concessions on other issues to give you the bogey issue that you really don't want, and you are spending time evaluating offers and making arguments for an issue that you know you do not want).

The Nibble

Negotiators using this tactic ask for a proportionally small concession (say, 1 to 2 percent of the total profit of the deal) on an item that hasn't been discussed previously in order to close the deal. Herb Cohen describes the nibble as follows: After trying many different suits in a clothing store, tell the clerk that you will take a given suit if he throws in a tie for free.[23] The tie is the nibble. Cohen claims that he usually gets the tie. In a business context, the tactic occurs like this: After negotiating a deal for a considerable amount of time and being close to an agreement, a negotiator asks to include a clause that hasn't been discussed previously and that will cost the other party a proportionally small amount. This amount is too small to lose the deal over, but large enough to upset the other party. And that is the major weakness with the nibble. It is a great motivator for revenge because many people feel that the party using the nibble has not bargained in good faith (as part of a fair negotiation process, all items to be discussed during the negotiation should be placed on the agenda early). Even if the party claims to "be very embarrassed about forgetting this item until now" and that she "must have this item or lose my job," the party who has been nibbled will not feel good about the process and will often seek revenge in future negotiations.

Chicken

This tactic is named after the 1950's contest, portrayed in the James Dean movie *Rebel without a Cause,* of driving cars at one another or towards a cliff until one person swerves to avoid disaster. The person who swerves is labeled a chicken and the other person is treated like a hero. Negotiators who use this tactic combine a large bluff with a threatened action to force the other party to chicken out and give them what they want. In labor–management negotiations, management may tell the union that if they do not agree to the current contract offer, management will close the factory and go out of business (or move to another state or country). Clearly this is a high-stakes gamble. Management must be willing to follow through on their threat—if the union calls their bluff and they do not follow through, they will not be believed in the future. However, how can the union take the risk and call the bluff? If management is telling the truth, they may actually close and move elsewhere. If management is using the chicken tactic and the union calls their bluff, management may feel a great deal of pressure to follow through with it. The real weakness with this tactic is that negotiation is turned into a high-stakes game where reality and postured negotiation positions are difficult to distinguish from each other. For instance, in the 1990s when organizations downsize and retrench by asking for givebacks from their employees, are they using the chicken tactic? Or would they really close their organizations? We frequently cannot know for sure because the circumstances must be grave in order for this tactic to be believable. But it is precisely when circumstances are grave that one may be most tempted to use this as a tactic rather than as a true reflection of the circumstances.

Intimidation

Many tactics can be gathered under the general label of intimidation. What they have in common is that they all attempt to force the other party to agree by employing various emotional ploys, usually anger and fear. For example, the other party may deliberately use anger to indicate the seriousness of a position. One of the authors of this book had the following experience:

> Once while I was negotiating with a car salesman, he lost his temper, destroyed his written notes, told me to sit down and listen to him, and explained in a loud voice that this was the best deal in the city and if I did not accept it that evening I should not bother returning to that dealership and wasting his time. I didn't buy the car and I

haven't been back, nor do I suspect have any of the students in my negotiation classes, to whom I relate this story every year! I suspect that the salesman was trying to intimidate me into agreeing to the deal and realized that if I went elsewhere his deal would not look as good. What he didn't realize was that I had asked the accountant at the dealership for further information about the deal and had found that he had lied about the value of a trade-in; he really lost his cool when I exposed the lie!

Another form of intimidation includes increasing the appearance of legitimacy. When there is a high degree of legitimacy, there are set policies or procedures for resolving disputes. Negotiators who do not have such policies or procedures available may try to invent them and impose them on the other negotiator and make the process appear legitimate. For example, policies that are written in manuals or preprinted official forms and agreements are less likely to be questioned than those that are delivered verbally.[24] For example, long and detailed loan contracts used by banks for consumer loans are seldom read completely.[25] The higher the appearance of legitimacy, the less likely the other party will be to question the process being followed or the contract terms being proposed.

Finally, guilt can also be used as a form of intimidation. Negotiators can question the other party's integrity or the other's lack of trust in them. The purpose of this tactic is to place the other party on the defensive so he or she is dealing with the issues of guilt or trust rather than discussing the substance of the negotiation.

Aggressive Behavior

There are tactics similar to intimidation that include various ways of being aggressive in pushing your position or attacking the other person's position. These tactics include the relentless push for further concessions ("You can do better than that"), asking for the best offer ("Let's not waste any more time. What is the most that you will pay?"), and asking the other party to explain and justify his or her proposals item by item or line by line ("What is your cost breakdown?"). The negotiator using these techniques is signaling a hard-nosed, intransigent position and trying to force the other side to make many concessions in order to reach an agreement.

Dealing with Typical Hardball Tactics

The negotiator dealing with a party who uses the hardball tactics described above has many choices about how to respond. A good strategic response to these tactics requires that the negotiator identify the tactic quickly and understand what it is and how it works. Most of the tactics are designed either to enhance the appearance of the bargaining position of the person using the tactic or to detract from the appearance of the options available to the other party. Choosing the best way to respond to a tactic depends on your goals and the broader context of the negotiation (who are you negotiating with? what are your alternatives and your BATNA?). No one response will work in all situations to meet your goals. We will now discuss some options that negotiators can use to respond to typical hardball tactics.[26]

Ignore Them

Although ignoring a hardball tactic may appear to be a "weak" response, in fact it can be a very powerful way to deal with hardball tactics. It takes a lot of energy to use some of these hardball tactics (good guy/bad guy, for instance), and while the other side is using energy to play these games, you can be using your energy to work on satisfying your needs. Not responding to a threat is often the best way of dealing with it. Pretend you didn't hear. Change the subject and get the other party involved in a new topic. Call a break, and upon returning, switch topics. All these options can deflate the effects of a threat and allow you to press on your agenda while the other party is trying to decide what trick to use next.

Discuss Them

Fisher, Ury, and Patton suggest that a good way to deal with hardball tactics is to negotiate the negotiation process (how you are to conduct the negotiations) before continuing to negotiate the substance of the talks.[27] Offer to change to less-aggressive methods of negotiating. Explicitly acknowledge that they are tough negotiators and that you can be tough too. Then suggest that you both change and try more productive methods that can allow you both to gain. Fisher, Ury, and Patton suggest that negotiators separate people from the problem and then be "hard on the problem, soft on the people." It doesn't hurt to remind the other negotiator of this from time to time during the negotiation.

Respond in Kind

It is always possible to respond to a hardball tactic with your own tactic. Although this response can frequently result in chaos and hard feelings, it is not an option that should be dismissed out of hand. Once the smoke clears, both parties will realize that they are skilled in the use of hardball tactics and may recognize that it is time to try something different. This tactic may be most useful when dealing with another party who is testing your resolve or as a response to exaggerated positions taken in negotiations. A participant in a recent negotiation seminar told one of the authors the following story about bargaining for a carpet in a northern African country:

> I knew that the value of the carpet was about $2,000 because I had been looking at carpets throughout my trip. I found the carpet that I wanted and made sure not to appear too interested. I discussed some other carpets with the vendor before moving on to the carpet that I really wanted. When I asked him the price of this carpet, he replied $9,000. I replied that I would give him *negative* $5,000. We bargained for a while and I bought the carpet for $2,000.

The purchaser in this negotiation clearly responded to a hardball tactic with one of his own. When asked if he felt comfortable with his opening bid, he responded:

> Sure. Why not? The seller knew the value of the carpet was about $2,000. If anything, he seemed to respect me when I bargained this way. If I had opened with a positive number I would have ended up having to pay more than the carpet was worth. And I really wanted the carpet.

Co-Opt the Other Party

One way to deal with negotiators who use aggressive hardball tactics is to try to befriend them before they use the tactics. This approach is built on the theory that it is much more difficult to attack a friend than an enemy. If you can stress what you have in common with the other party and find another element upon which to place the blame ("the system," "foreign competition"), then you may be able to sidetrack the other party before he even begins.

Summary

In this chapter we examined the basic structure of distributive, or competitive bargaining situations and some of the strategies and tactics used in distributive bargaining. The basic structure of distributive bargaining consists of setting your own opening, target, and resistance points. You soon learn the other party's starting points and find out her target points directly or through inference. Usually you won't know resistance points, the point beyond which a party will not go, until late in negotiation because the other party often carefully conceals them. All points are important, but understanding the resistance points is most critical. The spread between the parties' resistance points defines the bargaining range. If positive, it defines the area of negotiation, with each party working to get as much of the bargaining range for himself as possible. If negative, successful negotiation may be impossible.

It is rare that a negotiation includes only one item; more typically, there is a set of items referred to as a bargaining mix. Each item in a bargaining mix can have opening, target, and resistance points. The bargaining mix may provide opportunities for bundling issues together, logrolling, or mutually concessionary behavior.

Examining the structure of distributive bargaining reveals many options for a negotiator to achieve a successful resolution, most of which fall within two broad efforts: to influence the other party's belief in what is possible and to learn as much as possible about the other party's position, particularly about the resistance points. The negotiator's basic strategy is to conclude the final settlement as close to the other party's resistance point as possible. The tactics used to achieve this goal involve getting information about the opposition and its positions, convincing members of the other party to change their minds about their ability to achieve their own goals, and promoting your own objectives as desirable, necessary, or even inevitable.

Distributive bargaining is basically a conflict situation, wherein parties seek their own advantage—in part through concealing information, attempting to mislead, or using manipulative actions. All these tactics can easily escalate interaction from calm discussion to bitter hostility. Even so, negotiation is the attempt to resolve a conflict without force, without fighting. Further, to be successful, both parties to the negotiation must feel at the end that the outcome was the best that they could achieve and that it is worth accepting and supporting. Hence, negotiation is a process that requires not only skill, but also—and even more important—understanding and good planning.

End Notes

1. Walton and McKersie (1965).
2. Raiffa (1982).
3. Fisher and Ertel (1995).
4. For a more extensive treatment of this subject, see Walton and McKersie (1965, pp. 59–82).
5. Karrass (1974).
6. See Roth, Murnighan, and Schoumaker (1988) and Walton and McKersie (1965).
7. Jacobs (1951).
8. Cohen (1980).
9. See Tutzauer (1992).
10. See Chertkoff and Conley (1967); Donohue (1981); Hinton, Hamner, and Pohlan (1974); Komorita and Brenner (1968); Liebert, Smith, and Hill (1968); Pruitt and Syna (1985); and Weingart, Thompson, Bazerman, and Carroll (1990).
11. For further discussion of these points, see Pruitt (1981) and Tutzauer (1991).
12. See Putnam and Jones (1982) and Yukl (1974).
13. Northrup (1964) and Selekman, Selekman, and Fuller (1958).
14. Baranowski and Summers (1972), Crumbaugh and Evans (1967), Deutsch (1958), and Gruder and Duslak (1973).
15. Rubin and Brown (1975, pp. 277–78).
16. Froman and Cohen (1970), Neale and Bazerman (1991), and Pruitt (1981).
17. See Yukl (1974).
18. Walton and McKersie (1965).
19. Ibid., p. 82.
20. Pruitt (1981).

21. Walton and McKersie (1965).

22. See Aaronson (1989), Brooks and Odiorne (1984), Cohen (1980), and Schatzki (1981).

23. Cohen (1980).

24. Ibid.

25. Hendon and Hendon (1990).

26. For extended discussion of these points, see Ury (1991) and Fisher, Ury, and Patton (1991).

27. See Fisher, Ury, and Patton (1991) and Ury (1991).

3   STRATEGY AND TACTICS OF INTEGRATIVE NEGOTIATION

Introduction

Periodically, we read of tragic fires in restaurants, night clubs, or theaters that kill large numbers of people. Often there is panic; in the rush to escape, exits are blocked, trapping many and causing unnecessary deaths. People seem to act as if their lives depended upon being first out of the building. In contrast, most of us are taught from our earliest school days that there is ample time for everyone to leave a burning building safely if people move out in an orderly fashion. As children, we were urged to have a shared concern to get everyone out of the building, to collaborate rather than to compete. The need for orderly, cooperative behavior comes not from ideals, but from the reality that cooperation is often essential to survival.

The same principles are true for negotiation. In bargaining, there need not be winners and losers; everyone can be a winner. Rather than assume that all conflicts are win–lose events, negotiators can learn that win–win solutions are possible. These assumptions will lead them to search for the win–win options, and often they will find them. This win–win approach to negotiation is called *integrative negotiation.*

In distributive bargaining, the goals of the parties are initially irreconcilable—or at least they appear that way to the parties. Central to the conflict is the belief that there is a limited, controlled amount of key resources available—a "fixed pie" situation (see Chapter 5 for a discussion of cognitive biases in negotiation). Both parties may want to be the winner; both may want more than half of what is available. For example, both management (on behalf of the stockholders) and labor (on behalf of the rank and file) believe that they deserve the larger share of the company's profits. Both may want to win on the same dimension, such as the financial package or control of certain policy decisions. In these situations, their goals are mutually exclusive and hence lead to conflict.

TABLE 3.1   **Processes That Distinguish Integrative from Distributive Negotiation**

	Integrative Negotiation	*Distributive Negotiation*
Flow of information	Create a free and open flow; share information openly	Conceal information, or use it selectively and strategically
Understanding the other	Attempt to understand what the other side really wants and needs	Make no effort to understand the other side, or use the information to gain strategic advantage
Attention to commonalties and differences	Emphasized common goals, objectives, interests	Emphasize differences in goals, objectives, interests
Focus on solutions	Search for solutions that meet the needs of both (all) sides	Search for solutions that meet own needs or even block the other from meeting their needs

In contrast, in integrative negotiation the goals of the parties are not mutually exclusive. If one side pursues its goals, that does not necessarily preclude the other from achieving its goals. One party's gain is not necessarily at the other party's expense. The fundamental structure of an integrative negotiation situation is that it is possible for both sides to achieve their objectives.[1] Although the conflict may appear initially to be win–lose to the parties—and may create the same kind of competitive panic we described in the fire example—discussion and mutual exploration will usually suggest win–win alternatives. The strategy by which negotiators discover these alternatives is the focus of this chapter. Our description will draw heavily from the writings of several authors who have written about the integrative process in great detail.[2] In addition, we will note recent research findings that have affirmed the validity of particular strategies and tactics.

An Overview of the Integrative Negotiation Process

Past history, biased perceptions, and the truly distributive aspects of bargaining often make it remarkable that integrative agreements occur at all. But they do occur, largely because negotiators work hard to overcome the inhibiting factors and to assertively search for common ground. The following key processes are central to achieving almost all integrative agreements and are distinctively different from the processes pursued in distributive bargaining (see also Table 3.1).

Creating a Free Flow of Information

There is ample evidence from research indicating that effective information exchange promotes the development of good integrative solutions.[3] For this open dialogue to occur, negotiators must be willing to reveal their true objectives and to listen carefully to the other negotiator. In short, negotiators must create the conditions for a free and open discussion of all related issues and concerns. This willingness to share information is significantly different from a distributive bargaining situation, in which the parties distrust one another, conceal and manipulate information, and attempt to learn information about the other for their own competitive advantage.

Attempting to Understand the Other Negotiator's Real Needs and Objectives

As we noted earlier, negotiators differ in their values and preferences. What one side needs and wants may or may not be what the other side needs and wants. If you are to help satisfy another's needs, you must first understand them. Hence, throughout the process of sharing information about preferences and priorities, the parties must make a true effort to understand what the other side really wants to achieve. Again, this is in contrast to distributive bargaining, where the negotiator either makes no effort to understand what the other side really wants or uses this information to challenge, undermine, or even deny the other the opportunity to have those needs and objectives met.

Emphasizing the Commonalties between the Parties and Minimizing the Differences

To sustain a free flow of information and to make an effort to truly understand the other's needs and objectives, negotiators may also require a different outlook or frame of reference. (We will address frame of reference later in this chapter.) In distributive bargaining, the parties focus on achieving their own individual objectives. However, in integrative negotiation, individual goals may need to be redefined as best achievable through collaborative efforts that achieve a broader collective goal. Sometimes the collective goal is clear and obvious. For example, politicians in the same party may recognize that their petty squabbles must be put aside to assure the party's victory at the polls. The phrase "Politics makes strange bedfellows" suggests that the quest for victory can unite political enemies into larger coalitions that will be assured of political victory. Similarly, managers who are quarreling over cutbacks in their individual department budgets may need to recognize that unless all departments sustain budget cuts, they will be unable to change an unprofitable firm into a profitable one. At other times, the larger goal is not so clear, nor is it as easy to keep in sight. For example, a friend of ours was a consultant to a company that was closing down a major manufacturing plant and, at the same time, opening several others in different parts of the country. The company was perfectly willing to transfer employees to new plants and let them take their seniority with them up to the time of the announced move; the union agreed to this arrangement. However, conflict developed because some employees were able to transfer immediately whereas others were needed to close and dismantle the old plant. Because workers acquired seniority in the new plant based on the date they arrived (and seniority might affect decisions about layoffs, pay raises, etc.), those who stayed to close the old plant would have less seniority in the new plant compared to those who moved earlier. The union wanted everyone to go at the same time to avoid this inequity. Management was adamant that this was unworkable. In the resulting argument, both parties lost sight of their larger goal—to transfer all employees who wanted to move to the new plant with their seniority intact. Only by constantly stressing this larger goal were the parties able to maintain a focus on commonalties that eventually led to a solution. Transferred workers were allowed to select in advance the jobs they moved into, and their seniority was transferred to those jobs when the choice to move was made, not when the physical move actually occurred.

Searching for Solutions That Meet the Goals and Objectives of Both Sides

Finally, successful integrative negotiation requires that the negotiators search for solutions that meet the objectives and needs of both (all) sides. In this process, negotiators must be firm but flexible[4]—they must be firm about their primary interests and needs, but flexible about the manner in which these interests and needs are met through solutions. When the parties have traditionally held a combative, competitive orientation toward each other, they are more prone to be concerned only with their own objectives. In this competitive interaction, any concern with the other's objectives may be in one of two forms: first, to make sure that what the other obtains does not take away from one's own accomplishments; second, to attempt to block the other from obtaining objectives because of a strong desire to win and even defeat the opponent. In contrast, successful integrative negotiation requires each negotiator, not only to define and pursue her own goals, but also to be mindful of the other's goals and to search for solutions that will meet and satisfy the goals of both sides. Outcomes are measured by the degree to which they meet both negotiators' goals. They are *not* measured by determining whether one party is "doing better" than the other. If the objective of one party is to get more than the other, integrative negotiation is difficult at best; if both strive to get more than the other, integrative negotiation is impossible.

In summary, successful integrative negotiation requires a process fundamentally different from that of distributive negotiation. Negotiators must attempt to probe below the surface of their opponent's position to discover underlying needs. They must create a free and open flow of information, and they must use their desire to satisfy both sides as the perspective from which to structure their dialogue. If negotiators do not have this perspective—if they approach the problem and their opponent in win–lose terms—integrative negotiation cannot occur.

Key Stages in the Integrative Negotiation Process

There are four major steps in the integrative negotiation process: identifying and defining the problem, understanding the problem and bringing interests and needs to the surface, generating alternative solutions to the problem, and choosing a specific solution from among those alternatives.

Identify and Define the Problem

The problem identification step is often the most difficult one; this is even truer when several parties are involved. Consider the following example:

> In a large electronics plant, there was considerable difficulty with one of the subassemblies (component parts) used in the final assembly department. Various pins and fittings that held the assembly in place were getting bent and distorted. When this happened to a unit, it would be laid aside as a reject. At the end of the month, these rejects would be returned to be reworked by the department that built them. The material to be reworked often arrived at the subassembly department at a time when workers there were under pressure to meet end-of-the-month schedules; in addition, they were often low on parts. As a result, the reworking effort had to be done in a rush and on overtime. The extra cost of overtime and expediting the rush work presented an additional problem because it did not fit into the standard cost-allocation system. The manager of the subassembly department did not want the costs allocated to his overhead charge. The manager of the final assembly department insisted that he should not pay the additional cost because his unit did not cause the problem; he argued that subassembly should bear the cost because their poor work originally caused the problem. The subassembly department manager countered that the parts were in good condition when they left his area and that it was the poor workmanship in the final assembly area that created the damage. The actual costs were relatively small; what *really* concerned both parties was setting a long-term precedent for paying the costs of rework.

Eventually, an integrative solution was reached. During any given month, the subassembly department had a number of short slack-time periods. Arrangements were made to return damaged subassemblies in small batches, allowing them to be worked on during the slack periods. It also became clear that many people in the final assembly department did not fully understand the parts they were handling, which may have contributed to some of the damage that was all blamed on subassembly. Arrangements were made for some of these people to be temporarily transferred to the subassembly department during slack periods in order to learn more about that department and to pick up some of the rush orders in that department.

This example helps us to identify a number of key aspects of the problem definition process.[5]

1. Define the problem in a way that is mutually acceptable to both sides. Ideally, parties should enter the integrative negotiation process with few if any preconceptions about the solution and with open minds about the other negotiator's needs. As a problem is defined jointly, it should accurately reflect both parties' needs and priorities. Regrettably, this is not what we usually encounter. An understandable and widely held fear about integrative negotiation is that during the problem definition process, the other party is manipulating information and discussion in order to state the problem for his own advantage. For positive problem solving to occur, both parties must be committed to stating the problem in neutral terms. The problem statement must be mutually acceptable to both sides and not stated so that it favors the preferences or priorities of one side over the other. The parties may be required to work the problem statement over several times until each side agrees upon its wording.

2. Keep the problem statement clean and simple. The major focus of an integrative agreement is to solve the primary problem. Secondary issues and concerns should be raised only if they are inextricably bound up with the primary problem. Discipline is required to identify the less-important issues and keep them out of the picture. This approach is in stark contrast to the distributive bargaining process, in which the parties are encouraged to "beef up" their positions by bringing in a large number of secondary issues and concerns so they can trade these items off during the hard bargaining phase. If there are several issues on the table in an integrative negotiation, the parties may want to clearly identify the linkages among the issues and decide whether they will be approached as separate problems (which may be packaged together later) or redefined as one larger problem.

3. State the problem as a goal and identify the obstacles to attaining this goal. The problem should be defined as a *specific* goal to be attained (*what* we want to achieve). However, it is important for the parties to create this specific goal mutually, rather than having one side introduce it unilaterally. If only one side introduces it and defines it specifically, it will be perceived by the other as a distributive bargaining tactic. Moreover, problem definition should then proceed to specify what obstacles must be overcome for the goal to be attained. For example, in the previous example, the problem might be defined as "minimizing the number of rejects." This is not as clear and explicit as "cutting the number of rejects in half." Moreover, although this is a noble statement of a goal, greater progress could be made if the parties would specify what they need to know about how the product is made, how defects occur, what must be done to repair defects, and so on.

4. Depersonalize the problem. As we have pointed out earlier, when parties are engaged in conflict, they tend to become evaluative and judgmental. They view their own actions, strategies, and preferences in a positive light and the other party's actions, strategies, and preferences in a negative light. As a result, when negotiators attempt the integrative negotiation process, their evaluative judgments of the value or worth of the opponent's preferences can get in the way of clear and dispassionate thinking, simply because the other happens to own those preferences (see Chapter 5 for a discussion of reactive devaluation). Viewing the situation as "your point of view is wrong and mine is right" inhibits the integrative negotiation process because we cannot attack the problem without attacking the person who "owns" the problem. In contrast, by depersonalizing the definition of the problem—stating, for example, that "there is a difference of viewpoints on this problem"—both sides can approach the difference as a problem "out there," rather than as one they personally own.

5. Separate the problem definition from the search for solutions. Finally, we will repeat the maxim that every discussion of the problem-solving process stresses: Don't jump to solutions until the problem is fully defined. In distributive bargaining, negotiators are encouraged to state the problem in terms of their preferred solution and to make concessions from this most desired alternative. In contrast, the integrative negotiation process cannot work unless negotiators avoid premature solutions (which probably favor one side or the other). Negotiators should fully define the problem and examine all the possible alternative solutions.

Understand the Problem Fully—Identify Interests and Needs

Many writers on negotiation—most particularly, Roger Fisher and William Ury in their popular book *Getting to Yes*—have stressed that a key to achieving an integrative agreement is the ability of the parties to get at each other's *interests*.[6] Interests are different from positions in that interests are the underlying concerns, needs, desires, or fears behind a negotiator's position that motivate the negotiator to take that position. These writers argue that although negotiators may have difficulty satisfying each other's specific positions, an understanding of underlying interests may permit them to invent solutions that meet those interests. In this section, we will first define interests more fully, and then discuss how understanding them may be critical to effective integrative negotiation.

An example told by Fisher, Ury, and Patton reveals the essence of the difference between interests and positions:

> Consider the story of two men quarreling in a library. One wants the window open and the other wants it closed. They bicker back and forth about how much to leave it open: a crack, halfway, three-quarters of the way. No solution satisfies them both.
>
> Enter the librarian. She asks one why he wants the window open. "To get some fresh air." She asks the other why he wants it closed. "To avoid the draft." After thinking a minute, she opens wide a window in the next room, bringing in fresh air without a draft.[7]

As the authors point out, this is a classic example of the parties' negotiating over positions and failing to understand underlying interests. Their positions are "window open" and "window closed." If they continue to pursue positional bargaining, the set of possible outcomes can either be a victory for the one who wants the window open, a victory for the one who wants it shut, or some form of a compromise in which *neither* gets what he wants. Note that a compromise here is more a form of lose–lose than win–win for these bargainers because one party believes that he won't get *enough* fresh air with the window open halfway, whereas the other views it as a loss because *any* opening will create a draft. The librarian's questions transform the dispute by focusing on *why* each man wants the window open or closed: to get fresh air or to avoid a draft. Understanding these interests enables the librarian to invent a solution that meets the interests of both sides—a solution that was not at all apparent when they continued to argue over their positions.

In this description, the key word is *why*—why they want what they want. Interests are motivators—the underlying needs, concerns, and desires that lead us to set a particular position. When we begin negotiation, we usually lay our position or demands on the table; and as we have pointed out, this position or these demands have emerged from a planning process in which we decided what we wanted and then specified opening bids, targets, and walkaway points. In distributive bargaining, we trade these points and positions back and forth, attempting to achieve a settlement as close to our target as possible. However, in integrative negotiation, we need to pursue the negotiator's thinking and logic to determine the factors that motivated her to arrive at those points. The presumption is that if both parties understand the motivating factors for the other, they may recognize possible compatibilities in interests that permit them to invent positions which both will endorse as an acceptable settlement. Consider the following dialogue between a company recruiter and a job applicant over starting salary:

> *Recruiter:* What were you thinking about as a starting salary?
> *Applicant:* I would like $40,000.
> *Recruiter:* We can only offer $35,000.
> *Applicant:* That's not acceptable.

Thus far, the parties have only laid positions on the table. They are $5,000 apart. Moreover, the applicant may be afraid to positionally bargain (Chapter 2) with the new employer, whereas the recruiter may be afraid that the applicant—who she very much wants to hire—will walk out. Now let us revise their dialogue to help them focus on interests.

> *Recruiter:* $40,000 is a problem for our company. Can you tell me why you decided you wanted $40,000?
> *Applicant:* Well, I have lots of education loans to pay off, and I will need to pay for a few more courses to finish my degree. I can't really afford to pay these bills and help my family live comfortably for less than $40,000.
> *Recruiter:* Our company has a program to help new employees refinance their education loans. In addition, we also have a program to provide tuition assistance for new courses if the courses you need to take are related to your job. Would these programs help you with your problem?
> *Applicant:* Yes!

Thus, the recruiter was able to bring the applicant's interests—paying off education loans and future education costs—to the surface and offer a financial package that met the needs of both the recruiter's company and the applicant. Similarly, the applicant might have asked why the company could only pay $35,000 and discovered that it was company policy to not offer more than this to any applicant with the same qualifications. However, the question would also have revealed that the company can pay performance bonuses and would be willing to review the salary after six months on the job. This information may well enable the applicant to make $40,000 by the end of the first year, and thus have her financial goal met.

Types of Interests. David Lax and Jim Sebenius, in their book *The Manager as Negotiator,* have suggested that several types of interests may be at stake in a negotiation.[8] Each type of interest may also be intrinsic, in that the parties value it for its essence; or be instrumental, in that the parties value it because it helps them derive other outcomes in the future.

Substantive interests are the types of interests we have just been discussing. These are the interests that relate to the focal issues under negotiation—economic and financial issues such as price or rate, or the substance of a negotiation such as the division of resources. These interests may be intrinsic or instrumental; in the first case, we want something because it is intrinsically satisfying to us, whereas in the second case, it helps us achieve a longer-range goal. Thus, the job applicant may want $40,000 *both* because the salary affirms her intrinsic sense of personal worth in the marketplace, and also because it instrumentally contributes toward paying off her education loans.

Process interests are related to the way we settle this dispute. One party may pursue distributive bargaining because he sees negotiation as a competition and enjoys the strategic game of wits that comes from nose-to-nose, hard-line bargaining. Another party may be negotiating because she believes she has not been consulted in the past, and she wants to have some say in how a key problem is resolved. In this latter case, the issues under discussion may be less important to the parties than the opportunity for them to be asked their views and invited to the negotiating table.[9] Process interests can also be both intrinsic and instrumental. Thus, in the voice example, having a say may be intrinsically important to a group in order to affirm their legitimacy and worth and the key role they play in the organization; it can also be instrumentally important, in that if they are successful in gaining voice in this negotiation, they may also be able to demonstrate that they should be invited back into the negotiation on a wide variety of other related issues in the future.

Relationship interests mean that one or both parties value their relationship with each other and do not want to take actions that will harm or damage the relationship. Intrinsic relationship-interests value the relationship both for its existence and for the pleasure or fulfillment that sustaining the relationship creates. Instrumental relationship-interests exist when the parties derive positive benefits from the relationship and do not wish to endanger future benefits by souring it.

Finally, Lax and Sebenius point out that the parties may have *interests in principles.* These principles—what is fair, what is right, what is acceptable, what is ethical, or what has been done in the past and should be done in the future—may be deeply held by the parties and serve as the dominant guides to their action. (These principles are often the "intangibles" we described in Chapter 1.) These interests can also be intrinsic, valued because of their inherent worth, or instrumental, valued because they can be applied instrumentally to a variety of future situations and scenarios. Bringing these interests in principles to the surface will lead the parties to explicitly discuss the principles at stake and to invent solutions consistent with it. For example, suppose three students (who are also good friends) collaborate on an essay and submit it for a major prize competition. Two of the students contributed equally, and together they did 90 percent of the work. The three students win the prize of $300. The issue is how to split the prize money. Obviously, one way to split it is for each to take $100. But if they split it based on what they each contributed, the two hard-working students would get $135 each and the third student would get $30. However, separately or together, they may also decide that it is not worth fighting over the workload—they don't want to alienate their third friend, or the difference in money is trivial—and simply decide to split the prize into $100 parts. Only by discussing the interests at stake—principles about what is fair in this situation and their relationship—can they arrive at a solution that divides the prize, minimizes animosity, and maintains their relationship.

Some Observations on Interests. Based on this discussion, we may make several observations about interests and types of interests:

1. **There may be more than one type of interest in a dispute.** Parties can have more than substantive interests about the issues—they can also care deeply about process, the relationship, or the principles at stake. Note that "interests as principles" effectively cuts across substantive, procedural, and relationship interests as well, so that the categories are not necessarily exclusive.

2. **Parties can differ on the type of interests at stake.** One party may care deeply about the specific issues under discussion, whereas the other cares about how the issues are resolved—questions of principle or process. Bringing these different interests to the surface may enable the parties to see that in fact they care about very different things, and thus they can invent a solution that addresses the interests of both sides.

3. **Interests are often based in more deeply rooted human needs or values.** Several authors have suggested that frameworks for understanding basic human needs and values are most helpful for understanding interests. These frameworks suggest that needs are hierarchical and that satisfaction of the more basic or lower-order needs will be more vigorously argued and defended in negotiation. For example, Gerard Nierenberg, a

popular writer on negotiation, proposed a model of negotiation based on Maslow's well-known hierarchy of needs.[10] In this hierarchy, behavior to satisfy physiological and safety (security) needs will take precedence over higher-order needs such as recognition, respect, affirmation, and self-actualization. Others have suggested that combat in many international disputes is so intense because it reflects the deep underlying needs of the parties for nationalism, security, and the protection of ethnic and national identity. [11]

4. **Interests can change.** Like positions on issues, interests can change over time. What was important to the parties last week—or even 20 minutes ago—may not be important now. Interaction between the parties can put some interests to rest, but it may raise others. Thus, the parties must continually be attentive to changes in their own interests and the interests of the other side. As we will point out, when parties begin to talk about things in a different way—when the language or emphasis changes—it may indicate a change in interests.

5. **Getting at interests.** There are numerous ways to get at interests. Sometimes we are not even sure of our own interests. In these cases, we should be asking ourselves not only, "What do I want (from this negotiation)?" but also "What do I *really* want?" "Why is that important to me?" "What will achieving that help me do?" "What will happen if I don't achieve my objective?" Listening to your own inner voices—fears, aspirations, hopes, desires—is important to bring your own interests to the surface.

The same dialogue is essential in clarifying the other party's interests. Asking probing questions (why questions) and listening carefully to the other party's language, emotions, nonverbal behavior, and the like, are the essential keys to the process. We might also want to distinguish between intrinsic interests, which need to be satisfied as ends in themselves, and instrumental interests, which help to get other outcomes. In both cases, once we understand these interests, we may then be able to invent a variety of ways to satisfy them through alternatives that are also acceptable to us. The result is a mutually satisfactory solution.

Generate Alternative Solutions

The search for alternatives is the creative phase of integrative negotiations. Once the parties have agreed on a common definition of the problem and have understood each other's interests, they can generate a variety of alternative solutions in the next phase of negotiations. The objective is to create a list of options or possible solutions that solve the problem; selecting from among those options will be their task in the final phase.

A number of techniques have been suggested to help negotiators generate alternative solutions. These approaches fall into two general categories. The first approach requires the negotiators to redefine, recast, or reframe the problem (or problem set) so as to create win–win alternatives out of what earlier appeared to be a win–lose problem. In contrast, the second approach takes the problem as given and creates a long list of alternative options, from which negotiators can choose a particular option. In integrative negotiation over a complex problem, both approaches may be used and intertwined.

Generating Alternative Solutions by Redefining the Problem or Problem Set. The approaches in this category recommend that the parties specifically define their underlying needs and develop alternatives to successfully meet them. At least five different methods for achieving integrative agreements have been proposed.[12] Each of these approaches not only successfully refocuses the issues under dispute but also requires progressively more information about the other side's true needs and hence moves from simpler, distributive solutions to more complex, integrative ones. Each approach will be illustrated by the example of a husband and wife attempting to decide where to spend their two-week vacation. The husband wants to go to the mountains for the entire two weeks, whereas the wife wants to go to the seashore for the entire two weeks. A compromise solution—to spend a week at each place—is possible, but the husband and wife want to determine whether other solutions are possible.

Expand the Pie. Many conflicts begin with a shortage of resources. Each party believes that it is not possible for both sides to satisfy their interest because the available resources are limited and both parties cannot obtain their objectives under the current allocation. The simple solution is to add resources in such a way that both sides can achieve their objectives. If the married couple could persuade their employers to give them four weeks for their vacation they would expand the pie. Expanding the pie requires no information about the other party other than her position (and maybe her interests), and it is a simple way to solve resource shortage problems. In addition, the approach assumes that simply enlarging the resources will solve the problem. Thus, four weeks would be a very satisfactory solution if the husband and wife both liked the mountains and the beach but each preferred one or the other. However, expanding the pie would not be a satisfactory solution if their conflict were based on other grounds—for example, if the husband couldn't stand the beach or the wife wouldn't go to the mountains under any conditions.

Logroll. Successful logrolling requires that the parties establish (or find) more than one issue in conflict; the parties then agree to trade off these issues so one party achieves a highly preferred outcome on the first issue and the other person achieves a highly preferred outcome on the second issue. If the parties do in fact have different preferences on different issues, each party gets his most preferred outcome on his high priority issue and should be happy with the overall agreement. Thus, suppose that the husband and wife not only disagree about where to take their vacation, but also about the kind of accommodations. The husband prefers informal housekeeping cabins whereas the wife prefers a luxury hotel. If the wife decides that the formality of the accommodations is more important to her than the location, they may be able to agree on a luxury hotel in the mountains as a way to meet both their needs.

Logrolling is frequently done by trial and error, as the parties experiment with various packages of offers that will satisfy both sides. The parties must first establish which issues are at stake and then decide their individual priorities on these issues. If there are already at least two issues on the table, then any combination of two or more issues may be suitable for logrolling. If it appears initially that only one issue is at stake, the parties may need to engage in "unbundling" or "unlinking" of a single issue into two or more issues, which may then permit the logrolling process to begin.[13] Additional issues of concern may also be generated through the brainstorming processes described later in this chapter.

Use Nonspecific Compensation. A third way to resolve the conflict is to allow one person to obtain his objectives and pay off the other person for accommodating his interests. This payoff may be unrelated to the substantive negotiation, but the party who receives it nevertheless views it as adequate for acceding to the other party's preferences. In the vacation example, the wife could tell the husband that if he agrees to go to the seashore, she will buy him a new camera or a set of golf clubs. For nonspecific compensation to work, the person doing the compensating needs to know what is valuable to the other person and how seriously the other is inconvenienced (i.e., how much compensation is needed to make the other feel satisfied). She might need to test several different offers (types and amounts of compensation) to find out how much it will take to satisfy the other. This discovery process can turn into a distributive bargaining situation itself, as the husband may choose to set very high demands as the price for going along to the beach while the wife tries to minimize the compensation she will pay.

Cut the Costs for Compliance. Through cost cutting, one party achieves her objectives and the other's costs are minimized if he agrees to go along. In the vacation example, suppose that the husband really likes a quiet and peaceful vacation and dislikes the beach because of the crowds, whereas the wife really likes the beach because of all the activity. If peace and quiet is what the husband really wants, then he may be willing to go to the beach if the wife assures him that they will stay in a secluded place at the beach that is located far away from the other resorts. Unlike nonspecific compensation, where the compensated party simply receives something for going along, cost-cutting tactics are specifically designed to minimize the other party's costs and suffering. The technique is thus more sophisticated than logrolling or nonspecific compensation because it requires a more intimate knowledge of the other party's real needs and preferences (the party's interests, what really matters to him, how his needs can be more specifically met).

TABLE 3.2   Refocusing Questions to Reveal Win–Win Options

Expanding the Pie

1. How can both parties get what they are demanding?
2. Is there a resource shortage?
3. How can resources be expanded to meet the demands of both sides?

Logrolling

1. What issues are of higher and lower priority to me?
2. What issues are of higher and lower priority to the other?
3. Are issues of high priority to me low for the other, and vice versa?
4. Can I unbundle an issue—that is, make one larger issue into two or more smaller ones—that can then be logrolled?
5. What are things that would be inexpensive for me to give and valuable for the other to get that might be used in logrolling?

Nonspecific Compensation

1. What are the other party's goals and values?
2. What could I do for the other side that would make them happy and have them allow me to get my way on the key issue?
3. What are things that would be inexpensive for me to give and valuable for the other to get that might be used as nonspecific compensation?

Cost Cutting

1. What risks and costs does my proposal create for the other?
2. What can I do to minimize the other's risks and costs so that they would be more willing to go along?

Bridging

1. What are the other's real underlying interests and needs?
2. What are my own real underlying interests and needs?
3. What are the higher and lower priorities for each of us in our underlying interests and needs?
4. Can we invent a solution that meets both sides' relative priorities and their underlying interests and needs?

Find a Bridge Solution. Finally, by bridging, the parties are able to invent new options that meet each side's needs. Thus, if the husband reveals that he really wants to hunt and fish on his vacation, whereas the wife wants to swim, go shopping, and enjoy the night life, they may be able to discover a resort area that will satisfy all these desires. Successful bridging requires a fundamental reformulation of the problem such that the parties are no longer squabbling over their positions; instead, they are disclosing sufficient information to discover their interests and needs and then inventing options that will satisfy both parties' needs. Bridging solutions do not always remedy all concerns; the wife may not get the salt sea air at the resort, and the husband may spend more money than he wanted to. But both have agreed that taking their vacation together is more desirable than taking it separately (i.e., they have committed themselves to interdependence) and have worked to invent a solution that meets their most important needs. If negotiators fundamentally commit themselves to a win–win negotiation, bridging solutions are likely to be highly satisfactory to both sides.

As we stated earlier, the successful pursuit of these five strategies requires a high-quality information exchange between the parties. This information must either be volunteered or the parties must ask each other questions that will generate sufficient information to reveal possible win–win options. Table 3.2 presents a series of refocusing questions that may reveal these possibilities.[14]

Generating Alternative Solutions to the Problem as Given. In addition to the techniques mentioned above, there are a number of alternative approaches to generating possible solutions. These approaches can be used by the two negotiators or, alternatively, by involving a number of other parties (e.g., constituencies, audiences, bystanders). Several of these approaches are commonly used in small groups to facilitate group problem-solving. The success of these approaches relies on the principle that groups of people are frequently better problem solvers than single individuals, particularly because groups provide a wider number of perspectives on the problem and hence can invent a greater variety of ways to solve it. However, as we noted, groups must also observe the procedures for defining the problem, defining interests, and generating options that we have just identified, or the group process will quickly degenerate into a win–lose competition.

Brainstorming. Individuals are asked to work in small groups, generating as many possible solutions to the problem as they can. Someone records the solutions, without comment, as they are identified. Parties are urged to be spontaneous, even impractical, and not to censor any idea because they think it is unworkable or too expensive. Moreover, parties are required not to discuss or evaluate any solution as it is proposed, since discussion and evaluation will criticize ideas and stop the free flow of new ideas. The success of the brainstorming approach depends upon the free flow of ideas and the intellectual stimulation that should occur as these ideas are tossed around. Therefore, successful brainstorming and group generation and discussion of alternatives require that the following rules be observed:

1. *Avoid judging or evaluating solutions.* As we stated earlier, criticism inhibits creative thinking. In addition, some of the most creative

solutions come from ideas that initially seemed wild and impractical. Parties should impose a clear rule that no idea will be evaluated or ruled out until the group is finished brainstorming.

2. *"Separate the people from the problem."* Fisher, Ury, and Patton, and several others have noted that group discussion and brainstorming processes are often constrained because the parties take ownership of certain preferred solutions and alternatives.[15] Since competitive negotiators assume an offensive posture toward the other negotiator, they are unlikely to see the merits of a suggested alternative simply because the other person suggested it. In addition, when opponents act offensively, we may be so turned off by their behavior that we are unable to pay attention to what they are really saying. For effective problem solving to occur, negotiators must concentrate on attacking the problem and treat all possible solutions as equally viable, regardless of who initiated them. (This is easy to say but *very difficult* to do if you really dislike the other!) For example, if the parties try to depersonalize the suggestions by collectively listing them on a blackboard or flip charts, then they will be less likely to identify who originated any particular idea, and they may be in a better position to pick the solution that best solves the problem. Some other techniques for generating options may work better because they assure anonymity in suggesting ideas and minimize the likelihood that the interpersonal conflict will escalate.

3. *Be exhaustive in the brainstorming process.* Many times our best ideas come after a meeting is over or after a problem is solved. Sometimes, this happens because the parties were not persistent enough. Research has shown that when brainstormers work at the process for a long period of time, the best ideas are most likely to surface during the latter part of the activity:

Generating a large number of superior ideas apparently increases the probability of developing superior ideas. Ideas, when expressed, tend to trigger other ideas. And since ideas can be built one upon the other, those that develop later in a session are often superior to those without refinement or elaboration. What difference does it make if a lot of impractical ideas are recorded? They can be evaluated and dismissed rapidly in the next step of the win–win process. The important thing is to ensure that few, if any, usable ideas are lost.[16]

4. *Ask outsiders.* Often, people who know nothing about the past history of the conflict, or even about the issues, can suggest options and possibilities that have not been considered. Outsiders can provide additional input to the list of alternatives, or they can help orchestrate the process and keep the parties on track.

Nominal Groups. In the nominal group technique, negotiators must start with the problem as defined; each one then individually prepares a written list of possible solutions. Participants are encouraged to list as many solutions as they can. Then they meet in small groups and read their solutions aloud while a recorder writes them on flip charts or a blackboard. Particularly in a large group, this approach can generate a great number of possible options in a short period of time. These solutions can then be examined by all those working on the problem.

Surveys. The disadvantage of nominal groups is that they usually do not solicit the ideas of those who are not present at the negotiation. In addition, the nominal group technique can be time consuming. A different approach is to distribute a written questionnaire to a large group of people, stating the problem and asking them to list all the possible solutions they can imagine. This process can be conducted in a very short period of time. The liability, however, is that the parties cannot benefit from seeing and hearing the other people's ideas, a key advantage of the nominal group technique.

Summary. The two basic approaches to generating alternative solutions that we have discussed—generating options to the problem as given and generating options by redefining the problem—may give the impression that if bargainers simply invent enough different options, they will find a solution to solve their problem rather easily. Although identifying options sometimes leads to a solution, solutions are usually attained through hard work and pursuit of several related processes: information exchange, focusing on interests rather than positions, and firm flexibility.[17] Information exchange will allow the parties to maximize the amount of information available. Focusing on interests will allow the parties to move beyond opening positions and demands to determine what the parties *really* want, what needs truly *must* be satisfied. Finally, firm flexibility means that the parties must be firm with regard to the *ends* they want to achieve (i.e., interests), while remaining flexible on the *means* by which they are achieved. Firm flexibility recognizes that negotiators have one or two fundamental interests or principles that must be achieved, although a wide variety of positions, possible solutions, or secondary issues may get drawn into the negotiations. Negotiators need to be able to signal to the other side the positions on which they are firm and the positions on which they are willing to be flexible. There are several ways to communicate firm flexibility:[18]

1. Use contentious (competitive) tactics to establish and determine basic interests, rather than using them to demand a particular position or solution to the dispute. State what you want clearly.
2. At the same time, send signals of flexibility and concern about your willingness to address the other party's interests. "Acknowledge their interests as part of the problem."[19] In doing so, you communicate that you have your own interests at stake but are willing to try to address the other's as well.
3. Indicate a willingness to change your proposals if a way can be found to bridge the two parties' interests.

4. Demonstrate a problem-solving capacity. For example, use experts on a negotiating team or bring them in as consultants based on their expertise at generating new ideas.

5. Maintain open communication channels. Do not eliminate opportunities to communicate and work together, if only to demonstrate continually that you are willing to work with the other party.

6. Reaffirm what is most important to you through the use of deterrent statements—for example, "I need to attain this;" "This is a must; this cannot be touched or changed." These statements communicate to the other that a particular interest is fundamental to your position, but it does not necessarily mean that the other's interests can't be satisfied as well.

7. Reexamine any aspects of your interests that are clearly unacceptable to the other party and determine if they are still essential to your fundamental position. It is rare that negotiators will find that they truly disagree on basic interests.

Evaluation and Selection of Alternatives

The fourth stage in the integrative negotiation process is to evaluate the options generated during the previous phase and to select the best alternatives for implementing them. When the problem is a reasonably simple one, the evaluation and selection steps may be effectively combined into a single step. When confronted with complex problems or a large number of alternative options, however, the evaluation stage may take considerably longer. Negotiators will need to determine criteria for judging the options and then rank order or weigh each option against the criteria. Finally, the parties will be required to engage in some form of decision-making process, in which they debate the relative merits of each side's preferred options and come to agreement on the best options. The following guidelines should be used in evaluating options and reaching a consensus.[20]

Narrow the Range of Solution Options. Examine the list of options generated and focus on the options that are strongly supported by any negotiator. This approach is more positive than allowing people to focus on negative, unacceptable criteria and options. Solutions not strongly advocated by at least one negotiator should be eliminated.

Evaluate Solutions on the Basis of Quality and Acceptability. Solutions should be judged on two major criteria: how good they are, and how acceptable will they be to those who have to implement them. These are the same two dimensions that research has revealed to be critical in effective participative decision making in organizations.[21] Negotiators will evaluate the quality dimension by determining what is best, what is most rational, what is most logical. To the degree that parties can support their arguments with statements of hard fact, logical deduction, and appeals to rational criteria, their arguments will be more compelling in obtaining the support of others. Fisher, Ury, and Patton suggest that the parties "appeal to objective standards" for making decisions. This suggests that the parties are more likely to accept a solution they perceive as fair and equitable to all concerned. Thus, the parties should search for past decisions, precedents, arbitration decisions, or other objectively fair outcomes and processes that can be used as benchmarks for legitimizing the fairness of the current settlement. These criteria may be different from what the negotiators judge to be most rational or the best solution. When a specific solution must meet the criteria of both quality and acceptability (fairness), those evaluating the solution options may have to be prepared to make trade-offs between the two to ensure that both criteria are met.

Agree to the Criteria in Advance of Evaluating Options. Fisher, Ury, and Patton exhort negotiators to "insist on using objective criteria"—that is, to develop standards for deciding what is fair, correct, or "the right thing to do" in the situation.[22] Groups often follow this process when they have to narrow the choice down to a single alternative—for example, to pick a candidate for a new job—or to select the option most likely to succeed. If the parties first debate their criteria and determine which ones are most important, they will be able to decide on criteria independent of the consideration of any particular candidate or option. Then, when they consider the individual candidates or options, they will pick the best one based on these criteria, not on the individual preferences of one side or the other. If the parties agree, they may revise their criteria later to improve their choice, but this should only be done by the agreement of all negotiators.

Be Willing to Justify Personal Preferences. Why someone likes what he likes, or dislikes what he dislikes, is often hard to publicly justify. "Why do you like that?" "I don't know, I just do," is usually the reply. Moreover, negotiators gain little by requiring opponents to justify themselves—having to justify makes people angry and defensive. For example, if the topic under negotiation is what to have for dinner, and one party states that she hates clam chowder, no amount of persuasive effort is likely to change that person's opinion of clam chowder. Instead, the parties would be more productive if they accepted this information and attempted to explore other options for dinner. Yet what we prefer often has a more-deep-seated rationale—as we pointed out how interests, values, and needs often underlie positions. Thus, inquiries from the other party about why we prefer what we want *may* be an effort to probe behind a position and identify underlying interests and needs. So when others ask us why questions, they may elicit a little defensiveness; but the questioner should explain that the intent is to probe for possible underlying interests that might facilitate a collaborative settlement, rather than to produce a defensive restatement of one's preferences.

Be Alert to the Influence of Intangibles in Selecting Options. One side may favor some options because they help that negotiator satisfy some intangible—

gaining recognition, looking strong or tough to a constituency, feeling like he has won, and so on. As we pointed out, intangibles or principles can serve as strong interests for a negotiator. Intangibles can lead the negotiator to fight harder to attain a particular solution option if that option satisfies both tangibles and intangibles. Help the other party identify those intangibles and make them public as part of the evaluation process; the other party is likely to prefer options that satisfy those intangibles, and to the degree that you can live with them, agreeing to those options may be important concessions.

Use Subgroups to Evaluate Complex Options. Small groups may be particularly helpful when many complex options must be considered or when many people will be affected by the solution. Groups of six to eight people, composed of representatives from each faction, side, or subgroup, will be able to work more effectively than a large group. (See our earlier discussion of nominal groups for deciding on options, and Chapter 8 for a discussion of group negotiations.)

Take Time Out to Cool Off. Even though the parties may have completed the hardest part of the process—generating a list of viable options—they may become upset if communication breaks down, they feel their preferences are not being acknowledged, or the other side pushes too hard for a particular option. If the parties become angry, take a break. Negotiators should make their dissatisfaction known and openly discuss the reasons for it. Make sure the parties are back on an even emotional keel before continuing to evaluate the options. Finally, work as hard as possible to keep discussions on the specifics of the proposals, not on the people advocating them. Keep the people advocating a point of view separate from the options for settlement, and depersonalize the discussion as much as possible.

Explore Different Ways to Logroll. Earlier we discussed a variety of ways to invent options. Logrolling as a strategy is effective not only in inventing options, but also as a mechanism to combine options into negotiated packages. In addition to simply combining several issues into a package, Margaret Neale and Max Bazerman point out several additional ways to logroll:[23]

Exploit Differences in Risk Preference. Suppose two business partners are discussing a future business venture. One has little to risk at the moment and everything to gain from the future; the other has a lot on the line now that she does not want to risk losing if the future looks bad. If they simply agree to split profits in the future, the one with a large amount of current risk may feel very vulnerable. Logrolling around these interests can create a solution that protects one partner's current investment first and provides more long-term profits for the other partner.

Exploit Differences in Expectations. In the same example, the person with a lot to lose may also have pessimistic expectations about the future of the joint venture, whereas the person with little to lose may be more optimistic about it. The optimist may thus be willing to gamble more on the future profitability and payout, whereas the pessimist is willing to settle for a smaller but more assured payment. Like differences in risk, simple differences in expectations about what will happen can permit the parties to invent a solution that addresses the needs of both parties.

Exploit Differences in Time Preferences. Negotiators may have different time preferences—one may be more concerned about meeting short-term needs, whereas the other may be more interested in the long-term rewards of their relationship. Parties with short-term interests will need immediate gratification, whereas parties who look for long-term rewards may be willing to make short-term sacrifices to assure the long-term payoff. Parties with different preferences can invent solutions that address both the short-term and long-term interests.

Keep Decisions Tentative and Conditional until All Aspects of the Final Proposal Are Complete. Even though a rather clear consensus may emerge about the solution option(s) that will be selected, the parties should talk about the solution in conditional terms. This tentative tone allows any side to change or revise the final package at any time. Points agreed upon in earlier discussion are not firm until the entire package is determined. Parties do not have to feel that, because they gave up on an earlier option, they have burned their bridges behind them; rather, nothing is final until everything is final.

Minimize Formality and Record Keeping until Final Agreements Are Closed. Parties usually do not want to lock themselves into any specific language or written agreement until they are close to a consensus. They want to make sure that they will not be held to comments made and recorded in notes or transcripts. In general, the fewer the transcripts, minutes, or written records during the solution-generating phase, the better. In contrast, when the parties are close to consensus, one side should write down what they have agreed to. This document may then be used as a "single text"[24] passed around from party to party as often as necessary until all sides agree to the phrasing and wording of their agreement.

Factors That Facilitate Successful Integrative Negotiation

We have stressed that successful integrative negotiation can occur if the parties are predisposed to finding that mutually acceptable joint solution. Many other factors contribute to a predisposition toward problem solving and a willingness to work with the other toward finding the best solution. These factors are also the preconditions necessary for the integrative negotiation process.[25] In this section, we will review these factors in greater detail: the presence of a common goal, faith in one's own problem-solving ability, a belief in the validity of the other's position, the motivation and commitment to work together, trust, and clear and accurate communication.

Some Common Objective or Goal

When the parties believe they are likely to benefit more from working together than from competing or working separately, the situation offers greater potential for successful integrative negotiation. Three types of goals may facilitate the development of integrative agreements:

1. *A common goal,* by which all parties share the result equally, each one benefiting in a way that would not be possible if they did not work together. A town government and an industrial manufacturing plant may debate one another over the amount of taxes owed by the plant, but they are more likely to work together if the common goal is to keep the plant open and employ half the town's workforce.

2. *A shared goal,* by which the parties work toward a common end but benefit differently. For example, partners can work together in a business but not divide the profits equally. One may get a larger share of the profit because he contributed more experience or capital investment. Inherent in the idea of a shared goal is that parties will work together to achieve some output that will be shared. The same result can also come from cost cutting, by which the parties can earn the same outcome as before by working together, but with less effort, expense, or risk. This is often described as an "expandable pie" as contrasted to the assumption of a "fixed pie" (Chapter 5).

3. *A joint goal,* by which individuals with different personal goals agree to combine them in a collective effort. For example, people joining a political campaign can have different goals: one wants to satisfy personal ambition to hold public office, a second wants to serve the community, and a third wants to benefit from policies that will be implemented under the new administration. All will unite around the joint goal of helping the new administration get elected.

The key element of an integrative negotiation situation is the belief that all sides can benefit. Whether each side attains the same outcome or achieves different outcomes, all sides must believe that they will be better off by working in cooperation than by competing or working independently.

Faith in One's Own Problem-Solving Ability

Parties who believe they can work together usually are able to do so. Those who do not share this belief in themselves (and others) are less willing to invest the time and energy in the potential payoffs of a collaborative relationship and are more likely to assume a contending or accommodating approach to conflict. Expertise in the focal problem area strengthens the negotiator's understanding of all the problem's complexity, nuances, and possible solutions. Researchers have demonstrated that expert negotiators in a real estate problem—corporate real estate executives—achieved significantly better integrative agreements than amateurs. Expertise increases both the knowledge base and the self-confidence necessary to approach this problem with an open mind. Similarly, direct experience in negotiation increases the negotiator's sophistication in understanding the bargaining process and approaching it more creatively.[26]

A Belief in the Validity of the Other's Position

In distributive bargaining, negotiators invest time and energy in inflating and justifying the value of their own positions and debunking the value and importance of the other's position. In contrast, integrative negotiation requires negotiators to accept the other's attitudes, information, and desires as accurate and valid.[27] If you challenge the other party's views, the party may become angry, defensive, and hence unproductive in the problem-solving process. The purpose of integrative negotiation is not to question or challenge the other's viewpoint but to incorporate it into the definition of the problem and to attend to it as the parties search for mutually acceptable alternatives. In addition, these views are to be given value equal to one's own position and viewpoint.

The Motivation and Commitment to Work Together

For integrative negotiation to succeed, the parties must be motivated to collaborate rather than to compete. They need to be committed to a goal that benefits both of them rather than to pursuing only their own ends. Finally, they must be willing to adopt interpersonal styles that are more congenial than combative, more open and trusting than evasive and defensive, more flexible (but firm) than stubborn (but yielding). Needs have to be made explicit, similarities have to be identified, and differences have to be recognized and accepted. Uncertainties have to be tolerated and inconsistencies unraveled.

It might seem that for successful integrative negotiation to occur, each party should be as interested in the objectives and problems of the other as each is in his own—each must assume responsibility for the other's needs and outcomes as well as for her own. This is an incorrect interpretation; in fact, such a position is more likely to be dysfunctional. Parties who are deeply committed to each other and each other's welfare often do not work out the best solution, for several reasons. First, as close as the parties may feel to one another, they still may not fully understand one another's needs, objectives, and concerns, and thus they can fall into the trap of not meeting the other's objectives while thinking that they are. Further, parties strongly committed to each other are likely to yield more than they would otherwise; the result is that they may arrive at a joint outcome that is less satisfactory than if they had remained firm in pursuing their own objectives. Parties in negotiation maximize their outcomes when they assume a healthy, active self-interest in achieving their own outcomes, yet also recognize that they are in a collaborative, problem-solving relationship.[28] Motivation and commitment to problem solving can be enhanced in several ways:

- The parties can come to believe that they share a common fate; to quote Ben Franklin, "If we do not hang together, we will surely hang separately."
- The parties can demonstrate to one another that there is more to be gained by working together (to increase the payoffs or reduce the costs) than by working separately.
- The parties can emphasize that they may have to work together after the negotiations are over or they can recognize that they may be able to work together and continue to benefit from the relationship they have created.

In spite of these efforts, competitive and contentious behavior may persist. In Chapter 5, we will elaborate upon approaches that may be used to enhance the parties' predisposition toward cooperation and problem solving.

Trust

Although there is no guarantee that trust will lead to collaboration, there is plenty of evidence to suggest that mistrust inhibits collaboration. People who are interdependent but who do not trust each other will act defensively. Defensiveness usually means that they will not accept information at face value, but instead look for hidden, deceptive meanings. When people are defensive, they withdraw, withhold information, and try to protect themselves. Defensive people also attack the other's opponent's statements and perceived position, seeking to defeat the other rather than to work together. Either of these responses is likely to make the negotiator hesitant, cautious, and distrustful of the other, undermining the negotiation process.[29]

Generating trust is a complex, uncertain process; it depends in part on how the parties behave and in part on the parties' personal characteristics. When people trust one another, they are more likely to accurately communicate their needs, positions, and the facts of the situation. In contrast, when people do not trust one another, they are more likely to engage in positional bargaining, use threats, and commit themselves to tough positions.[30] As with defensiveness, this behavior is likely to contribute to an unproductive conflict spiral and to lead to more distributive negotiations. To develop effective trust, each negotiator must be willing to signal to the other that each chooses to behave in a cooperative manner; moreover, each must believe that this behavior is a signal of the other's honesty and a similar mutual commitment to a joint solution.[31]

A number of key factors contribute to the development of trust between negotiators. First, we are more likely to trust someone we perceive as similar to us or holding a positive attitude toward us. Second, we often trust people who are dependent upon us because we are in a position to help or hurt them (and they frequently can do the same to us). Third, we are more likely to trust people who initiate cooperative, trusting behavior. Acting in a cooperative, trusting manner serves as an invitation to others, especially if the invitation is repeated despite initially contentious behavior from the opponent . Finally, we are more likely to trust negotiators who act reasonably and make some concessions. The more other people's behavior communicates that they are holding firm in their fundamental commitment to their own needs at the same time as they are working toward a joint solution, the more we are likely to find their conduct trustworthy, in the spirit of the best joint agreement.[32]

Given that trust has to be built during the negotiation, opening moves are crucial. The more that the opening statements and actions of a party are perceived as open, nonthreatening, and oriented toward mutual gains, the more trust and cooperation is engendered in the other party.[33] Once a cooperative position is established, it is more likely to persist. If cooperative behavior can be established at the very beginning, there is a tendency for parties to lock in to this cycle and make it continue. Finally, these opening moves not only set the tone for the negotiation but also begin the momentum of the negotiation. The longer the cycle of trust and cooperation continues, the easier it should be to restore should the cycle break down.[34]

Clear and Accurate Communication

The next precondition for high-quality integrative negotiation is clear and accurate communication. First, negotiators must be willing to share information about themselves.[35] They must be willing to tell what they want—and, more important, they must be willing to state why they want it in specific, concrete terms, avoiding generalities and ambiguities. Second, the opponents must understand the communication. At a minimum, they must understand the meaning we attach to our statements; hopefully, they also attach the same meaning to the facts that we do. Others at the negotiating table can frequently identify ambiguities and breakdowns in communication. If someone on a bargaining team makes a confusing statement, others can try to clarify it. When one person on the other side does not grasp a difficult point, someone else from the same side will often be able to find the words or illustrations to bring out the meaning. This understanding is the responsibility of both sides. The communicator must be willing to test whether the other side has received the message that was intended. Similarly, the listener must engage in active listening, testing to make sure that what they received and understood is the message that the sender intended.

If multiple communication channels are available (i.e., opportunities for the two sides to communicate in ways other than formally across the negotiation table), they will provide alternative ways to clarify the formal communication or to get information through if the formal channels break down. Conversations over coffee breaks, separate meetings between chief negotiators outside the formal sessions, or off-the-record contacts between key subordinates are all alternatives to the formal channel.

When there are strong negative feelings or when one or more parties are inclined to dominate, negotiators may create formal procedures for communication. Under these circumstances, negotiators should follow a procedure that gives everyone a chance to speak. For example, the rules of most debates limit statements to five minutes, and similar rules are often adopted in contentious open meetings or public hearings. In addition, the parties may agree to stick to a previously agreed upon agenda so everyone can be heard and each person's contribution can be noted. Other ways to ensure effective communication processes in negotiation are covered extensively in Chapter 6. In addition, in Chapter 10, we will describe ways that third parties can help facilitate disabled communication processes.

Summary

We identified six major factors that are fundamental preconditions for successful integrative negotiation: some form of shared or common goal, faith in one's own ability to solve problems, a belief in the validity and importance of the other's position, the motivation and commitment to work together, trust in the opposing negotiator, and the ability to accurately exchange information in spite of conflict conditions. If the parties are not able to successfully meet all these preconditions, they will need to resolve these problems as the integrative negotiation process evolves.

Chapter Summary

In this chapter, we have reviewed the strategy and tactics of integrative negotiation. The fundamental structure of integrative negotiation is that the parties are able to define goals that allow both sides to achieve their objectives. Integrative negotiation is the process of defining these goals and engaging in a set of procedures that permits both sides to maximize their objectives.

The chapter argues that a collaborative, problem-solving, integrative approach to negotiation is the best way to approach a conflict in which the best solution is one which achieves the objectives of all parties best represented by a high level of concern for having both sides achieve their own objectives. Successful integrative negotiation requires several preconditions. First, the parties must be able to understand each other's true needs and objectives. Second, they must be able to create a free flow of information and an open exchange of ideas. Third, they should attempt to focus on their similarities, emphasizing their commonalties rather than their differences. Finally, they should search for solutions that meet the goals of both sides. This is a very different process from distributive bargaining, described in Chapter 2.

For the integrative negotiating process to occur successfully, several preconditions are necessary. First, the process will be greatly facilitated by some form of common goal or objective. This goal may be one that the parties both want to achieve, one they want to share, or one they could not possibly attain unless they worked together. Second, they must share a motivation and commitment to work together, to make their relationship a productive one. Third, the parties must be willing to believe that the other's needs are valid. Fourth, they must be able to trust one another and to work hard to establish and maintain that trust. Finally, there must be clear and accurate communication about what each one wants and an effort to understand the other's needs. Instead of talking the other out of his or her needs or failing to acknowledge them as important, negotiators must be willing to work for both their own needs and the other's needs in order to find the best joint arrangement. Given these preconditions, the integrative negotiating process is most likely to be successful.

The three major stages in the integrative negotiation process are problem identification, generating solutions, and choosing a specific solution. For each of these stages, we proposed a number of techniques and tactics to make the process successful. In spite of all of these suggestions, the process is not as easy as it seems for parties locked in conflict, defensiveness, and a hard-line position. Only by working to create the necessary conditions for integrative negotiation can the process occur with relative ease and success. In Chapters 4 and 5, we will discuss a number of ways in which parties can defuse hostility, defensiveness, and the disposition toward hard-line negotiating so as to create the conditions for successful integrative negotiation.

End Notes

1. Walton and McKersie (1965).
2. Walton and McKersie (1965); Filley (1975); Fisher, Ury, and Patton (1991); Pruitt (1981, 1983); Carnevale and Pruitt (1992); Pruitt and Carnevale (1993).
3. Pruitt (1981) and Thompson (1991).
4. Fisher, Ury, and Patton (1991) and Pruitt and Rubin (1986).
5. See Filley (1975) and Shea (1983) for fuller treatments of these points.
6. Fisher and Ury (1981); see also Fisher, Ury, and Patton (1991).
7. Fisher, Ury, and Patton (1991, p. 40); story originally told by Follett (1940).
8. Lax and Sebenius (1986).
9. See chapter 5 of Sheppard, Lewicki, and Minton (1992) for a more detailed discussion of the role of voice in organizations.
10. Nierenberg (1983).
11. Burton (1984).

12. See Pruitt (1981, 1983), Pruitt and Lewis (1975), Neale and Bazerman (1991), and Pruitt and Carnevale (1993).

13. *Unbundling* is the term used by Lax and Sebenius; *unlinking* is used by Pruitt.

14. These questions were drawn from Pruitt and Rubin (1986) and Pruitt and Carnevale (1993).

15. Fisher, Ury and Patton (1991); Walton and McKersie (1965); and Filley (1975).

16. Shea (1983, p. 57).

17. Fisher, Ury, and Patton (1991) and Pruitt (1983).

18. Pruitt (1983) and Fisher, Ury, and Patton (1991).

19. Fisher and Ury (1981, p. 55).

20. Filley (1975), Pruitt and Carnevale (1993), Shea (1983), and Walton and McKersie (1965).

21. See the work on how leaders should use participative decision making by Vroom and Yetton (1973).

22. Fisher, Ury, and Patton (1991).

23. Neale and Bazerman (1991).

24. Fisher, Ury, and Patton (1991).

25. Pruitt (1981, 1983) and Filley (1975).

26. Neale and Northcraft (1986) and Thompson (1990a).

27. Fisher, Ury, and Patton (1991).

28. Kelley and Schenitzki (1972); Fry, Firestone, and Williams (1979); Rubin and Brown (1975).

29. Gibb (1961).

30. Kimmel et al. (1980).

31. See Lewicki and Bunker (1995) for a discussion of steps required to repair trust.

32. Solomon (1960), Bonoma et al. (1969), Gahagan et al. (1969), Gruder and Duslak (1973), Heller (1967), Kleinke and Pohlan (1971), Rubin and Brown (1975), Deutsch (1973), and Lewis and Weingart (1985).

33. Crumbaugh and Evans (1967), Michelini (1971), Oskamp (1970), and Sermat and Gregovich (1966).

34. Pilisuk and Skolnick (1978), Komorita and Mechling (1967), Sermat (1967), Swinth (1967), Lewicki and Bunker (1995). See also our discusion of "GRIT" in chapter 5.

35. Neale and Bazerman (1991).

4 PRENEGOTIATION ESSENTIALS

Other things being equal, the negotiator who plans better does better. This chapter addresses the planning and related activities that must occur before actual negotiation. The flow of these processes is represented in Figure 4.1.

FIGURE 4.1

The Negotiation Preparation Flow

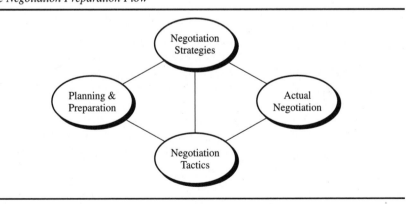

Strategy, Tactics, and Planning

Planning encompasses the considerations and choices we make about tactics, resource use, and contingent responses in pursuit of the overall strategy—how to proceed and how to use what we have to get what we want. It is clear that planning produces strategies and tactics, but how are strategy and tactics related? Although the line between strategy and tactics may seem hard to define, one major difference is that of scale, perspective, or immediacy.[1] Tactics are short-term, adaptive moves designed to enact or pursue broader (or higher level) strategies, which in turn provide the stability, continuity, and direction for tactical behaviors. Tactics are subordinate to strategy; they are structured, directed, and driven by strategic considerations.

Types of Strategy

Strategies vary on a number of different dimensions, including voluntariness, structure, informational locus, and opportunism.

Voluntariness. A voluntary strategy is based on choice: what to pursue, how to pursue it, or even whether to have a strategy at all. Alternatively, a strategy may be imposed on the parties, who are charged with pursuing it by their superiors or by external forces such as regulatory agencies. Voluntary and imposed strategies differ primarily in the amount of involvement or discretion the directed party has in designing, pursuing, or amending the strategy. The more voluntary the strategy, the more you empower the other side by allowing them to buy in and create co-ownership of the final product. However, if you expect strong opposition from the other side, you may want to move toward imposition.

Structure. Strategies also may be more or less structured. When structure levels differ, the trade-off is between control and adaptation. Highly structured strategies provide firm guidelines, controls, and a sense of direction and certainty; close adherence to such strategies, however, may prevent negotiators from responding and adapting to new information and opportunities that were unknown or undervalued when the original strategy was formulated. Having too little structure fails to provide the control necessary to guide decisions and direct the application of scarce resources. The dangers here, then, involve the extremes of too much structure or too little.

Informational locus. Strategies prepared before negotiations begin are often unilateral, or one-sided, in that they reflect a certainty about one's own strategy, but only an educated guess (if that) about the other party's strategy. Improved information may emerge as the negotiation proceeds, making strategic corrections or adaptations advisable and possible. Negotiators who are able to adapt their intended strategies early in a negotiation appear to achieve better outcomes as a result.[2]

Opportunism. Not having a particular strategy is itself a form of strategy. When done intentionally, this may be called an opportunistic, adaptive, or emergent

FIGURE 4.2

A Choice Model of Negotiation Strategy

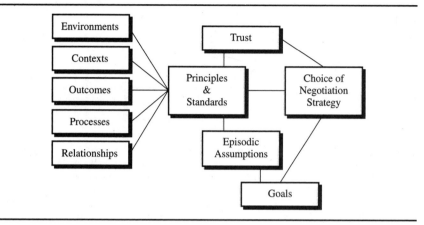

approach, and it enables negotiators to evaluate and exploit opportunities as they recognize them.[3] Extreme forms of this strategy can be dangerous. Too little responsiveness to changing information and situations may bind negotiators to strategies that no longer work.

A Choice Model of Negotiation Strategy

A general model of the process of choice of negotiation strategy includes at least five elements:

- Driving factors.
- Principles and standards.
- The role of trust.
- Assumptions about the episodic nature of the process.
- Negotiation goals.

These elements relate to each other as shown in Figure 4.2.

Let's examine this process starting from actual strategic choice (the right side, or "business end," of the model).

Negotiation Strategy Choices. The focus here is on the unilateral choice of a strategy. *Unilateral* denotes making a choice without the active involvement of the other party. A reasonable effort to find out about the other party and to incorporate that information into the choice of a negotiation strategy is *always* useful. A negotiator's unilateral choice of strategy is reflected in the answers to

FIGURE 4.3

Choosing an Initial Negotiation Strategy

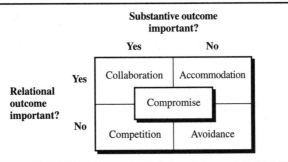

Adapted from G.T. Savage, J.D. Blair, and R.J. Sorenson, "Consider Both Relationship and Substance When Negotiating Strategically," *Academy of Management Executive*, (vol. 3, 1989, pp. 37–48).

two simple questions: how much concern does the actor have for achieving the substantive outcomes at stake in this negotiation? How much concern does the negotiator have for the current and future quality of the relationship with the other party? The answers to these questions result in the mix of strategic alternatives suggested in Figure 4.3.

Situational Strategies. The power of this framework lies in requiring the negotiator to first determine the relative importance and priority of the two dimensions (substance and relationship) in the desired settlement. As Figure 4.3 shows, answers to these two simple questions suggest at least five types of initial strategies for negotiators: avoidance, competition, accommodation, compromise, and collaboration. Let's look at each of these, in turn.

Avoidance is an option if neither achieving a particular substantive outcome nor enhancing (or maintaining) a relationship is very important. By definition, avoidance is non-negotiation; however, it may serve a number of strategic negotiation purposes. A number of situations are conducive to avoidance:

- All your needs and interests can be met without negotiating.
- The desired ends are not worth the often-considerable time and effort of negotiation.
- There are one or more acceptable alternatives to a negotiated agreement.
- Your BATNA (see Chapter 2) is weak or nonexistent.
- You have the developmental responsible for teaching or allowing a peer or subordinate to build negotiation skills.

Competition is an option when there is an overpowering interest in achieving substantive outcomes—getting *this* deal, winning *this* negotiation, with little or no regard for the effect on the relationship and subsequent exchanges with the other party. Competition is also known as distributive, or win–lose, bargaining (see Chapter 2 for more detail regarding the competitive model of negotiation).

Accommodation may be an option when there is a strong interest in achieving only the relationship outcomes—preserving or enhancing a good relationship with the opponent. Like competition, accommodation is a win–lose strategy, though with a mirror image. It involves an imbalance of outcomes but in the opposite direction ("I lose, you win" as opposed to "I win, you lose"). Accommodation is often used when the major goal of the exchange is to build or strengthen the relationship with the other party, and the accommodator is willing to make a sacrifice regarding the substance of the negotiation. Some level of accommodation may also be advisable if it is desirable for the negotiation relationship to extend beyond a single episode (see "Episodic Assumptions" in Figure 4.2). In such cases, it is usually expected that, over multiple negotiation episodes, some sort of balance will be achieved and maintained between the negotiating parties.

Compromise may seem like an option that allows the balancing of both parties' needs and interests—a "meeting in the middle," as it were. It is telling that Figure 4.3 shows compromise in the middle of the diagram, at the halfway point of a line connecting competition and accommodation. It is worth noting that compromise, often perceived as a win–win approach, is still a *win–lose* strategy—a settlement midway between the win–lose extremes of "I get" and "they get." Compromise, in fact, is often confused with, and mistaken for, collaboration, the strategy that truly involves mutual gain and creative resolution. Parties choosing compromise should recognize that it often represents an easy—and often premature—end to the negotiation process. True compromise should be seen for what it is: an amalgamation of competition and accommodation, two distributive strategies.

Collaboration becomes an option (in fact, the *preferred* option) when *both* substance and relationship are important. In this case, the negotiator should pursue a collaborative (also called an integrative, or win–win) strategy. Too often, collaboration is confused with compromise. True collaboration involves thorough and rigorous preparation *and* execution. Rather than simply "splitting the difference," collaborative negotiators use communication, creativity, and understanding to fashion agreements that maximize joint gains (see Chapter 3).

Taken together, competition, accommodation, and collaboration constitute the basic "action/engagement" strategies available to negotiators. Table 4.1 summarizes these three types of strategies, comparing and contrasting them across a number of dimensions.

As Table 4.1 shows, there are both positive and negative aspects to all three strategies. If applied blindly, thoughtlessly, or inflexibly, any of the three has certain predictable drawbacks. For instance, if the other party believes that a negotiator is going to pursue a collaborative strategy without regard to the opponent's behavior, then the opponent can manipulate and exploit the collaborator and take advantage of the good faith and goodwill being demonstrated. An excessive collaborative effort can also lead negotiators to cease being accountable to their constituencies in favor of pursuit of the negotiation process for its own sake (see Chapter 7 for a discussion of negotiator–constituency dynamics). Inflexible

TABLE 4.1 **Characteristics of Different Negotiation Engagement Strategies**

Aspect	Competition (Distributive Bargaining)	Collaboration (Integrative Negotiation)	Accommodative Negotiation
Payoff Structure	Usually a fixed amount of resources to be divided	Usually a variable amount of resources to be divided	Usually a fixed amount of resources to be divided
Goal Pursuit	Pursuit of own goals at the expense of those of others	Pursuit of goals held jointly with others	Subordination of own goals in favor of those of others
Relationships	Short-term focus; parties do not expect to work together in the future	Long-term focus; parties expect to work together in the future	May be short-term (let the other win to keep them happy) or long-term (let the other win to encourage reciprocity in the future)
Primary Motivation	Maximize own outcome	Maximize joint outcome	Maximize others' outcome or let them gain to enhance relationship
Trust and Openness	Secrecy and defensiveness; high trust in self, low trust in others	Trust and openness, active listening, joint exploration of alternatives	One party relatively open, exposing own vulnerabilities to the other
Knowledge of Needs	Parties know own needs, but conceal or misrepresent them; neither party lets the other know real needs	Parties know and convey real needs while seeking and responding to needs of the other	One party is overresponsive to other's needs so as to repress own needs
Predictability	Parties use unpredictability and surprise to confuse other side	Parties are predictable and flexible when appropriate, trying not to surprise	One party's actions totally predictable, always catering to other side
Aggressiveness	Parties use threats and bluffs, trying to keep the upper hand	Parties share information honestly, treat each other with understanding and respect	One party gives up on own position to mollify the other
Solution Search Behavior	Parties make effort to appear committed to position, using argumentation and manipulation of the other	Parties make effort to find mutually satisfying solutions, using logic, creativity, and constructiveness	One party makes effort to find ways to accommodate the other

TABLE 4.1 Characteristics of Different Negotiation Engagement Strategies (*concluded*)

Aspect	Competition (*Distributive Bargaining*)	Collaboration (*Integrative Negotiation*)	Accommodative Negotiation
Success Measures	Success enhanced by creating bad image of the other; increased levels of hostility and strong in-group loyalty	Success demands abandonment of bad images and consideration of ideas on their merit	Success determined by minimizing or avoiding conflict and soothing all hostility; own feelings ignored in favor of harmony
Evidence of Unhealthy Extreme	Unhealthy extreme reached when one party assumes total zero-sum game; defeating the other becomes a goal in itself	Unhealthy extreme reached when one subsumes all self-interest in the common good, losing self-identity and self-responsibility	Unhealthy extreme reached when abdication to other is complete, at expense of personal and/or constituent goals
Key Attitude	Key attitude is "I win, you lose"	Key attitude is "What's the best way to address the needs of all parties?"	Key attitude is "You win, I lose"
Remedy for Breakdown	If impasse occurs, mediator or arbitrator may be needed	If difficulties occur, a group dynamics facilitator may be needed	If behavior becomes chronic, party becomes negotiationally bankrupt

Adapted and expanded from Robert W. Johnston, "Negotiation Strategies: Different Strokes for Different Folks," *Personnel* 59 (March–April 1982), pp. 38–39. Used with permission of the author.

adherence to a competitive strategy, either through intent or because the negotiator tends to see all negotiations as competitive, can have the effect of driving even the most collaborative negotiators to compete, in a defensive effort. Finally, accommodative strategies may have drawbacks in that they may generate a pattern of constantly giving in to the opponent to keep him happy or to avoid a fight. This pattern establishes a precedent that is hard to break. It could also lead to a false sense of well-being due to the satisfaction that comes with the harmony of a good relationship, which may completely ignore all the giveaways on substance.

It is also useful to remember that these strategies are presented here in pure form, which is at odds with the mixture of issues and motivations that actually characterize the conduct of most negotiations.[4] Just as most conflicts are neither purely competitive or cooperative, neither are negotiation strategies. Actual strategies should reflect the mixture and diversity created by the driving factors and other components of the choice model (see Figure 4.2).

Principles and Standards. The second major component in our model (see Figure 4.2) involves guidelines for desires and expectations about how the negotiation relationship will be established, conducted, and continued. Principles and standards have a major effect on the choice of negotiation strategy in that they help classify behaviors, procedures, and outcomes as acceptable or unacceptable. Examples of principles include:

- A commitment to tell the truth and maintain integrity.
- A commitment to be polite and civil to each other (control our temper, respect each other's intelligence and capabilities).
- Beliefs about when competition or collaboration is appropriate to pursue.
- A belief that each side ought to take care of itself and not be concerned with how the other side is doing in the negotiation.

Principles help determine what approaches negotiators choose, avoid, or ignore; they are often personal values related to cooperation or competition and the way one believes people should be treated. In contrast, standards help set boundaries for negotiation outcomes, processes, and behaviors by providing ways to choose among the various options that make up the broader, more basic personal principles. For example, negotiators frequently talk about fairness as a standard, using it either to decide what outcomes are fair or to decide what processes should be used to achieve those outcomes. Yet the real standards are the ways that fairness can be determined. For example, in distributing outcomes, the standard may be that everyone gets the same outcome (an equality standard), that people should get different outcomes if they work harder or contribute more (an equity standard), or that outcomes should be based on what people "need" (a need standard).[5] Objective standards may also be used to decide how to divide or allocate outcomes, but deciding on which objective standard will be used or how it will be applied can also be a critical part of the negotiation itself.[6]

Negotiation Goals. Negotiators should specify their goals and objectives clearly. This includes stating all the goals that are to be achieved in the negotiation, determining their priority, identifying potential multigoal packages, and evaluating the possible trade-offs among them. Goals may also include intangibles such as maintaining a certain precedent or getting an agreement that is satisfactory to both sides (see Chapter 1).

Effects of Goals on Choice of Strategy. Four aspects of the impact of goals on negotiation are important to understand:

- Wishes are not goals, especially in negotiation. Wishes may be closer to interests or needs that motivate goals (see Chapter 3), but they are not goals themselves.
- *Our* goals are linked to the *other's* goals; the linkage between the two parties' goals defines an issue to be settled.
- There are boundaries or limits to what our goals can be. If what we want exceeds these limits (i.e., what the other party is capable of or willing to give), we must either change our goals or end the negotiation—goals must be reasonably attainable.
- Effective goals must be concrete or specific, and preferably measurable. The less concrete and measurable they are, the harder it is to communicate to the other party what we want, to understand what she wants, and to determine whether any particular outcome satisfies our goals.

Most goals are quite tangible, as they address directly such questions as purchase price, timing, and terms. No less important are the many intangible goals that accompany tangible goals. Intangible goals might include things such as "enhancing my reputation with my friends" or "maintaining my friends' image of me as a shrewd negotiator."

Episodic Assumptions. Some goals can be attained in the short term, in a single negotiation session. However, because such goals are also pursued infrequently (such as when we make a major expenditure for a car or a home), we tend to view the negotiation as a single episode—a single defined event, without future consequences. This episodic assumption has, in turn, a distributive effect on negotiation strategy choice; the relationship with the other party tends to be ignored completely in favor of a simplistic concern for achieving only the substantive outcome. *The sole pursuit of a substantive goal often tends to support the choice of a distributive, or competitive, strategy.*

Other negotiation goals, often more complex or more difficult to define, may require initiating a sequence of negotiation episodes. In these cases we expect that progress will be made incrementally, and that progress may depend on the prior establishment of a strong relationship with the other. Examples here might include a substantial increase in a line of credit with your bank or credit union, or the establishment of a most-favored-nation status with an important trading partner. Such relationship-oriented goals should motivate the negotiator toward an integrative strategy choice; the relationship with the other party should be valued as much as (or even more than) the substantive outcome. Thus, relational goals tend to support the choice of an integrative, or collaborative, strategy.

Trust. Trust is a complex concept in itself. In negotiation, trust is more specifically derived from past experience with another person, knowledge of that person's actions with other opponents, and expectations regarding how likely this person is to behave cooperatively in an upcoming interaction.[7] Trust acts on strategic negotiation choice both directly and indirectly (through the formation and consideration of principles and standards). The direct effect involves deciding how much the other party in a specific negotiation can be trusted to do (or not do). The effect on choice is direct in that it reflects beliefs about a particular, impending exchange. Trust also affects choice indirectly, through its direct effect on the negotiator's principles and standards. Beliefs and expectations about trust color and shape principles and standards in a global or general sense, and through them provide a filter, or test, that the negotiator applies to strategy choice. The difference between the direct and indirect effects of trust on strategy choice reflect what should or ought to happen (i.e., general beliefs about negotiation propriety and order), and what most likely will happen with a particular opponent, respectively. As most of us have experienced, it is possible to perceive a difference between beliefs and expectations ("I'd really prefer to be open and trusting, but I don't think I can afford to do that with this particular party"). It is also possible to face dilemmas between what we believe we should do and other, less-admirable behaviors that violate our standards—but which we might be able to get away with at little or no cost.

Driving Factors. How negotiators interpret, act on, or react to these elements generates the principles and standards that ultimately drive their choice of negotiation strategy.

Environments are the general settings within which events take place. In negotiation, environments include communities, industries, family groups, corporations, and so forth. Environments differ in the cultural and behavioral norms that shape the conduct of negotiations and determine what is appropriate and inappropriate conduct and action. They can affect the climate, or tone, of negotiations.

Contexts are the various situational settings that mark actual negotiation episodes within any given environment. For instance, within a given industry, management may negotiate frequently with suppliers, customers, regulatory agencies, and labor organizations. Each of these represents a different context within this single environment, and the contexts may differ from each other in ways that affect norms and expectations of outcomes, processes, and relationships.

Outcomes are the effects that results from past negotiations have on subsequent exchanges. These include the results of a given negotiation on both the current substantive issues (e.g., "We gave up more on price last time than we should have, so we intend to do better on price next time"), and on the current relationship between the negotiating parties ("They really gouged us on price last time; I don't think they really care about us as valued customers").

Processes are the vehicles, methodologies, and behaviors by which the negotiation takes place—the "how" of the activity or the play of the game. Processes can have both an environmental and a historical effect. Environmentally, processes reflect and predict the negotiation climate and norms that are generally expected (e.g., whether the negotiation involves formality and reserved manners, or informality and easygoing behavior). Historically, specific past processes have an effect on future exchanges in much the same way as goals, as mentioned above.

Relationships are the connections and associations among the negotiating parties, as well as those among the parties and their various constituencies. For example, a customer may have trouble expecting anything different out of a supplier who has been very powerful in the past and who has always dictated the price and product availability to the customer. Frequently, negotiators also must be concerned with their relationships back home, considering expected norms and appearances, or constituency effects. Constituency expectations and accountability often drive negotiators to do (or not do) things in dealing with other negotiators that would not be issues if the constituencies did not exist or made no demands (e.g., "You'd better bargain tough for us with management this time; no contract, no work!"). (See Chapter 7.)

Summary

Negotiation strategy choice is affected by four key elements: trust level, principles and standards at stake, negotiating goals, and episodic assumptions about what will happen in the upcoming negotiation. Several of these elements also have an impact on each other. Principles and standards are affected by five key driving factors: environmental factors, negotiation contexts, prior outcomes, prior processes employed to achieve those outcomes, and the status of the relationship with the opponent and with other key parties. Thus, strategy choice is the result of a complex number of interrelated factors.

Managing the Planning Process

On the surface, the drama and theatrics of face-to-face confrontation can easily create the impression that negotiation success lies in persuasiveness, eloquence, clever maneuvers, and occasional histrionics. Although these tactics make the process interesting (and at times even entertaining), the foundation for success in negotiation is the planning that takes place prior to the actual interaction process.

Many Negotiators Are Poor Planners!

Regrettably, systematic planning is not something that most of us do willingly. Managers, for example, are much more inclined to take action than to spend time reflecting about conditions and planning.[8] Time constraints and work pressures make it difficult to set aside the time to plan adequately. For many of us, planning is boring and tedious, easily put off in favor of getting into the action quickly. In addition to devoting insufficient time to planning, negotiators frequently fail because of several weaknesses in their planning processes:

- Negotiators fail to set clear objectives that can serve as standards by which to evaluate offers and packages. When something has to give, or when the other party makes a proposal that rearranges the component elements of a settlement, a negotiator who does not have clear objectives is not in a position to evaluate the new possibilities quickly and accurately. As a result, she may agree to something she later finds is not to her advantage. Alternatively, the negotiator may become confused and defensive and delay the process, causing the other party to lose patience.

- If negotiators have not done their homework, they may not understand the strengths and weaknesses of their positions or recognize weaknesses in other parties' arguments. As a result, they may not be able to formulate convincing arguments to support their own position or rebut their opponent's arguments.

- Negotiators cannot simply depend upon being quick and clever during the give and take of negotiation. Should the other party plan to win by stalling and delaying, holding to a position to wear you down, other approaches will be necessary. Being glib and eloquent in presenting your position is not helpful when the other party assails that position as illegal, inefficient, or ineffective.

Guarding against potential shortcomings in the planning process is necessary, but it's not enough.[9] Effective planning also requires hard work on a number of specific steps:

1. Defining issues.
2. Assembling issues and defining agendas.
3. Defining interests.
4. Consulting with others.
5. Managing goal setting.
6. Identifying your own limits.
7. Developing supporting arguments.
8. Analyzing the other party.

Defining the Issues

In identifying the issues at stake, an analysis of the conflict situation will usually be the first step. A negotiation usually involves one or two major issues and several minor ones. In a negotiation, a complete list of the issues at stake is best derived from these sources:

- An analysis of the conflict problem.
- Our own past experience in similar conflicts.
- Gathering information through research.
- Consultation with experts.

Before considering ways to manage our list of issues, a word of caution is necessary. Defining the key issues may be quite complex and elusive. For example, suppose a manager gets signals from his boss that his performance is not up to par, yet whenever he tries to confront the boss to discuss the problem and secure a realistic performance appraisal, the boss won't talk directly about the problem (which raises the manager's anxiety even further). Although the conflict in this situation is evident, the issues are elusive and complex. The central issue for the employee is the performance appraisal and why the boss won't give it. Maybe the boss is uncomfortable with doing the performance appraisal process or has a problem confronting other people about their behavior. Perhaps the boss is so preoccupied with her own job security that she doesn't even realize the impact she is having on her subordinate. In a situation like this one, where the issues are important but somewhat elusive, the manager needs to be clear about both what the issue is (in this case, getting a clear performance evaluation *and* getting the manager to talk about it) and how to initiate a productive discussion.

Assembling Issues and Defining the Bargaining Mix

The next step in planning is to assemble all the issues we have defined into a comprehensive list. The combination of lists from each side in the negotiation determines the bargaining mix (see Chapter 2). In generating a list of issues, there may be a tendency to put too much on the table at once, to raise too many issues. This may happen if the parties do not talk frequently or if they have lots of business to transact. However, provided that all the issues are real, it often turns out that a longer list of issues makes success more likely, rather than less likely. Larger bargaining mixes give us more possible components and arrangements for settlement, thus increasing the likelihood that a particular package will meet both parties' needs and therefore increasing the likelihood of a successful settlement.[10] At the same time, larger bargaining mixes can lengthen negotiations because there are more possible combinations of issues to consider, and combining and evaluating all these mixes makes things very complex.

Once issues are assembled on an agenda, the next step for the negotiator is to prioritize them. In assigning priorities to issues, the negotiator must do two things:

- Determine which of the issues are most important and which are minor in importance.
- Determine whether the issues are connected. If they are not, they can be easily added or subtracted; if they are, then settlement on one will be linked to settlement on the others and making concessions on one issue will inevitably be tied to making concessions on the other.

Defining Your Interests

After defining the issues, you must address the underlying interests and needs. If issues help us define what we want, then getting at interests requires us to ask why we want it. Asking these why questions usually surfaces critical values, needs, or principles that we want to achieve in the negotiation. These interests can be:

- Substantive (directly related to the focal issues under negotiation).
- Process-based (related to the manner in which we settle this dispute).
- Relationship-based (tied to the current or desired future relationship between the parties).
- Based on principles and standards (tied to intangibles or referring to the informal norms by which we will negotiate and the benchmarks we will use to guide us toward a settlement). (see Chapter 1.)

Consulting With Others

Having determined the relative importance of the issues, having evaluated the bargaining mix, and having ascertained the underlying interests and needs, negotiators at this stage frequently consult with others—particularly if the negotiator represents some constituent group or organization. This may seem premature to new negotiators, but experienced negotiators know that one negotiator alone cannot determine the issues on an agenda. Considerable consultation—and negotiation—must often occur between the negotiator and her constituents, and between the negotiator and the opponent, before formal deliberations begin.

Consulting with constituencies. If a negotiator is bargaining on behalf of others, they must be consulted so their concerns and priorities are included in the mix. A negotiator who is representing a constituency is often accountable to that constituency and must include and pursue their wishes in proposals. When negotiating for a large constituency, such as an entire company or union or a community, the process of consulting with the constituency can be elaborate and exhaustive. Many times the negotiator may also recognize that the constituency's wish list is unrealistic and unobtainable; negotiators will then be required to negotiate with their constituency over what should be put on the agenda and what is realistic to expect.

Consultation with the other side—clarifying issues, discussing agenda, negotiating ground rules. Consultation with the other side prior to actual negotiation is all too frequently neglected. A bargainer may draw up a firm list of issues and even establish specific goals well before the initial negotiation meeting. This process is valuable because it forces the bargainer to think through her position and decide on objectives. However, there is also potential risk in this process: the bargainer may define new issues to bring to the table that the other party is unprepared to discuss, or she may define priorities that cannot realistically be achieved. Many professional negotiators (labor negotiators, diplomats, etc.) often exchange (and negotiate) the list of issues in advance so that they can first agree to what will be discussed (the agenda) before actually engaging the substance of those issues.

However, preliminary consultation with the opponent does not always happen. When it does not, one side can dictate the negotiating issues, or the agenda itself (*what* issues we are discussing) becomes intertwined with the actual discussion of the issues themselves. In collaborative negotiation in particular, the agenda should be developed through mutual agreement and consultation prior to the actual discussion of the issue. In addition to negotiating the agenda, it may also be useful to prenegotiate other elements of the negotiation protocol—in effect, to negotiate about how to negotiate. There are several key elements to this protocol; each can have a subtle effect on the negotiation process and outcome:

- *The location of negotiation.* Negotiators tend to do better on their home turf—their own office, building, and city. They know the space, they feel more comfortable and relaxed, they have direct access to all the amenities—secretary, research information, expert advice, computer, and so on. In cross-cultural negotiations (see Chapter 12), language and cultural differences may come into play, and the parties may have to travel across many time zones. If negotiators want to minimize the advantage that comes with home turf, then they need to select neutral territory in which neither party will have an advantage. In addition, negotiators can choose the degree of formality of the environment.

- *The time period of negotiation.* If negotiators expect long, protracted deliberations, they might want to negotiate the time and duration of sessions. When do we start? How long do we meet? When do we need to end? When can we call for coffee breaks or time to caucus with our team?

- *Other parties who might be involved in the negotiation.* Is the negotiation between the principals only? Does one or both sides want to bring experts or advisors with them? What role will these outsiders play? Does one or both sides want to be represented by an agent who will negotiate for them? If so, will the principal be there? Or will the agent only consult her later? Is the media involved, and what role might they play?

- *What might be done if negotiation fails.* What will happen if we deadlock? Will we go to a third-party neutral (see Chapter 10)? Might we try
  some other techniques (see Chapter 5 for many suggestions on getting
  negotiations back on track)?

In new bargaining relationships, discussions on these procedural issues are
often used as tests to determine how the negotiation on the substantive issues will
proceed. Success in such procedural negotiations may make it easier to reach
agreement later, on the substantive issues.

Prioritizing—Defining the Relative Importance of Our Issues

The next step in negotiation planning is to determine the relative importance of
issues. Once negotiation begins, parties can easily be swept up in the rush of
information, arguments, offers, counteroffers, trade-offs, and concessions. For
those who are not clear in advance about what they want (and what they can do
without), it is easy to lose perspective and agree to suboptimal settlements, or to
get hung up on points that are relatively unimportant. When negotiators do not
have priorities, they may be more likely to yield on those points aggressively
argued by the other side, rather than to yield on the issues that are less important
to their own side.

Priorities can be set in a number of ways. One simple way is for the negotiator to rank order the issues by asking, "What is most important?" "What is second most important?" and "What is least important?" An even simpler process is
to group issues into categories of high, medium, or low importance. When setting
priorities (i.e., ranking issues), remember to pay attention to both tangibles *and*
intangibles. More than one negotiator has received a rude shock when her constituency has rejected a settlement because it ignored the intangibles or dealt with
them suboptimally in the final agreement.

Assessing the other's priorities. You may be able to learn what issues are
important to the other side, or what their real interests might be—*why* they want
what they say they want. By comparing this assessment against our own, we can
begin to define areas where there may be strong conflict (we both have a high priority for the same thing), simple trade-offs (we want the same group of things but
in differing priorities), or no conflict at all (we want very different things and both
sides can easily have our objectives and interests met).

Setting Goals: Understanding Limits

What happens if the other party in a negotiation refuses to accept some proposed
items for the agenda or states issues in such a way that they are far below our
resistance point? Negotiators should reassess these issues and decide how
important they really are. Can they be dropped? Can they be postponed and
taken up later? If the answer is no, then the other side has to consider whether

or not to proceed. If needs can be addressed adequately without negotiation, or if the likely costs of negotiation (including the investment of time) exceed the likely gains, it may be appropriate to forgo negotiation altogether (i.e., to choose an avoidance strategy).

The goal-setting process. Once the issues have been defined, a tentative agenda has been assembled, and others have been consulted as appropriate and necessary, the next step is to define goals on the key issues in the bargaining mix.

Where to start—optimistic, realistic, or pessimistic? In setting goals, we need to consider four key points: the target point (at which we realistically expect to achieve a settlement), the resistance point (the least acceptable settlement point, or the point below which we are likely to reject a deal), the alternative or BATNA (the point where we may have an alternative settlement with another negotiator, or where we may go it alone), and the asking price or opening bid (representing the best deal we can possibly hope to achieve). In goal setting, the question arises of where planning should start: at the most optimistic point, the likely target point, or the most pessimistic resistance point?

Goal setting forces positive thinking about objectives. Negotiators attempt to become aware of the other party—how they may behave, what they will probably demand, and how the negotiators feel about dealing with them. However, it is possible to devote too much attention to the other party, spending too much time trying to figure out what the other side wants, how to meet those demands, and so forth. If negotiators focus attention *totally* on the other side to the exclusion of themselves, they may plan their entire strategy as a reaction to the other's anticipated conduct. Such loss of initiative usually means trouble for the reactive negotiator.

Goal setting usually requires packaging among several issues and objectives. Because most negotiators have a mixture of bargaining objectives, they must consider the best way to achieve satisfaction across these multiple issues. This returns us to our earlier definition of the issues, the bargaining mix, and an understanding of the other's bargaining mix. Negotiators propose settlements that will help them achieve realistic or optimistic targets on the more important issues; they may then balance these areas by setting more conservative targets for items less important to them.

Goal setting requires an understanding of trade-offs and throwaways. Our discussion of packaging raises another possible problem. What do we do if the other party proposes a package that puts issues A, B, and C in our optimistic range, puts item D in the realistic range, puts E at the pessimistic point, and does not even mention item F, which is part of our bargaining mix? Is item F a throwaway item that we can ignore? If it is not a throwaway item, is it relatively unimportant and worth giving up in order to lock in agreement on A, B, and C in the optimal range? Suppose the other party had given us two proposed packages, the one described above and a second one that places items A and E in the optimistic range, items B and F in the realistic range, and C at the pessimistic point but ignores D. Would the first or the second package be more attractive?

To evaluate these packages, a negotiator needs to have some idea of what each item in the bargaining mix is worth in terms that can be compared across issues. The bargainer needs some way of establishing trade-offs. This is sometimes a difficult thing to do because different items or issues will be of different value to the bargainer and will often be measured in different terms.

Even though it may not be possible to find a common dimension (such as dollar value) to compare issues in the bargaining mix or to compare tangibles with intangibles, many negotiators have found it convenient to scale all items on some common dimension. The premise is that even if the fit is not perfect, any guide is better than none. Moreover, particularly if intangibles are a key part of the bargaining mix, negotiators must know the point at which they are willing to abandon the pursuit of an intangible in favor of substantial gains on tangibles. Translating every issue into dollars is one way to facilitate these comparisons.

Developing Supporting Arguments—Doing Research

One important aspect of actual negotiations is to be able to present a case clearly and to marshal ample supporting facts and arguments. Another is to be able to refute the other party's arguments with counterarguments. Because of the breadth and diversity of issues that can be included in negotiations, it is impossible to specify all the procedures that can be used to assemble information. There are, however, some good general guides that can be used:

- What facts support my point of view? What substantiates or validates this information as factual?
- With whom may I consult or talk in order to help me elaborate or clarify the facts? What records, files, or data sources exist that support my arguments?
- Have these issues been negotiated before by others under similar circumstances? Can I consult those negotiators to determine what major arguments they used, which ones were successful, and which were not?
- What is the other party's point of view likely to be? What are their interests? What arguments are they likely to make? How can I respond to those arguments and seek more creative positions that go further in addressing both sides' issues and interests?
- How can I develop and present the facts so they are most convincing? What visual aids, pictures, charts, graphs, expert testimony, and the like can be helpful or make the best case?

Analyzing the Other Party

Gathering information about the other party is a critical step in preparing for negotiation. Several key pieces of background information will be of great importance in aiding in our own preparation:

- The other party's current resources, interests, and needs.
- The other party's objectives.
- The other party's reputation and negotiation style.
- The other party's BATNA.
- The other party's authority to make an agreement.
- The other party's likely strategy and tactics.

Let's look at each of these in more detail.

The other party's current resources, interests, and needs. A negotiator will learn much about the other party at the negotiating table, but he should gather as much information as possible in advance through research and homework. Determination of which data are the most relevant will depend on the negotiation and who the other party is. You might study the other party's business history. An analysis of that person's previous negotiations, successful and otherwise, will provide useful clues. Financial data about the organization might be obtained through channels such as Dun and Bradstreet, financial statements, newspapers, files, company biographies, stock reports, and public records of legal judgments. You might investigate the other party's inventories. Sometimes you can learn a great deal simply by visiting the other party or talking to his friends and peers and asking questions. Another way to learn is to ask questions of people who have done business with the other party.

The other party's objectives. How do we understand and appraise the other party's goals? Although we may speculate about one another's goals and objectives, most of us do not gather information systematically—although we should. One of the best ways to get this information is directly from the other party. Professional negotiators often exchange information about goals or initial proposals days or even weeks before negotiations begin. If this does not occur, then the negotiator should plan to collect this information at the parties' first meeting.

The other party's reputation and style. As noted earlier, the other party's past negotiating behavior is a good indication of how they will behave in the future. If a bargainer has had no prior experience with the other person, talking to those who have dealt with that party in the past can be very valuable. There is a potential danger in drawing conclusions from this information, however. Assuming that the other party will act in the future the way they have been described as acting in the past is just that—an assumption. People can and do act differently in different circumstances at different times. Although past behavior is a reasonable starting point for making assumptions, people do change. Our impression of the other party's reputation may be based upon several factors:

- How their predecessors have negotiated with us in the past.
- How they have negotiated with us in the past, either in the same or in different contexts.
- How they have negotiated with others in the past.

These different bases for our assumptions have different degrees of relevance and therefore different degrees of usefulness for predicting future behavior. We can use the information to prepare, to alert ourselves to what might happen, but we should also act with caution and actively look for new information that confirms or denies the validity of our assumption. There is always the danger, however, that invalid assumptions will lead a negotiator into unfortunate self-fulfilling prophecies. That is, there is often a tendency to seek and recognize information *confirming* our desires and assumptions, while failing to seek or recognize information that *counters* them.

A negotiator who assumes the other party is going to be demanding and aggressive may decide that "the best defense is a good offense" and open with aggressive demands and belligerent behavior. The other party may accept this behavior in stride, or they may decide to reply in kind, even though they initially intended to be cooperative. Of course, when the other party does fight back, the first negotiator's assumptions seem to be confirmed.

The other party's BATNA. As part of the preparation process, we have stressed that negotiators need to understand their own alternative or BATNA. The alternative offers the negotiator a viable option for agreement if the current negotiation does not yield an acceptable outcome. Similarly, we should attempt to understand the quality of the other party's BATNA. If he has a strong and viable BATNA, the other party will probably be confident in negotiation, set high objectives, and be willing to push hard for those objectives. In contrast, if he has a weak BATNA, then he will be more dependent on achieving a satisfactory agreement with us, and we may be able to drive a harder bargain because the other party's alternative is unsatisfactory.

The other party's authority. When negotiators represent others, their power to make agreements may be limited. In fact, their ability to carry out negotiations may be restricted in many ways. Sometimes a constituency tells negotiators that they cannot make any agreements; often they can only pass on proposals from the constituency or collect information and take it back to their superiors. There are many reasons for limiting a negotiator's authority. Negotiators kept on a short leash cannot be won over by a persuasive presentation to commit their constituency to something that is not wanted. They cannot give out sensitive information carelessly. Although these limitations may actually be helpful to a negotiator, they can also be frustrating!

Summary

Preparation is of primary importance in negotiation. We presented a basic model of negotiation strategy choice, and suggested that strategy choice is determined by the interplay of five components: goals, principles and standards, trust, episodic assumptions, and a list of driving factors that includes environments, contexts, outcomes, processes, and relationships.

Having described our model, we then discussed the various aspects of managing the planning process. We propose that negotiation success is largely a function of careful planning. A negotiator who carefully plans will make an effort to do the following:

- Realize that different negotiation situations might call for different basic strategies, as well as varying levels of concern for the substantive and relational aspects of the negotiations.
- Clarify the goals and objectives that he would like to achieve.
- Understand and define the key issues and interests at stake in the negotiation and be able to specify which ones are important and which she would like to achieve.
- Consult with others—constituents and possibly opponents—to shape and refine the agenda of issues, interests, and goals.
- Understand the fundamental predictability of the negotiation process so he can strategically plan how to achieve his goals and objectives and how one's limits should be defined.
- Understand the other party and how the other party's personality, history, and negotiating style are likely to affect the strategy.
- Develop the key supporting arguments and information to build a persuasive case for achieving objectives.

If a negotiator is able to consider and evaluate each of these factors, the negotiator will know what he wants and will have a clear sense of direction on how to proceed. This sense of direction, and the confidence derived from it, will be the single most important factor in affecting negotiating outcomes.

End Notes

1. See Quinn (1991).
2. Thompson and Hastie (1990a).
3. Mintzberg (1991).
4. See Lax and Sebenius (1986).
5. See Sheppard, Lewicki, and Minton (1992) for a comprehensive discussion of fairness standards.
6. See Fisher, Ury, and Patton (1991).
7. See Pruitt and Carnevale (1993) for a summary of negotiation research findings.
8. See Mintzberg (1973) and Sheppard, Blumenfeld-Jones, Minton, and Hyder (1994).
9. See Richardson (1977), Asherman and Asherman (1990), Dan Bernstein's *Negotiator Pro,* (1995).
10. See Rubin and Brown (1975).

5 DEALING WITH NEGOTIATION BREAKDOWNS

As we have noted several times, negotiation is a conflict management process, and all conflict situations have the potential for becoming derailed. The parties become angry or entrenched in their positions. Perceptions become distorted and judgments are biased. Communication decreases in effectiveness and is used instead to accuse and blame the other. The other party's negotiation style does not enable us to reach agreement. The parties cannot find a middle ground where agreement is possible. In short, destructive conflict processes override the negotiation, and the parties cannot proceed.

This chapter focuses on three key areas where negotiation breakdowns may occur. First, we focus on the techniques available to the parties themselves to get negotiations back on track. Second, we examine processes that can be used to convert a negotiation situation from a more distributive bargaining process to a more integrative negotiation process. Finally, we explore strategy and tactics that can be used to control or manage difficult behavior in an opponent.

General Conflict Management by the Parties Themselves

The alternatives posed in this chapter are designed to respond to the following dynamics:

- The atmosphere is charged with anger, frustration, and resentment. Mistrust and hostility are directed at the opposing negotiator.
- Channels of communication, previously used to exchange information and supporting arguments for each side's position, are now closed or constrained. Each side attempts to use communication channels to

criticize and blame the opponent, while simultaneously attempting to close off the same type of communication from her opponent.

- The original issues at stake have become blurred and ill-defined, and perhaps new issues have been added. Negotiators have become identified with positions on issues, and the conflict has become personalized. Even if a negotiator were ready to make a concession to the other side, he would not make it due to a strong dislike for the other party.

- The parties tend to perceive great differences in their respective positions. Conflict heightens the magnitude of these differences and minimizes areas of perceived commonalty and agreement. The parties see themselves as further apart than they may actually be, and they do not recognize areas where they may be in agreement.

- As anger and tension increase, the parties become more locked into their initial negotiating positions. Rather than searching for ways to make concessions and move toward agreement, the parties become firmer in stating their initial demands, and they resort to threats, lies, and distortions to force the other party to comply with those demands. The opponent usually meets these threats with counterthreats and retaliation.

- If there is more than one person on a side, those on the same side tend to view each other more favorably. They see the best qualities in the people on their side and minimize whatever differences exist, yet they also demand more conformity from their team members and will accept a more militant, autocratic form of leadership. If there is dissension in the group, it is hidden from the opposing party; group members always attempt to present a united front to the other side.

Reducing Tension And Synchronizing De-Escalation

Unproductive deliberations usually become highly emotional. Parties are frustrated, angry, and upset. They are strongly committed to their viewpoints and have argued strenuously for their preferred alternatives, seeing themselves as firm, principled, or deserving. The other side, behaving the same way, is seen as stubborn, bullheaded, inflexible, and unreasonable. The longer the parties debate, the more likely emotions will overrule reason—name-calling and verbal assaults on the other replace logic and reason. When the dispute becomes personalized, turning into a win–lose feud between individuals, negotiation loses all hope of productivity. Several approaches for controlling conflict are specifically directed at defusing volatile emotions.

Tension release. Tension is a natural by-product of negotiations. Consequently, negotiators should be aware that it is bound to increase, and they should know how to act to address or diminish it. Some negotiators who are sensitive to increases in tension know how to make a witty remark or crack a joke that causes laughter and releases tension. Others know that it is sometimes appropriate to let the other become angry and ventilate the pent-up anger and frustration, without having to respond in kind. Skilled negotiators also know that by listening to the other person and allowing the expression of feelings, the catharsis will vent emotion and clear the air and may permit negotiations to return to a calmer pace.

Acknowledgment of the other's feelings: Active listening. When one party states her views and the other openly disagrees, the first negotiator often hears the disagreement as more than *just* disagreement. She may hear a challenge, a put-down, an assertion that the statement is wrong or not acceptable, an accusation of lying or distortion of the facts, or another form of personal attack. Whether or not this is the message that was intended is unimportant; the negotiator has to deal with the way it was received. Understandably, such misinterpretations escalate conflict.

There is a difference between accurately hearing what the other party has said and agreeing with those statements. When conflict escalates, accurate listening frequently becomes confused with agreeing and accepting. Situations like this may be effectively handled by letting the other person know that you have heard and understood both the content and the emotional strength of the message. This technique is called active listening, and it is frequently used in interviews and therapy settings as a way of encouraging a person to speak more freely.[1] Rather than challenging and confronting the other negotiator's statements by bolstering your own statements (and position), you respond with statements that probe for confirmation and elaboration on the other's first statements. Comments may include these: "You see the facts this way," "You feel very strongly about this point," or "I can see that if you saw things this way, you would feel threatened and upset by what I have said." These statements do not indicate that you *agree* with these statements; rather, they communicate only that you have accurately heard and understood the other person.

Separation of the parties. The most common approach to letting tempers cool down is to break off face-to-face relations. Declare a recess, call a caucus, and agree to adjourn and come back together later when the parties have had a chance to unwind. The parties should acknowledge explicitly that the purpose of the caucus is to allow tempers to cool so the dialogue will become less emotional. Each party should also agree to return with a renewed effort to make deliberations more productive—either by simply regaining composure, or by attempting to address the issue that created the anger in a new or different way.

Separation of the parties may occur for short periods of time such as a few minutes or hours, or it may be planned to last for several days or weeks. Variations in the time period are related to the level of hostility, as well as to unique situational circumstances. Parties may use the time to check with their constituencies, gather new information, and reassess their position and commitments.

Synchronized de-escalation: GRIT. Conflict situations are dynamics—they change constantly. Charles Osgood, writing about the Cold War and disarmament, suggested a unilateral strategy for conflict de-escalation called GRIT (**G**raduated and **R**eciprocated **I**nitiatives in **T**ension Reduction).[2] The party who desires to de-escalate a conflict initiates the action, deciding on some small concession that each side could make that would signal both sides' good faith and desire to de-escalate. The concessions should be large enough so it can be read as an unambiguous signal of a desire to change the relationship, but not so large that if only one side followed through, that side would make itself weak or vulnerable. The unilateral action should then be publicly announced to the other side:

1. Stating exactly what the concession is.
2. Stating that the concession is part of a deliberate strategic policy to reduce tension.
3. Stating that the other side is explicitly invited to reciprocate in some specified form.
4. Stating that the concession will be executed on some stated time schedule.
5. Stating that each party commits to execute the concession without knowing whether the other will reciprocate.

The party that initiated the de-escalation then executes the concession. The specific concession should be something that is obvious, unambiguous, and subject to easy verification. Making it public and symbolic will help.

If the opposing party does not respond, then the initiator goes through with the action and repeats the sequence again, selecting a simple, low-risk concession in an effort to attract the other into synchronized de-escalation. If the other does respond, then the initiator proposes a second action, slightly riskier than the first, and once again initiates the sequence. For example, Bill could agree to clean the bathroom again or have Alice show him where she is unsatisfied with his cleaning efforts. As the synchronized de-escalation takes hold, the parties can both propose larger and riskier concessions that will bring them back into a productive negotiating relationship.

GRIT strategies are efforts to change the nature of relationships—from hostile and mistrusting, with each side attempting to punish the other, to more open and trusting, in which one side initiates a trusting gesture, and each side rewards the other's gestures with more cooperative efforts. This mutual reward sequence will help to de-escalate the conflict and often leads to a positive, productive climate for negotiation.

Improving the Accuracy of Communication

The second step in conflict reduction is to ensure that both parties accurately understand the other's position. As stated earlier, when conflict becomes more heated, communication efforts concentrate on managing emotions and directing the next assault at the other. Effective listening declines. We think we know what the other side is going to say, and we do not care to listen to it anymore. In intense conflict, listening becomes so diminished that the parties are frequently unaware that their positions may have much in common. According to Anatol Rapoport, this is the "blindness of involvement," because it inhibits the development of trust and the problem-solving process.[3] Several approaches can be used to rectify this situation.

Role reversal. Role reversal is one way of helping each side see things from the other's perspective. One party attempts to put herself in the other's shoes, looking at the issue from the other's perspective. You can reverse roles simply by playing out scenarios in your imagination, by asking a friend or colleague to assume the other role and act out a dialogue, or, more effectively, by including role reversal as part of a unilateral strategy preparation process. Although role reversal will not tell exactly how the other party thinks and feels about the issues, the process can provide useful and surprising insights about how the other party might see, feel, and think about things.

Imaging. Like role reversal, imaging is also a method for gaining insight into the other party's perspective. In the imaging process, parties in conflict are asked to engage in the following four distinct activities:

- To describe how they see themselves.
- To describe how the other party appears to them.
- To state how they think the other party would describe them.
- To state how they think the other party sees themselves.

The parties then exchange this information. Parties first compare how they described themselves, then how they would describe the other and how they think the other party would describe them, and lastly, how they think the other would describe themselves. The differences between the two sets of statements are frequently surprising because they reveal dissimilarities and inconsistencies. Imaging usually produces animated discussion as the parties clarify and substantiate what they have said or heard. A common result is that the parties recognize that many apparent differences and areas of conflict are not real and begin to better understand those that are real.

Controlling Issues

A third major difficulty that inhibits parties from resolving conflict is that as conflict intensifies, the size and number of the issues expand. As conflict escalates, it snowballs; bits and pieces of other issues accumulate into a large, unmanageable mass. Although smaller conflicts can be managed satisfactorily one at a time, larger conflicts become unwieldy and less amenable to easy resolution. The problem for negotiators in escalated disputes, therefore, is to develop strategies to contain issue proliferation and reduce the dispute to manageable proportions.

There are six major approaches to "fractionating" conflict, or reducing a large conflict into smaller parts:

- Reduce the number of parties on each side.
- Control the number of substantive issues involved.

- State issues in concrete terms rather than as principles.
- Restrict the precedents involved, both procedural and substantive.
- Search for ways to fractionate the big issues.
- Depersonalize issues, separating them from the parties advocating them.[4]

Let's examine each of these approaches.

Reduce the number of parties on each side. When conflict escalates, both parties seek to build alliances for strength or to bring their constituencies into the dispute; either they increase the number of parties at the negotiation or they bring more clout to the table. Additional parties, such as lawyers, experts, or parties with more formal authority, are often brought into negotiations for the information or the clout they can provide. Because the sheer number of parties at the table can make negotiations considerably more complex (more parties equal more perspectives on the issues, more time needed to hear each side, more opportunities for disagreement, etc.), negotiation ground rules should provide ways to limit the number of parties. One way to control conflict size is to return the dispute to the original negotiating parties. The fewer actors present, or the more the conflict can be limited to two individuals, the more likely the parties will be to reach a favorable settlement.

Control the number of substantive issues involved. A second way to control the size of a conflict is to keep the number of issues small enough to manage. When conflict escalates, the size and number of issues proliferate. Some conflicts escalate to the point where there are too many issues to manage constructively. At the same time, limiting negotiations to a very few issues also raises problems. Single-issue conflicts are frequently harder to manage because they quickly lead to win–lose polarization over the issue. In such circumstances, it is often desirable to expand the number of issues so both sides can see themselves as having gained something, and thus achieve a win–win solution. You can expand the number of issues by defining the issue more broadly so resolution can benefit both sides or by coupling the issue with another issue so each party can receive a preferred settlement on one of the issues. We discussed bundling and packaging issues, the bargaining mix, and inventing options in Chapters 2 and 3.

State issues in concrete terms rather than as principles. A third way that conflict issues become difficult to control is when events or issues are treated as matters of principle. Small conflicts can rapidly become intractable disputes when their resolution is not treated as an isolated event, but instead must be consistent with a broader policy or principle. Because any deviation from policy is viewed as a threat to that policy, and because it is far more difficult to change broad policy than to make a concession on a single issue, negotiations are immediately problematic. For example, an employee needs to take her child to the doctor during her work hours and requests an excused absence from the company. The company does not have a policy that permits employees to take time off for this reason, and the employee's supervisor tells her she has to take sick leave or vacation time instead. "It's a matter of principle," management asserts. Resorting to arguments of principle and policy is often a strategic defense by high-power parties against any change from the status quo; however, the longer discussion remains at the level of policy or principle, the less likely those disputes can be successfully resolved. There are, of course, times when a single event is properly seen as indicative of a new principle or policy. That being the case, negotiations should be arranged to address the policy or principle specifically. Many times, people are reluctant to address principles because they know negotiations over principles are difficult and lengthy. However, to attempt to negotiate a concrete issue when the negotiation really involves the hidden agenda of a major principle only results in frustration. If this occurs, it is wise to face the issue and raise it directly. There are at least two strategies to do so:

- *Question whether the issue needs to be addressed at the principle or policy level.* Inquire about the link between the specific issue and the broader policy or principle. If none exists and if one party wants to look at the matter from a policy or principle level, suggest that the immediate concrete issue be handled and discussed separately from the underlying principle or policy. If need be, the parties can agree that the concrete issue can be settled in this instance, with no expectation as to how the policy will later be established.
- *Point out that exceptions can be made to all policies, and that principles and policies can be maintained even if minor deviations are agreed to under special circumstances.* The parties may be willing to agree that this specific negotiation might be one of those times.

Restrict the precedents involved, both procedural and substantive. The final type of issue magnification occurs when the parties treat concessions on a single issue as violations of some substantive or procedural precedent. When a substantive precedent is at stake, one party will imply that to concede on this issue at this time will render him vulnerable to conceding on the same issue, or a similar issue, in the future. To return to our previous example, the manager is likely to argue that if she grants the employee an excused absence in this case, when no policy exists, then she will be obligated to grant every other employee the same request. Belief in the domino theory is strong. The high-power party, who supports the precedent, believes that if she gives in to this request, rather than nipping the problem in the bud, there will be no end to the number and types of requests she may get for excused absences in the future. In contrast, procedural precedents are at stake when parties agree to follow a process they haven't followed before. For example, a procedural precedent may be set when the parties agree to negotiate in a relationship that previously has not been characterized by negotiation, or where one has more power than the other. In the same employment example, the manager may not want to give the employee the excused absence because the employee did not submit any proof that she was, in fact, taking a child to the doctor.

Issues of precedent are usually as thorny to control as issues of principle. Once again, a negotiator trying to move a conflict toward de-escalation and resolution should try to keep from translating single issues into major questions of precedent. Focus the dialogue on the key issue and persist in arguments that concessions on this issue at this time do not necessarily dictate any precedents—substantive or procedural—for the future.

Search for ways to fractionate the big issues. Also called salami tactics, these are ways to slice a large issue into smaller pieces. Issues that can be expressed in quantitative terms are easy to slice. For example, compensation demands can be cut up into pennies-per-hour increments, or lease rates can be reduced to pennies per square foot. When trying to fractionate issues of principle or precedent, use the time horizon—when the principle goes into effect or how long it lasts—as a way to fractionate the issue, or vary the number of different ways that the principle may be applied. Thus, for example, the company may devise a family emergency leave policy, under which a manager may allow a period of no longer than three hours (without a formal application process), and no more often than once a month, for illness in the employee's immediate family.

Depersonalize issues: separating them from the parties advocating them. Positional bargaining tends to create conflict over both the issues and the relationship between negotiators. People become identified with positions on issues, and vice versa. Effective negotiation requires separating the issues from the parties, not only by working to establish a productive relationship between the parties (leaving only the issue conflict at stake), but also by trying to resolve the issues without regard to the people. Authors Fisher, Ury, and Patton extensively elaborate on this point, suggesting that effective integrative negotiation is "tough" on the negotiating problem but "soft" on the people.[5]

Establishing Commonalties

As we noted earlier, parties in escalated conflict tend to magnify perceived differences and to minimize perceived similarities. The parties tend to see themselves as farther apart and having less in common than may actually be the case. Therefore, a fourth major action that parties can take to de-escalate conflict is to establish commonalties or to focus on common objectives. Several approaches are possible: establishing common goals, focusing on common enemies, agreeing to follow a common procedure, and establishing a common framework for approaching the negotiation problem.

Superordinate goals. Superordinate goals are common goals; both parties desire them, but are unable to achieve them without cooperating with each other. In a corporation, for example, people do different jobs (e.g., marketing, manufacturing) that have different objectives, yet they must work together (e.g., to get the product to the customer) or the corporation will not survive.

Common enemies. A common enemy is a negative form of superordinate goal. The parties find new motivation to resolve their differences to avoid intervention by a third party or to pool resources to defeat a common enemy.

Agreement on rules and procedures. A third way parties can establish commonalties is by mutual agreement about the rules by which negotiations will be conducted. These ground rules include the following:

- Determining a site for a meeting.
- Setting a formal agenda as to what may and may not be discussed, and agreeing to abide by that agenda.
- Determining who may attend the meetings.
- Setting time limits for the individual meeting and for the overall negotiation session.
- Setting procedural rules, such as:

  Who may speak.

  How long they may speak.

  How issues will be approached.

  What facts may be introduced.

  How records of the meeting will be kept.

  How agreements will be affirmed.

  What clerical or support services are required.

- Finally, the parties may agree to set aside a short period of time during negotiations to critique "how they are doing."[6]

Integrative frameworks. Superordinate goals, common enemies, and mutual commitment to rules are factors outside the boundaries of the dispute; they transcend the specific issues and bring the parties together in unified action. However, superordinate goals and common enemies do not establish the foundation for long-term cooperation; when the common goal or common enemy is removed, the parties may find that they have no greater basis for resolving their dispute than they did before. Hence, other mechanisms must be pursued to establish a common ground for agreement.

There are two primary vehicles for developing commonalties in disputes: first, focusing on similarities between the parties rather than on differences; second, searching for ways to cognitively redefine the dispute to accommodate all parties' interests. Maximizing similarities is simply a process of refocusing the parties' attention on what they have in common, rather than where they disagree. As noted earlier, conflict processes tend to highlight perceived differences and magnify the importance of these differences. The longer the parties are in dispute, the more they quibble about the differences and the more they recognize other differences that are then drawn into the dispute. One way to control this escalation is to reemphasize what the parties have in common, such as objectives, purposes, overall philosophies and viewpoints, long-range goals, and styles of operation. Another is to review what they have accomplished together, either in the current negotiation or in prior engagements. Reemphasizing the commonalties tends to put the differences back into their proper perspective, and it de-emphasizes the importance of differences. This process either defuses the emotionality tied to the differences or creates a positive emotional bond based on similarities that will allow differences to be bridged.[7]

Integrative frameworks are ways of redefining the issues to create a common perspective from which initial positions appear more compatible. Successful negotiators focus on "interests," not positions.[8] By defining negotiated issues in terms of positions, parties tend to simplify complex phenomena by defining a single point and then refusing to move from it. To create movement, parties must establish ways of redefining the conflict so that they can explore compatible interests. There are several ways to create integrative frameworks out of polarized positions:[9]

- *Dimensionalize the problem.* Instead of treating the conflict as distinctly different categorical viewpoints, treat it as points along a continuum.

- *Increase the number of dimensions.* Multiple dimensions allow one party to win on one dimension and the other to win on another. Increasing the number of dimensions increases the possibility that the parties can identify a dimension on which they can more easily reconcile their differences.

- *Construct an ideal case.* Sometimes parties are in dispute because each is proposing a solution that meets only her own needs, but not those of the other. One way to break this deadlock is constructing an ideal case that would meet the needs of both sides, then creatively devising ways that both parties could ideally have their needs met, and then determining how that ideal scenario might be attained.

- *Search for semantic resolutions.* Particularly in conflicts where the parties are negotiating over words and ideas, conflict intensifies over key words, phrases, and expressions. Discovering how parties attach different meanings to some words, or exploring language that can accommodate both sides, is another alternative for achieving an integrative framework.

Making Preferred Options More Desirable to the Opponent

A final alternative method that parties can use to increase the likelihood of agreement is to make their desires and preferences appear more palatable to the other. Several approaches to this exist:[10]

- *Give them a "yesable" proposal.* Rather than emphasizing her own position and letting the other party suggest alternatives that she can approve or overrule, a negotiator can direct her efforts to understanding the other side's needs and devising a proposal that will meet those needs (i.e., one to which the only answer possible is yes).

- *Ask for a different decision.* Rather than making demands more general, negotiators can to make demands more specific. Negotiators must determine what specific elements of their demands are most palatable or offensive to the other party, then use this information to refine the demand (i.e., reformulate, repackage, reorganize, rephrase, split, divide, or make it more specific).

- *Sweeten the offer rather than intensifying the threat.* This is a matter of placing the emphasis on the positive rather than the negative. Promises and offers can be made more attractive in a variety of ways: maximizing their attractive qualities and minimizing their negative ones, showing how they meet the other party's needs, reducing the disadvantages to them of accepting an offer, making offers more credible (i.e., we will do what we promise to do), or setting deadlines on offers so they expire if not accepted quickly.

- *Use legitimacy or objective criteria to evaluate solutions.* Negotiators on both sides should be able to demonstrate that their demands are based on sound facts, calculations, and information, and that preferred solutions are consistent with those facts and information. The more this information is open to public verification and demonstrated to be within the bounds of fairness and legitimacy, the more convincing it will be that the position is independent of the negotiator who advocates it, and the more persuasive the position will be in achieving a settlement.

Specific Remedies: Traps, Challenges, and Processes

In this section, we address three other ways that negotiation can break down:

- Traps that we often set for ourselves.
- Challenges that occur when dealing with particularly difficult opponents.
- Processes for building more productive, resilient relationships.

Negotiation Traps

Negotiators often become their own worst enemies. This is most likely to happen when they engage in behaviors and thought processes that make negotiation more difficult and less productive than it can be.[11] These include:

- Irrational escalation of commitment.
- The belief that the issue under negotiation is a "fixed pie."
- Anchoring and adjustment in decision making.
- Issue and problem framing.
- Availability of information.

- The "winner's curse."
- Negotiator overconfidence.
- The law of small numbers.
- Biased causal accounts.
- The tendency to ignore others' cognitions.
- A process called reactive devaluation.

We will discuss each of these in more detail.

Irrational escalation of commitment. Negotiators sometimes maintain commitment to a course of action, even when that commitment constitutes irrational behavior on their part. This desire for consistency is often exacerbated by a desire to save face, to maintain an impression of expertise or control in front of others. No one likes to admit error or failure, especially when doing so may be perceived as a weakness in front of the other party. One way to combat these tendencies is to have an advisor, someone who is not consumed by the play of the game, provide a reality check. Such checks can warn negotiators when they inadvertently begin to behave irrationally.

Mythical "fixed pie" beliefs. Although some negotiations are categorized correctly as distributive or win–lose, many negotiators tend to assume that *all* negotiations constitute a fixed-pie, or zero-sum game. Negotiators often approach negotiation opportunities that are integrative in nature as zero-sum, win–lose, fixed-pie exchanges. Such beliefs assume that the possibility for integrative settlements and mutually beneficial trade-offs doesn't exist, and this belief suppresses any efforts to search for such settlements and trade-offs. Negotiators can minimize this fixed-pie belief through procedures for inventing options (see Chapter 3).

Anchoring and adjustment. Traps in this area are related to the effect of the standard (or anchor) against which subsequent adjustments (gains or losses) are measured during negotiation. The choice of an anchor (e.g., an initial offer or an intended goal) might well be based on faulty or incomplete information and thus be misleading in itself. However, once this initial anchor is defined, parties tend to treat it as real and valid and use it as a benchmark to adjust all other judgments relative to it. Goals in negotiation, *whether realistically or carelessly set,* can also serve as anchors. These anchors may be visible or invisible to the other party, and the person who holds them may do so consciously or unconsciously. Thorough preparation and the use of a devil's advocate or reality check can help prevent errors of anchoring and adjustment.[12]

Framing. By a frame, we mean the subjective mechanism through which we evaluate and make sense out of situations, leading us to pursue or avoid subsequent actions. The framing process can cause us to exhibit certain behaviors while ignoring or avoiding others, leading us to seek, avoid, or be neutral about risk in decision making and negotiation. It is in evaluating risk that framing most affects negotiators; framing can make negotiators more or less risk averse or risk seeking. If a negotiator is more risk averse, she may accept any viable offer put on the table simply because she is afraid of losing it. However, if the negotiator is more risk seeking, she should be willing to pass up an offer, choosing instead to wait for a better offer or for possible future concessions.

This positive/negative framing process is not inconsequential. Negotiations in which the outcomes are negatively framed tend to produce fewer concessions, reach fewer agreements, and perceive outcomes as less fair than positively framed negotiations. Remedies for framing effects are similar to those mentioned above (e.g., better information, thorough analysis, and reality checks) but are more difficult to achieve (and thus, more critical) because frames are often tied to deeply held matters of personal value and belief or other anchors that we cannot detect.

Availability of information. In negotiation, the availability trap operates when information that is presented in more vivid, colorful, or attention-getting ways becomes easier to recall, and thus more central and critical in evaluating events and options. Information presented through a particularly clear chart, diagram, or formula (even if it is overly simplified) might be used more readily than data that are confusing, detailed, or hard to understand. Availability of information also affects negotiation through the use of established "search patterns." If we have a favorite way of collecting information or key things we tend to look for, we will use these patterns repeatedly and perhaps overvalue the information that comes from them. In sum, negotiators run the risk of letting availability overwhelm the need for and benefits of thorough analysis.

The "winner's curse." The *winner's curse* is a term that describes the discomfort and misgivings that typically accompany a negotiation win that comes too easily. Too quick a capitulation on the other party's part often leaves the winner wondering, "Could I have gotten this for less?" or "What's wrong with the item/product/option?" In dealing with the winner's curse, the value of thorough investigation and analysis cannot be underestimated; they provide the negotiator with an independent verification of the worth of the settlement. Negotiators can also try to secure performance or quality guarantees from the other party to ensure against the subject of the outcome being faulty or defective.

Overconfidence. Overconfidence in your own judgments—the tendency to believe in your ability to be correct or accurate more often than is really true—has a double-edged effect. First, overconfidence can solidify the degree to which you support a position or option that may actually be incorrect or inappropriate. Second, overconfidence in your own judgment can lead you to discount the worth or validity of others' judgment, in effect shutting down other parties as sources of information, interests, and options necessary for a successful integrative negotiation. An awareness of this tendency and a commitment to more thorough planning seem to be the appropriate remedies.

The law of small numbers. The law of small numbers has to do with the tendency to draw big conclusions from small sample sizes. In negotiation, the law of small numbers applies to the way negotiators learn (and extrapolate) from their own experience. If that experience is limited in time or in scope (e.g., all one's prior negotiations have been hard-fought and distributive), the tendency is to project those norms and behaviors on future negotiations—often with disastrous effect. The smaller the prior sample (i.e., the more limited the negotiation experience), the greater the possibility that past lessons will be erroneously used to imply what will happen in the future. The remedy here is to broaden your experience and be cautious about using *only* your own experience to deduce the future. In addition, including expert negotiators in the planning process assures that we challenge the assumptions underlying our strategic and tactical planning.

Biased causal accounts. This is the process by which bias creeps into our accounts of what caused the current situation, and it is frequently a problem when the purpose of the negotiation is to work out the current problem. Research in this area suggests that causal accounts can have strong effects on the choices involved in the planning and conduct of negotiations.[13] Better information (less biased and more objective) can help prevent and correct poor attributions of what causes what.

Ignoring others' cognitions. Negotiators often just don't bother to ask the other party what they see and think, thus forcing themselves to work with faulty or incomplete information, and thus producing faulty results. Failure to consider others' cognitions allows negotiators to simplify their thinking about otherwise complex processes (usually leading to a more distributive strategy), causing a failure to recognize the contingent nature of their behaviors and responses. The emotional drives at work here can be very deep-seated, and they can only be avoided if negotiators explicitly focus on accurately understanding the other party's interests, goals, and perspective.

Reactive devaluation. Reactive devaluation is the process of devaluing the other party's concessions simply because your opponent made them.[14] This devaluation may be based in emotionality ("I just don't like that so-and-so") or on distrust fostered by past experience. Reactive devaluation leads us to minimize the magnitude of a concession made by a disliked other, reduces our willingness to respond with a concession of equal size, or motivates us to want to seek even more once a concession has been made. It may be minimized by maintaining an objective view of the process (or charging someone on your side to do so and to remind you of it periodically), by clarifying each side's preferences on options and concessions before making any, or by using a third party to mediate or facilitate concession-making processes (see Chapter 10).

Challenges When Dealing with Other Negotiators

Whether or not negotiators lay traps for themselves, they always run the risk of encountering parties who, for any of a number of reasons, are difficult negotiators. This section addresses methods negotiators can use when meeting such challenges, discusses some of the difficult negotiator types one might come across, and explains the skills and behaviors needed to defend against such parties and convert them to a more productive negotiation process, or both.

In trying to move from win–lose to win–win negotiations, at least three challenges exist:

- What to do when the other side uses distributive tactics (i.e., "dirty tricks").
- What to do if the other side is more powerful.
- What to do if the other side is just generally difficult to deal with.

Responding to the other side when they use dirty tricks. By the term *dirty tricks,* we mean the distributive tactics that one side applies in a negotiation to put pressure on the other side to do something that is probably not in their best interest to do. We discussed some of these tactics in Chapter 2; to briefly summarize here, a party can respond in any of these ways:

1. *Respond in kind.* Responding in kind, though, is likely to escalate the conflict, and it is not consistent with the principles we are proposing here.
2. *Ignore them.* A tactic ignored is, essentially, a tactic "defanged": Unfortunately, some bargainers simply do not get the message that you want something different to happen.
3. *Call them on it.* Let your opponents know you recognize what they are trying to do when they use dirty tricks by pointing the tactic out and raising it to the level of open discussion. The embarrassment value of such an observation is often sufficient to make negotiators disavow the tactic and abandon it.
4. *Offer to change to more productive methods.* Announce that you have noted your opponent's behavior and suggest a better way to negotiate. The logic of this advice lies in the assumption that, once the "trickster" understands that you know what he is doing and that continuing this behavior will entail certain costs (including the possibility that you will walk away from the negotiation), he will respond to your suggestion for a more integrative exchange.

Responding to the other side when they are more powerful. Relative power alone can be a good predictor of how a conflict will evolve. Other things being equal, when power is unequal, victory goes, typically, to the more powerful party. Power imbalances in negotiation can represent clear dangers to the satisfaction of personal needs and to the collaborative process:

- High-power parties tend to pay little heed to the needs of lower power parties, who either settle with their needs unmet or use disruptive, attention-getting tactics that make collaboration very difficult.
- Lower-power parties are not usually in a position to bring about integrative processes, which require a tolerance of change and flexibility. Lower power parties have less to give, typically, and therefore less potential for flexibility.

When dealing with an opponent with more power, negotiators have at least four alternatives:

1. Protect themselves.
2. Cultivate their BATNA.
3. Formulate a "trip wire" alert system.
4. Correct the power imbalance.

Negotiators can *protect themselves* by keeping in mind their real interests, that negotiation may be the preferred approach to getting those interests met, and that excessive accommodation to the high-power party will not serve them well over the long term. However, overcontrol may deprive you of creativity and flexibility, which are critical components to the design of an integrative arrangement, or limit your ability to use information that emerges during the exchange.

Negotiators should always *know and cultivate their BATNA*, which represents the best they can accomplish without negotiation or an alternative deal. Many negotiators bargain without a clear definition of their BATNA, which limits them to what can achieve in the current negotiation.

A clear, strong BATNA may also be reinforced by additional safety measures. Low-power negotiators are also advised *to formulate a "trip wire" alert system* which serves as an early warning signal when bargaining enters the safety zone—close to the walkaway option or the BATNA. The trip wire tells the negotiator to exercise special caution and pay increased attention to the negotiation in progress, as his options are becoming more constrained. Given that negotiations often become intense and engrossing at such points, it might be appropriate to assign a friendly party, even a co-negotiator, to attend to the trip wire and to notify the involved negotiator at the critical time.

The foregoing options involve dealing with an existing power imbalance. A final option for dealing with more powerful parties is to *correct the imbalance*. Three approaches to this are possible:

1. Lower-power parties taking power.
2. High-power parties giving power.
3. Third parties managing the transfer and balance of power

Typically, the first approach, *power taking*, is not feasible in negotiations. The disruptive or attention-getting actions required for lower-power parties to take power, typically, contribute to a competitive exchange. The third approach *is* feasible, and it represents a strategy used often by mediators and other third parties (see Chapter 10). The middle, remaining approach is for the high-power party to give power to the other party in order to achieve a power balance. Such actions include sharing resources, sharing control over certain processes or outcomes (e.g., agendas, decisions), focusing on *common* interests rather than solely on their (high-power) interests, or educating the lower-power party as to the power they do have and how to use it more effectively. Why, though, would high-power parties ever choose to give power away? The answer is complex. First, sharing power may facilitate a better integrative process. Second, even if one party does have power over the other, the best the high-power party can hope for is compliance rather than enthusiastic cooperation. Finally, no power imbalance exists forever, and when the low-power party does gain a power base or a BATNA, they are likely either to sever the relationship or to look for some form of revenge.

Responding when the other side is being difficult. When the other side presents a clearly problematic pattern of difficult behavior, two possibilities exist. You may be dealing with a negotiator who does not know any better way to negotiate, or you may be dealing with a type of difficult person whose behaviors are consistent both within and outside of the negotiation context. In most cases you won't know enough about the other to make the distinction. In the following section, we will review two main approaches for dealing with difficult opponents. The first suggests a broad-based approach that may be used with any difficult opponent, including an opponent using dirty tricks. The second suggests different strategies for dealing with opponents with particularly difficult styles.

Ury's "breakthrough approach." In his book *Getting Past No,* William Ury suggests a five-stage process which sees obstacles set by the opponent as challenges that you can address by specific strategies.[15] This process involves creating a favorable negotiation environment by (*a*) regaining your mental balance and controlling your own behavior and (*b*) helping the other party achieve similar balance and control, then (*c*) changing the game from a distributive one to an integrative one and (*d*) overcoming the other party's skepticism by jointly crafting a mutually satisfactory agreement and (*e*) achieving closure through firm, evenhanded use of your negotiating power.

Ury suggests that his approach operates on the principle of acting "counterintuitively" in that it requires you to do the opposite of what you might naturally do in difficult situations. He proposes a five-step process for this counterintuitive pattern of responding (see Table 5.1):

1. Don't React—Go to the Balcony. The natural reaction to difficulty is to strike back, give in, or break off negotiations. The resulting challenge to this obstacle is "not to react," thereby avoiding the destructive effect reacting naturally would have on the process. Instead, "going to the balcony"—that is, psychologically removing yourself from the interaction so that you become an observer to your own interaction with the other—allows you to:

- Distance yourself from the dispute, and from your emotions.
- Create breathing space, allowing you to cool off.
- Have an opportunity for you to see the situation in *context and to remind yourself why you were there in the first place.*

2. Disarm Them—Step to Their Side. Negativity and attack in negotiation tend to breed more of the same—tensions heighten and damaging exchanges tend to escalate. The negotiator's challenge here is to act

TABLE 5.1   **Managing Difficult Negotiators**

Steps	Barriers to Cooperation	Challenges	Strategies
1	Your natural reaction to their competitive behavior	Don't react	Go to the balcony
2	Other's negative emotions	Disarm them	Step to their side
3	Others' competitive bargaining	Change the game	Don't react, reframe
4	Others' skepticism about benefits of agreement	Make it easy for them to say yes	Build them a golden bridge
5	Others' perceived power	Make it hard for them to say no	Bring them to their senses, not their knees

counterintuitively—to deflect or sidestep the other party's negativity, disarming them through positive, constructive communication.

3. Change the Game—Don't Reject: Reframe. We have seen how improper framing of a problem can be a powerful trap for negotiators. Given the obstacle of the other party's competitive bargaining, the challenge at this stage is to change the game by proactively reframing their tactics by:

- Asking open-ended, problem-solving questions.
- Reinterpreting their tactics in less confrontational, more collaborative terms.
- Directly and openly negotiating the rules of the game.

4. Make It Easy to Say Yes—Build Them a Golden Bridge. The four most common objections from the other party are:

1. It's not their idea (i.e., "not invented here").
2. It doesn't address one of their basic interests.
3. It might cause them to lose face or look bad to some important constituency.
4. It requires too big an adjustment for them (i.e., "too much, too fast").

The proposed strategy is to close this gap by "building a golden bridge," to entice them to "cross over" to agreement by:

- Involving them in the actual design of an inclusive agreement.
- Satisfying as many of their unmet needs as you can (without jeopardizing the basic fabric of the agreement).
- Recognizing and being empathetic to the range of personal and organizational demands and expectations that they face.

- Helping them to save face and deal with their constituencies by providing justifications for the agreement.
- Walking them through complex agreements step by step and not rushing closure until they are ready.[16]

5. Make It Hard to Say No—Bring Them to Their Senses, Not Their Knees. Throughout the first four steps, the other party may maintain an abiding belief in the value of their superior power or wits. Having made it easy for them to say yes, you must now address the challenge of making it hard for them to say no. The components of this strategy are these:

- Tend to your BATNA, strengthening it and making sure the other parties know what it is.
- Help them think about the consequences of no agreement.
- If necessary, actually use your BATNA, being careful to anticipate and defuse their reaction to what may seem (to them) to be a punitive move on your part.
- Keep sharpening their choice—refer back to the attractive terms that got them to "cross the bridge" and help them maintain their focus on the advantages of completing the deal.
- Fashion a lasting agreement, thinking through and planning for implementation.

Responding to difficult people. Sometimes, problems in negotiation can be traced to difficulties in the other's behavioral style. Several points are important in this event. First, *all of us* are difficult to deal with at times; this is different from those characters who are *invariably* difficult and whose behaviors conform to predictable, identifiable patterns. Second, what is difficult behavior to one person is not difficult to another. One's definition of "difficult" behavior may say as much about the receiver as it does about the sender. Third, difficult people do what they do because it "works for them"—it gives them control, feels comfortable, and lets them get their way. We reinforce the difficult behavior by giving in to it, which provides the difficult person ample reason to behave in the present and future in ways that were useful in the past. Another reason why difficult people continue their difficult ways is because they honestly are unaware of the long-term costs to people and organizations who must contend with them. We provide here basic advice for coping with invariably difficult negotiators—as opposed to giving in to them, accepting their behavior, or getting them to change their values, beliefs, or attitudes. There are three stages in this process:[17]

1. Recognize the behavior for what it is.
2. Understand why the behavior exists and tends to persist.
3. Cope to produce effective behavior—for you, and for them.

Once you go through these stages and decide to try to cope with difficult people, six basic steps are involved:

1. *Assess* the situation realistically:
   a. Is the difficult behavior in character for this party, or are they just having a bad day?
   b. Is your reaction appropriate and proportional, or are you overreacting?
   c. Is there an identifiable trigger for the behavior? Did you do something to set off the other party?
   d. Will direct, open discussion solve the behavioral problem? If not, formulate a coping plan.

2. *Stop wishing* difficult people were different. (Wishing people were different, or blaming them, may only exacerbate the problem rather than solving it.)

3. *Get some distance* between you and the difficulty.
   a. Label the problem—characterize it so you can identify a way to respond.
   b. Understand the problem—determine what might have caused it, or what triggers it.

4. *Formulate* a relevant coping plan.

5. *Implement* the plan assertively.

6. *Monitor* your effectiveness and *modify* your plan accordingly.

Summary

Through any number of different avenues—breakdowns in communication, escalation of anger and mistrust, polarization of positions and refusal to compromise, or simply the inability to invent options that are satisfactory to both sides—negotiations often break down. This chapter reviewed actions that the parties can take to return to a productive dialogue, focusing on methods that parties can try without outside assistance.

If these methods do not work, the assistance of outside parties can be secured (see Chapter 10).

End Notes

1. See Rogers (1961).
2. See Osgood (1962).
3. See Rapoport (1964).
4. Fisher (1964).
5. Fisher, Ury and Patton (1991) and Pruitt and Rubin (1986).
6. This mechanism effectively designates a selected time for the parties to evaluate their own progress in negotiation. It provides time to reevaluate ground rules,

change procedural mechanisms, or perhaps even change negotiator behavior. This process orientation may provide the opportunity for the parties to self-correct the procedural mechanisms that will allow them to make greater progress on their substantive disagreements (Walton, 1987).

7. See Fisher (1964).

8. See Fisher, Ury, and Patton (1991).

9. See Eiseman (1978).

10. Ibid.; also see Fisher, Ury, and Patton (1991).

11. Adapted from Neale and Bazerman (1991) and Bazerman and Neale (1992).

12. Ibid.

13. See Bies and Moag (1986); Bies and Shapiro (1987); Bies, Shapiro, and Cummings (1988); Einhorn and Hogarth (1986); and Shapiro (1991).

14. See Stillenger, Epelbaum, Keltner, and Ross (1990).

15 See Ury (1991).

16. Ibid.

17. For a more detailed explanation of these processes, see Bramson (1991, 1992).

6   COMMUNICATION IN NEGOTIATION

Negotiation is a communicative process involving the exchange of views, ideas, and perspectives. This chapter examines "at the table" negotiation through the use of "phase models," then discusses a communication model of interpersonal exchange, emphasizing the mechanisms by which messages are encoded, sent, received, and decoded. Finally, we will address tools that might be used when communication processes go awry.

Key Issues Regarding Negotiation Phases

We begin with the three-stage model that traces back to the pioneering work of Ann Douglas.[1] For simplicity's sake, we call these three stages the beginning, middle, and end of the negotiation process. Within each state, certain processes are critical:

Beginning: Perceptual error, attributions and biases, framing.

Middle: Offering sequences and issue development, evolution of framework and detail, linguistics and the role of language, listening skills, the use of questions.

End: Decision making, avoiding decision traps, achieving closure.

The Beginning Stage

The beginning, or initiation, stage of negotiation is marked by the delineation and diagnosis of issues, agendas, and bargaining ranges, and by the social exchange necessary to develop the bargaining relationship. It is also the point at which the negotiator balances what was (and is) versus what might be (if things come out as hoped or planned). Parties approach the present tasks of negotiation guided, in large part, by their perception of past situations, attitudes, and behaviors. Expectations of future outcomes and other parties' future behaviors are based, in large part, on this perceptual baggage, gained through direct or vicarious experience and observations that negotiators bring with them. Two common pieces of baggage that can be problematic are attributional errors and frames. Both are affected by the process of perception.

The Role of Perception

Perception is the process by which individuals tune in to their environment (see Figure 6.1).[2] This is likely to be strongly affected by the receiver's current state of mind or comprehension of earlier communications. Our perceptions of other parties and of the environment where we operate, and our own dispositions are likely to affect how we ascribe meanings. Moreover, these same perceptions are likely to affect our ability to ascertain the other's message—to determine exactly what they are saying and what they mean.

Perception is a complex physical and psychological process, a "sense-making" procedure through which individuals interpret their environment so they can make appropriate responses to it. The body's physical senses—sight, hearing, taste, touch, and smell—receive cues from various environmental stimuli. Most environments are extremely complex; they present a large number and variety of stimuli, each having many different properties such as magnitude, color, shape, texture, and relative novelty. The sensing process quickly becomes overwhelming, so perception becomes selective, focusing on some stimuli while tuning out others. Once attention and recognition have occurred, recognition translates into reactive behavior. This part of the process is called *perceptual organization*; once we recognize stimuli, we must make appropriate responses to them. The message of a hot stove, transmitted from our fingertips to the brain, should lead us to quickly withdraw our fingers before we are burned.

Factors That Shape and Distort Social Perception

The typical stimuli used as examples are rather simple—sounds, visual images of size and shape, and so on. We can see how variations in these stimuli can be applied to negotiation, particularly in positioning arguments, using visual media in presentation and the like. However, the impact of perception on communication and negotiation outcomes is much more dramatic when we consider the perceptions of other people. People as perceptual stimuli are more complex than simple sights, sounds, or colors. They have many physical characteristics—height, weight, age, gender, race, dress, and speech patterns (how articulate they are with words, whether they speak with an accent, what tone of voice they use) that affect our perception. People also differ in their emotional expressiveness—how they

FIGURE 6 .1

The Perception Process

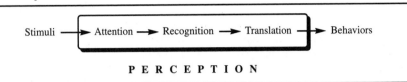

Stimuli ⟶ Attention ⟶ Recognition ⟶ Translation ⟶ Behaviors

P E R C E P T I O N

communicate with facial gestures, body posture, hand movements, or even tone of voice.

Not only are people complex stimuli; the social context of the perceptual event can be a stimulus that affects perception as well. The nature of the negotiation issues or the previous experience of the parties can define the situation as a competitive or a cooperative one. Collaborative or cooperative processes often tend to increase sensitity to similarities and commonalties. Competitive processes, however, tend to minimize similarity sensitivity, while increasing sensitivity to threats and differences. Therefore, representing the relationship between the parties as competitive or cooperative can lead the parties to misjudge the opposition or to misdiagnose the negotiation situation. These perceptions subsequently affect attitudes toward the other party, communication processes between the parties, and their strategic approaches to the negotiating task.

Perceptual Distortion in Negotiation

The perceiver's own needs, desires, motivations, and personal experiences may be likely to create a predisposition about the target in an upcoming negotiation. These predispositions are most troublesome when they lead to biases and errors in perception and in subsequent communication. Five major perceptual errors are typical: stereotyping, halo effects, selective perceptions, projections, and perceptual defenses.

Stereotyping is a very common distortion of the perceptual process. Stereotyping occurs when attributes are assigned to people solely on the basis of their membership in a particular social or demographic group. We assign the individual to groups based on one piece of perceptual information (e.g., young or old); then we assign characteristics of some other group members to this individual (e.g., "this person is old; old people are conservative; therefore, this person is conservative"). There is no factual basis for the conclusion—it is based on the generalization of qualities that have been ascribed to the larger group—and the error is compounded by applying traits we associate with the category to this single individual. The simple process of using some criterion, even an arbitrary one, to divide people into groups allows group members to begin to define themselves as "we" and the other group as "they," and then to make evaluative comparisons and judgments between them. Direct competition for resources among groups, or conflicting values and ideologies, will significantly heighten the stereotyping process.

Halo effects in perception are similar to stereotypes. Rather than using a target individual's group membership as a basis for classification, halo effects occur when we generalize about a wide variety of characteristics based on one characteristic of an individual.[3] A smiling person may be judged to be more honest than a frowning or scowling person, even though there is no necessary relationship between a smile and honesty. Halo effects are most likely to occur in perception when we have very little knowledge of a person along some dimension (and hence generalize about that person from our knowledge of him in other contexts), when we know a person well, or, when our judgements about that person have strong moral implications.[4] Halo effects are as common as stereotypes in negotiation—we are likely to form rapid impressions of new opponents based on very limited initial information, such as their appearance, group membership, or initial statements. We also maintain these judgments as we get to know people better, fitting each piece of new information into some consistent pattern that may tend to resist change, even given clearly disconfirming information.

Selective perception occurs when the perceiver singles out certain information that supports or reinforces a prior belief and filters out information that does not confirm that belief. As mentioned above, selective perception has the effect of perpetuating stereotypes or halo effects—we form quick judgments about individuals on the basis of limited information and filter out further evidence that might disconfirm the judgment. An initial smile from the opponent, which leads the perceiver to believe that the opponent is honest, might also lead him to ignore those statements by the opponent indicating that she intends to be competitive and aggressive. If the perceiver interprets the same smile as a smirk, the perceiver may ignore the opponent's statements that she wants to establish an honest and cooperative relationship. In both cases, the perceiver's own biases—the predisposition to view the smile as honest or dishonest—are likely to affect how he selects and interprets the other's cues.

Projection occurs when an individual ascribes to others characteristics or feelings he possesses himself. Projection usually arises out of a need to protect our own self-concept. People have a strong need to see themselves as consistent and in a positive light; therefore, if they perceive negative attributes, they tend to ascribe them to others. It is extremely common for negotiators to claim that they want to be cooperative and develop a positive relationship with the other negotiator, but that the opponent is behaving uncooperatively and untrustingly. Such assertions often keep the negotiator from admitting to herself that *she* really wants to be deceptive and dishonest. It is easy to see how such projection can lead to both self-fulfilling logic and highly destructive behavior.

Perceptual defense is also a result of the instinct for self-preservation, helping us to defend ourselves by screening out, distorting, or ignoring information that we find threatening or otherwise unacceptable. We are likely to deny, modify, distort, or redefine information that doesn't fit our self-image or our image of others to bring it into line with our earlier judgment. We may refuse to believe that a person we respect may engage in unethical negotiation behaviors; we perceive ourselves as moral and therefore are likely to deny that we have ever done anything seriously wrong.

Framing

The second key issue in perception is framing. In the communications context, framing helps explain how bargainers conceive of current events in light of past experiences. Framing (and reframing, i.e., reevaluation of information and positions) are tied to information processing, message patterns, linguistic cues, and socially constructed meanings.[5] This concern with framing is captured by three approaches in the negotiation literature: cognitive heuristics, frame categories, and issue development. The first two belong in this section on the beginning stage of negotiation; the third, issue development, falls in the middle stage, and we will discuss it there.

The *cognitive heuristics* approach to framing derives from the growing work in behavioral decision theory (BDT). In this context, a frame denotes a decision maker's conception of the acts, outcomes, and contingencies associated with a particular outcome, involving perceptions of loss or gain, risk orientation, and the evaluative use of reference points. Applying this to negotiation suggests that such biases may limit negotiator effectiveness, especially regarding a negotiator's level of risk aversion. Two effects have been suggested: negotiators are not usually indifferent to risk, but they should not necessarily trust their intuitions regarding risk. In other words, negotiators may overreact to a perceived loss when they might react more positively to the same situation if it is framed as a perceived gain.[6]

The second aspect of framing that affects this stage is *frame categories*. Merging cognitive views of framing with linguistic analysis, the frame category approach is similar to "scripting" negotiations. A variety of types of frames may exist:

- *Substantive* (what the negotiation is about).
- *Loss/gain* (the risks or benefits of various outcomes).
- *Characterization* (different expectations and evaluations of others' behaviors and outcomes).
- *Process* (how the negotiation will or should proceed).
- *Aspiration* (regarding the parties' underlying needs and interests).
- *Outcome* (the parties' preferred positions or solutions).[7]

It is possible, even likely, that negotiators will have (and apply) two or more of these frames. When different negotiators apply different or mismatched frames, they will find the bargaining process ambiguous and frustrating. In such situations, it may become necessary to reframe, to assist the other party to do so, or (ideally) to establish a common frame or set of frames within which the negotiation communication and exchange may be conducted more productively.

Negotiators can reframe by trying to see the situation in a different way or from a different perspective. For instance, they can constructively reframe a problem by defining it in terms that are broader or narrower, bigger or smaller, riskier or less risky, or subject to a longer or shorter (i.e., looser or tighter) time.

Attributional Error

In the most general sense, social perception is the process through which people come to understand each other. Starting with the raw data of other persons, a given situation, and their behavior therein, we apply or impose our own analyses and explanations of what they do. These, in turn, become "scripts," or preconceptions of what is likely to occur in a situation, based on a process of classification and analogy. For example, we may expect to have to deal with tough, competitive bargaining accompanied by distributive tactics (such as the old "limited authority" ploy, "I'll have to talk to the sales manager") when we buy a new automobile, based largely on our personal experience or experiences related to us by others. The advent of "one price, no haggle" auto sales by a growing number of dealers may not conform to our established schema, and we may be uncomfortable or unprepared when we encounter this new process for the first time—or we may be very comfortable if we really don't like to negotiate for a new car! The attributions we make based on these perceptions and scripts are correct only insofar as we factor in new experiences as we encounter them, and as long as the base data remain undistorted. In particular, we are often guilty of distorting data through attribution error or bias.

Perceptual error may also be expressed in the form of a bias, or distortion in the evaluation of data. For instance, the false-consensus effect is a tendency to overestimate the degree of support and consensus that exists for our own position, opinions, or behaviors.[8] If consensus information is available, but expressed in numerical probabilities (e.g., one chance in a hundred), many observers neglect to use the information, falling subject to a bias called the base rate fallacy. Either of these biases could seriously damage a negotiation effort—that is, negotiators subject to them would make faulty judgments regarding tactics or outcome probabilities.

Perceptual Error: A Summary

It cannot be stated strongly enough that perceptual distortions are frequently at the heart of breakdowns in communication between conflicting individuals. Stereotypes, halo effects, selective perceptions, and perceptual defenses bias and distort the information we receive. Perceptual biases tend to cast our own position and behavior in more favorable terms and the other person ("the opponent") in more negative terms. These biases affect expectations about an opponent and lead to assumptions about opponents (their position, their willingness to cooperate or make concessions, etc.). Finally, these assumptions may then cause us to assume a competitive, defensive stance early in a negotiation. The tragedy in this chain of events is that if these initial assumptions are incorrect, there may be no way for us to correct them—by the time we are in a position to accurately judge the predisposition of the other party, they may have interpreted our own competitive mood and defensive posture as offensive and antagonistic. This problem is likely to be most acute between groups that have had long-standing, hostile relationships: unions and management that have been plagued by bitter strikes, ethnic groups with long-standing disagreements, and so forth. To break this self-fulfilling perceptual spiral, individual negotiators (and their constituencies) must take clear-cut, specific, and public actions to signal to their adversaries a desire to change to cooperative behavior.

The Middle Stage

The middle or problem-solving stage of negotiation is the most dynamic stage—it is marked by movement, process, interaction, and exchange. There are four key elements here: offer sequences, the evolution of framework and detail, the role of language, and the complementary processes of listening and questioning.

Offer Sequences

According to some observers, perhaps the most important communications in a bargaining session are those that convey the disputants' offers and counteroffers. A communicative framework for negotiation is based on at least three assumptions:

- The communication of offers is a dynamic process (the offers that are made change or shift over time).
- The offer process is interactive; bargainers influence each other and a variety of internal and external factors (e.g., time limitations, reciprocity norms, BATNAs, or constituency pressures) drive the interaction and motivate a bargainer to change his or her offer.[9]

Another way of saying this is that the dynamic, interactive process of offer–counteroffer, similar in form to the "tit for tat" process of responding to the other's strategy choice and subject to certain situational and environmental constraints, "herds" the negotiation exchange down a playing field, eventually narrowing the bargaining range and funneling it toward an eventual settlement point. In short, offer sequences provide both direction and impetus during the middle stage of a negotiation.

Issue development, a related process, focuses on the way issues change during the negotiation process. Issues are shaped by, among other things, arguments attacking the significance or stability of problems or the workability of solutions, the ways parties "make cases" to others concerning the logic or propriety of needs or positions, and the management and interaction (e.g., addition, deletion, packaging, etc.) of multiple issues on the negotiation agenda.[10]

Framework and Detail

One approach to understanding the middle stage of negotiation is recognizing that the focus is on evolving a general *formula* for a negotiation agreement, and then working out a number of the more specific *details*.[11] This process can be viewed as having three-stages:

- *Diagnosis*, in which the parties recognize the need for change or improvement, review relevant history, and prepare positions.
- *Formula*, in which they attempt to develop a shared perception of the conflict, including common terms, referents, and fairness criteria.
- *Detail*, in which they work out operational details consistent with the basic formula.

In actual use, the model may be more flexible than this description suggests; in some settings or cultures, the stages may even be pursued in a different order.

Linguistics and the Role of Language

What a negotiator says and how she says it may well have an effect on the conduct of negotiations, where language operates at two levels: the logical level (for proposals or offers) and the pragmatic level (semantics, syntax, and style). The meaning conveyed by a proposition or statement is a combination of a logical, surface message and other, pragmatic (i.e., hinted or inferred) messages. In other words, it is not only what is said that matters, but how it is said, and what additional, veiled, or subsurface information is intended, conveyed, or *perceived* in reception. By way of illustration, consider threats. We often react not only to the substance of a statement, but also (and possibly more strongly) to the unspoken messages.

Whether the intent is to command and compel or to sell, persuade, or gain commitment, middle-stage linguistics would seem to depend on adequate command of technique by the speaker, as well as on clear understanding and decoding of the intended message(s) by the listener (see Figure 6.2 later in this chapter). As it turns out, chances for miscommunication abound. Speakers may be untrained, incompetent, ineffective, or overwrought; they may simply be inarticulate. Furthermore, speakers' use of idioms or colloquialisms are often problematic, especially in cross-cultural negotiations. The meaning conveyed might be clear to the speaker, but confusing to the listener (e.g., "I'm willing to stay until the last dog is hung"—a statement of positive commitment on the part of some regional Americans, but probably confusing at best to those with different cultural backgrounds, even within the United States). Even if the meaning is clear, the choice of word or metaphor may convey a lack of sensitivity or create a sense of exclusion, as is often done when males convey strategic business concerns by using sports metaphors ("Well, it's fourth down and goal to go; this is no time to drop the ball"). Intentional or not, the message received or inferred by females may be that they're excluded from the club.

Listening Skills and the Use of Questions

Given the many ways communication can be disrupted and distorted, we can only marvel at the amount that actually gets accomplished. We contend that failures and distortions in perception and communication are the single most dominant contributor to breakdowns and failures in negotiation. Research cannot directly confirm this assertion because the processes of perception and communication are so intertwined with other major factors, including commitment to one's own position and objectives, the nature of the negotiating process, the use of power and power tactics, and the negotiators' personalities. Nevertheless, we have found in many simulated and actual negotiations that parties whose goals are compatible and whose overriding objectives are the same still may not reach agreement because of their misperceptions of the opponent or because of breakdowns in the communication process.

A number of techniques have been suggested for improving the accuracy and efficiency of communications in negotiation. Either third parties or the parties to negotiation themselves can "tutor" communication—that is, help the parties learn to communicate accurately and appropriately. There are several techniques that the parties themselves can use to ensure that some of the typical perceptual and communication blocks are not confounding their ability to reach satisfactory agreement. Chief among these are the use of questions, active listening, and role reversal.

The Use of Questions. One of the most common techniques for clarifying communications and eliminating noise and distortion is the use of questions. Questions are essential elements in negotiations for securing information; asking good questions enables a negotiator to secure a great deal of information about the opponent's position, supporting arguments, and needs.[12] Questions can be divided into two basic classifications: those that are manageable and those that cause difficulty (see Table 6.1).

As Table 6.1 shows, most unmanageable questions are likely to produce defensiveness and anger in the opponent. Although they may yield information, they are likely to make the other party feel uncomfortable and less likely to provide more information in the future.

TABLE 6.1   Questions in Negotiations

Manageable Questions	*Examples*
Open-ended questions—ones that cannot be answered with a simple yes or no. *Who, what, when, where,* and *why* questions.	"Why do you take that position in these deliberations?"
Open questions—invite the other's thinking.	"What do you think of our proposal?"
Leading questions—point toward an answer.	"Don't you think our proposal is a fair and reasonable offer?"
Cool questions—low emotionality.	"What is the additional rate that we will have to pay if you make the improvements on the property?"
Planned questions—part of an overall logical sequence of questions developed in advance.	"After you make the improvements to the property, when can we expect to take occupancy?"
Treat questions—flatter the opponent at the same time as you ask for information.	"Can you provide us with some of your excellent insight on this problem?"
Window questions—aid in looking into the other person's mind.	"Can you tell us how you came to that conclusion?"
Directive questions—focus on a specific point.	"How much is the rental rate per square foot with these improvements?"
Gauging questions—ascertain how the other person feels.	"How do you feel about our proposal?"

Unmanageable Questions	*Examples*
Close-out questions—force the other party into seeing things your way.	"You wouldn't try to take advantage of us here, would you?"
Loaded questions—put the other party on the spot regardless of her answer.	"Do you mean to tell me that these are the only terms that you will accept?"
Heated questions—high emotionality, trigger emotional responses.	"Don't you think we've spent enough time discussing this ridiculous proposal of yours?"
Impulse questions—occur "on the spur of the moment," without planning, and tend to get conversation off the track.	"As long as we're discussing this, what do you think we ought to tell other groups who have made similar demands on us?"
Trick questions—appear to require a frank answer, but really are "loaded" in their meaning.	"What are you going to do—give in to our demands, or take this to arbitration?"
Reflective trick questions—reflects the other into agreeing with your point of view.	"Here's how I see the situation—don't you agree?"

From Gerard Nierenberg, *Fundamentals of Negotiating* (New York: Hawthorn Books, 1973), pp. 125–26. Used with permission of the author.

TABLE 6.2 Questions for Tough Situations

The Situation	*Possible Questions*
"Take it or leave it" ultimata.	"If we can come up with a more attractive alternative than that, would you still want me to 'take or leave' your offer?"
	"Do I have to decide now, or do I have some time to think about it?"
	"Are you feeling pressure to bring the negotiation to a close?"
Pressure to respond to an unreasonable deadline.	"Why can't we negotiate about this deadline?"
	"If you're under pressure to meet this deadline, what can I do to help remove some of that pressure?"
	"What's magical about this afternoon? What about first thing in the morning?"
The other party uses highball or lowball tactics.	"What's your reasoning behind this position?"
	"What would *you* think I see as a fair offer?"
	"What standards do you think the final resolution should meet?"
An impasse.	"What else can either of us do to close the gap between our positions?"
	"Specifically what concession do you need from me to bring this to a close right now?"
	"If it were already six weeks from now and we were looking back at this negotiation, what might we wish we had 'brought to the table?'"
The other party is torn between accepting and rejecting your proposal.	"What's your best alternative to accepting my offer right now?"
	"If you reject this offer, what will take its place that's better than what you know you'll receive from me?"
	"How can you be sure that you will get a better deal elsewhere?"
The other party asks if the offer you just made is the same as that offered to others.	"What do you see as a fair offer, and given that, what do you think of my current offer to you?"
	"Do you believe that I think it's in my best interest to be unfair to you?"
	"Do you believe that people can be treated differently, but still all be treated fairly?"
You are feeling pressured, controlled, or manipulated.	"Shouldn't we both walk away from this negotiation feeling satisfied?"
	"How would you feel if our roles were reversed, and you were feeling the pressure I'm feeling right now?"
	"Are you experiencing outside pressures to conclude these negotiations?"

Adapted from *What to Ask When You Don't Know What to Say,* by Sam Deep and Lyle Sussman.© 1993. Used by permission of the publishers, Prentice Hall/A Division of Simon & Schuster, Englewood Cliffs, NJ.

Negotiators can also use questions to manage difficult or stalled negotiations. Aside from their typical uses for collecting and diagnosing information or assisting the other party in addressing and expressing needs and interests, questions can also be used *tactically* to pry a negotiation out of a stall or an apparent dead end. Table 6.2 identifies a number of such situations and suggests specific questions for dealing with them.[13] The value of such questions seems to be in their power to assist or force the other party to face up to the effects or consequences of their behaviors, whether intended and anticipated or not.

Active Listening. One technique for gaining more information is to ask questions; however, as we pointed out in the previous section, frequent questions, particularly when the communication is emotionally charged, may contribute to defensiveness. The questioner should encourage the other party to elaborate voluntarily on his earlier statements, rather than making the communicator feel cross-examined by multiple questions. Another method of gaining more information is by listening. There are three major forms of listening: passive listening, acknowledgment, and active listening. Active listening and reflecting are terms that are commonly used in the helping professions such as counseling and therapy. Those practicing in these fields recognize that communications are frequently loaded with multiple meanings and that the counselor or therapist must try to "tease out" these different meanings without making the communicator angry or defensive.

Passive listening is merely the reception of the message, providing no feedback to the sender about the accuracy or completeness of reception. Listening is the key process in the reception and decoding stage of communication (see Figure 6.2). Sometimes passive listening is enough in itself to keep a communicator sending information. Some people like to talk and can't handle long silences. Negotiators who have an opponent with this characteristic may find that their best strategy is to sit and listen and let the other party eventually talk himself into, or out of, a position on his own.

Acknowledgment is the second form of listening, slightly more active than complete passivity. When acknowledging, the receiver occasionally nods her head, maintains eye contact, or interjects responses like "I see," "Mm-hmm," "Interesting," "Really," "Sure," "Go on," and the like. These responses are sufficient to keep the communicator sending messages, but the sender often misinterprets the acknowledgments as the receiver's agreeing with the position, rather than simply receiving the message.

Active listening is the third form of listening. When the receiver is actively listening, he restates or paraphrases the sender's message in his own language. Some examples include these:

Sender: I don't know how I am going to untangle this messy problem.
Receiver: You're really stumped on how to solve this one.
Sender: Please, don't ask me about that now.

FIGURE 6.2

A Model of the Communication Process

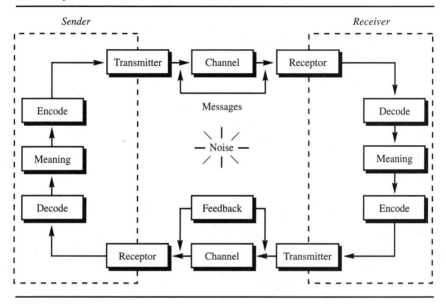

Adapted from E. Shannon and W. Weaver, *The Mathematical Theory of Communication* (Urbana, IL: University of Illinois Press, 1948.) Reprinted by permission of the University of Illinois Press.

Receiver: Sounds like you're awfully busy right now.
Sender: I thought the meeting today accomplished nothing.
Receiver: You were very disappointed with our session.[14]

Successful "reflective responding" (active listening) is characterized by:

- A greater emphasis on listening than on talking.
- Responding to personal rather than abstract points (personal feelings, beliefs, and positions rather than abstract ideas).
- Following the other rather than leading him into areas we think we should be exploring (exploring his frame of reference rather than forcing ours upon him, at least until we fully understand his position).
- Clarifying what the other has said about his own thoughts and feelings rather than close questioning or telling him what we believe he should be thinking or feeling.
- Responding to the other's feelings in his communication.[15]

This active listening technique has generally been recommended more for counseling communications such as employee counseling and performance improvement. In negotiation, it may appear initially that active listening is unsuitable because, unlike counseling sessions, the receiver does have a position of her own and usually does feel strongly about the issues. By recommending active listening, we are not suggesting that the receiver should automatically adopt or agree with her opponent's position and abandon her own. Rather, we are suggesting that active listening is a skill that encourages other parties to talk more fully about their frames of reference, that is, the position they are taking. When they do so, we may better understand the nature of their interests, the factors and information that support it, and the ways that the opponent's position can be compromised, reconciled, or negotiated in accordance with our own preferences and priorities.

Role Reversal. Communication distortions may be eliminated through role reversal, or "walking a while in the other's shoes." Continually arguing our own position in debate may lead to a self-reinforcing cycle of argumentation that prohibits us from recognizing the possible compatibilities between our own position and the other party's. In our description of active listening we suggested that one objective was to gain a better understanding of the other party's perspective or frame of reference, rather than only advocating our own. Active listening, however, is still a somewhat passive process. Role-reversal techniques allow us to understand others' positions by actively arguing them *to their satisfaction!* In doing so, negotiators more fully understand others' positions, perhaps come to accept their validity, and discover ways that both positions can be modified to make them more compatible.

A number of studies have examined the impact and success of the role-reversal technique. In general, research on role reversal supports the following conclusions:

- Role reversal is effective in producing cognitive changes (greater understanding of the opponent's position) and attitude changes (perceived similarities between the two positions).
- When the parties' positions are fundamentally compatible with one another, role reversal is likely to produce better results; when the parties' positions are fundamentally incompatible, role reversal may sharpen the perceptions of incompatibility *and inhibit positive attitude change.*
- Although role reversal may induce greater understanding of the opponent's position and highlight areas of possible similarity, it is not necessarily more effective overall as a means of inducing agreement between parties.[16]

In sum, role reversal may be a useful tool for reducing the distortions in communication that prohibit accurate understanding of, and appreciation for, the other position in negotiation. However, such understanding may not necessarily lead to an easier resolution of the conflict, particularly when accurate communication reveals a fundamental incompatibility in the positions of the two sides.

The End Stage

What the end stage lacks in a unique contribution to the flow of negotiation, it often makes up for in frustration. The successful completion of a negotiation often seems "so near, yet so far away." At this stage, negotiators must attend to two key issues simultaneously: the avoidance of fatal mistakes, and the achievement of satisfactory closure in a constructive manner.

The Avoidance of Fatal Mistakes. Achieving closure in a negotiation involves, in large part, making decisions to accept offers, to compromise priorities, to trade off across issues with the other party, or some combination of these elements. Such decision-making processes can be broken down into four key elements: framing, gathering intelligence, coming to conclusions, and learning from feedback. Framing was discussed earlier in this chapter, and gathering intelligence was discussed in Chapter 4. The process of coming to conclusions is specifically an end-stage element, but the dynamics of this process are not primarily communicative and have not been addressed specifically in the chapters on distributive and integrative negotiation. The fourth element, that of learning (or failing to learn) from feedback, is largely communicative in nature, involving "keeping track of what you expected would happen, systematically guarding against self-serving expectations, and making sure you review the lessons your feedback has provided the next time a similar decision comes along."[17] There are 10 "decision traps" that can ensnare decision makers, resulting in suboptimal decisions. Although some of these traps occur in earlier stages of the negotiation (you will recognize a few from our discussion in the previous chapter), we suspect that a number of them may occur at the end of a negotiation when parties are in a hurry to wrap up loose ends and cement a deal. The traps include:

1. *Plunging in*—reaching a conclusion to a problem before identifying the essence or crux of the problem (e.g., forcing negotiations into the end stage prematurely by pushing for a quantitative or substantive resolution to a problem that has been incompletely defined or is basically relational in nature).

2. *Overconfidence in one's own judgment*—blocking, ignoring, or failing to seek factual information that might contradict one's own assumptions and opinions (e.g., strictly adhering to a unilateral strategy, regardless of other information that emerges during the course of the negotiation).

3. *Frame blindness*—perceiving, then solving, the wrong problem, accompanied by overlooking options and losing sight of objectives because they do not fit the frame being used (e.g., forcing resolution of a complex, mixed-motive dispute into some simplistic, concrete measure of performance such as money).

4. *Lack of frame control*—failure to test different frames to determine if they fit, or being unduly influenced by the other party's frame (e.g.,

agreeing to a suboptimal outcome because the other party has taken advantage of our aversion to the risk of going home empty-handed).

5. *Shortsighted shortcuts*—use of heuristics, or rules of thumb, such as using convenient (but misleading) referent points (e.g., accepting the other party's commitment to turning over a new leaf when past experiences suggest that they are really unlikely to do so).

6. *Shooting from the hip*—managing a great deal of information in your head, rather than adopting and using a systematic process of evaluation and choice (e.g., proceeding on gut feelings or eye contact alone in deciding to accept a resolution, trusting that problems will not occur or that they will be easily worked out if they do).

7. *Group failure*—not managing the group process effectively; instead, assuming that smart and well-intentioned individuals can invariably produce a durable, high-quality group decision (e.g., to move stalled decisions in a group might take a vote on accepting a resolution, thereby disenfranchising the minority who do not vote for the resolution and stopping the deliberative process short of achieving its integrative possibilities).

8. *Fooling yourself about feedback*—failure to use feedback correctly, either to protect your ego or through the bias of hindsight (e.g., dealing with the embarrassment of being outmaneuvered by the other party because of a lack of good information or a failure to rigorously prepare).

9. *Not keeping track*—assuming that learning occurs automatically and thus not keeping systematic records of decisions and related outcomes (e.g., losing sight of the gains and deals "purchased" with concessions and trade-offs made during the negotiation, or not applying the lessons of one negotiation episode to future negotiations).

10. *Failure to audit one's own decisions processes*—failure to establish and use a plan to avoid the traps mentioned here or the inability or unwillingness to fully understand your own style, warts and all (e.g., doggedly adhering to a flawed or inappropriate approach to negotiation, even in the face of frequent failures and suboptimal outcomes).[18]

Achieving Closure. Advice from the field of sales negotiations in particular, advises about communication during the end stage.[19] Experts there enjoin negotiators to know when to shut up to avoid surrendering important information needlessly or making "dumb remarks" that push a wavering party away from the agreement they may be almost ready to endorse. The other side of this is to "beware of garbage and the garbage truck" by recognizing the other party's faux pas and dumb remarks for what they are and refusing to respond to them or be distracted by them. Negotiators must also watch out for last-minute hitches (such as nit-picking or second-guessing by parties who didn't participate in the bargaining process, but who have the right or responsibility to review it), by expecting such hitches

---

Criteria for Judging the Quality of the Agreement

Is there a preamble in which the intent of the agreement is spelled out clearly?

Are all the issues of interest to all parties addressed?

Are all the proposals workable?

Have all parties affected by the agreement been consulted?

For each point of agreement, is it crystal clear what you have agreed to, including what is to be done, by whom, by what time, and how?

Does the agreement in total make sense?

Is the agreement reasonable and equitable?

Have you considered the major barriers to fulfilling the agreement?

Do you have a vehicle for managing disagreements arising out of this agreement? Is it clear to all parties what this vehicle is and how to use it?

---

and being prepared to handle them with some aplomb. Finally, we must point out the importance of reducing the agreement to written form—writing "the contract." The party that writes the contract is in a position to achieve clarity of purpose and conduct for the deal. As for the communicative quality of the final, written agreement, a reasonable checklist is presented in the box.[20]

Summary

In this chapter, we have taken a multifaceted look at the role of communication in negotiation. In particular, we examined two perspectives: the structural perspective, provided by phase and stage models of negotiation, and the perceptual processes and phenomena that occur within these phases.

In the beginning stage, the key behaviors and activities include the clarification of issues and agendas and the demarcation of the playing field—the bounded area of interests and potentials within which the negotiation will unfold. Critically important to this beginning stage is the process of social perception, including the potential for perceptual distortion (such as stereotyping, halo effects, selective perception, and projection). Also important are the effects of framing and of the mistakes that can accrue from attributional biases.

The middle stage is marked by the exchange of offers and the evolution of a framework and the detail that fleshes out the negotiation and moves it toward closure. Interests and expectations are expressed, bargaining ranges are narrowed, and the parties move toward settlement. Communicative behaviors in this stage include providing clear information regarding one's own interests, proactively seeking information about the other's interests, and listening actively as those interests are expressed. This active listening requires a strong commitment to hearing the other party effectively and authentically, and it may be enhanced by empathic behaviors such as role reversal.

Finally, the end stage is marked by efforts to bring the negotiation to conclusion. At this stage, the parties must be careful to avoid a number of potential decision traps in their haste to reach a settlement and wrap up the details. Parties must also take care to write the agreement down and create a draft that contains language endorsed by both sides.

End Notes

1. See Douglas (1957, 1962).
2. See Holmes and Poole (1991).
3. See Cooper (1981).
4. See Bruner and Tagiuri (1954).
5. See Putnam and Holmer (1992).
6. See Neale and Bazerman (1991, 1992a).
7. See Gray and Donnellon (1989).
8. See Ross, Greene, and House (1977).
9. See Tutzauer (1992).
10. See Putnam and Homler (1992).
11. See Zartman (1977) and Zartman and Berman (1982).
12. See Nierenberg (1973).
13. See Deep and Sussman (1993).
14. See Gordon (1977).
15. See Athos and Gabarro (1978).
16. See Johnson (1971) and Walcott, Hopmann, and King (1977).
17. Russo and Schoemaker (1989, p. 3).
18. Ibid.
19. See Karrass (1985).
20. Adapted from Sheppard (1993).

7 SOCIAL CONTEXT OF NEGOTIATION

Probably one of the most influential factors in negotiations—and yet one that is the most poorly understood—is the nature of the negotiator's social environment. The social environment includes all parties who are present at the negotiation, those who help to plan it in advance or are affected by the outcome of negotiation (even though they are not actually negotiating), and different types of observers to the negotiation.

The purpose of this chapter is to examine negotiations which occur in a larger social context. Much of what we have said in the previous chapters has implied that two negotiators are acting alone and on their own, in a rather limited time frame, to arrive at an agreement. However, we will show in this chapter that a negotiator who is only representing her own interests will behave very differently from one who is negotiating as the representative of others. When there are more than two parties at the table, or when parties negotiate in front of other people, or when they represent the interests of others than themselves, the dynamics of negotiation definitely change.

The Social Context of Negotiation

The major theme of this chapter is that the number of parties in a negotiation dramatically affects the negotiation process. The greater the number of individuals, groups, and organizations that are involved in a negotiation or have a stake in its outcomes, the greater the number of possible interactions between the parties, the greater are the number of roles that can be played, and thus the more complex the flow of interaction becomes.

FIGURE 7.1

A Negotiation Dyad

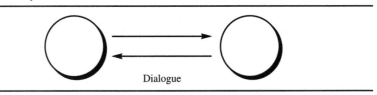

Dialogue

It is important to understand that although we have attempted to clearly delineate these different roles, in fact, negotiating parties may take on more than one role during the course of a negotiation. We will now explore the structural dynamics of the different roles, first examining the simplest form (two individual negotiators) and then describing how the social structure becomes more complex as additional parties and roles are added.

Two Individual Negotiators

In social structure terms, the simplest form of negotiation occurs when only two individuals are involved. Each individual is responsible for representing only her own needs and interests in the negotiation (see Figure 7.1). For example, consider a student who sets off to purchase a stereo system from another student on campus. The preferences of each party (asking price of the seller, amount the buyer can afford to pay, condition of the equipment, strength of the desire to buy or sell the system, etc.) will be determined wholly by the two individuals themselves. The price that they agree on—and any other terms and conditions of the sale, such as whether a few CDs are thrown in free—will be determined solely by the parties themselves through their deliberations.

Additional Negotiators

The first way that a negotiation situation becomes more complex is by adding more negotiators. Although each is only responsible for stating his or her own positions and needs, the agreement has to reflect the views of all the parties (although some may actually be shut out of the final deal). In the previous example, if two students want to buy the stereo and they both show up at the seller's door at the same time, then the seller must decide how to deal with them—separately or together (see Figure 7.2). The buyers may get into a bidding war with each other or the seller might get greedy because his stereo seems to be very attractive, raise his price, and then have both of the buyers walk away. If the situation was different—if, for example, the two buyers were roommates who were going to share the stereo—different negotiating dynamics might occur. When there are more than two negotiators in the event, negotiations instantly become more complex, and the likelihood increases that various subgroups may get together in some form of coalition.

FIGURE 7.2

A Seller and Two Buyers

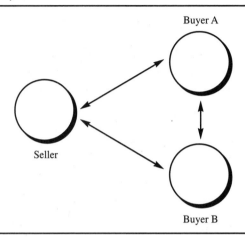

Group and Team Negotiations

In the above example, the negotiating parties were primarily engaged in a bilateral negotiation—that is, one or more buyers were negotiating with a seller for the stereo system. However, there is another form of multiparty negotiation, in which *more* than two parties with separate interests are all present in the negotiation and must come to some agreement (see Figure 7.3). For example, let us assume that four roommates had bought the stereo system; they have now decided to sell it, possibly to split the profit or possibly to invest in a more advanced system. Each has a different preference for what the roomates should do: Andy wants to sell it and simply split up the money because he wants to buy a new bike for himself; Aaron wants to sell it and buy a newer but inexpensive stereo system; Chuck wants to sell it and buy a super-high-quality system that will require each of them to chip in a lot more money; Dan doesn't want to sell it at all and thinks the whole idea is dumb. In this situation, the parties must figure out how to satisfy enough of them to make a decision. We will explore these within-group negotiations as a separate process in the next chapter.

Constituencies, Representatives, Audiences, and Bystanders

In the above situations, all parties were at the negotiating table. We shall now turn to consider the roles played by those parties who are *not* at the table, but whose interests are represented by someone else (their delegate, representative, or agent), who will be affected by the outcome in some way, or who are observing the negotiating process and perhaps offering comments, critique, or evaluation of

FIGURE 7.3

A Multiparty Negotiation

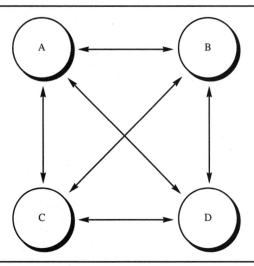

FIGURE 7.4

Pairs of Negotiators in Teams

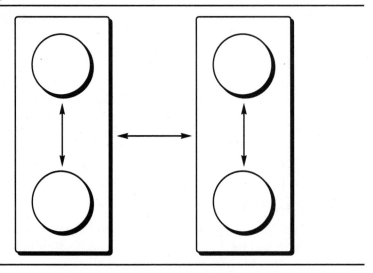

the process or outcome. Under these conditions, the negotiators at the table will begin to redirect their behavior away from the opponent to pay some attention to these "outsiders" as well. We will broadly describe the attention paid to these additional parties—regardless of who they are—as *audience* effects.

There are many different kinds of audiences and audience effects. Initially, we will include *all* the roles we delineated above—other members of a negotiating team, constituencies, bystanders, and even neutrals—as audiences because they all tend to serve the function of observers, commentators, or stakeholders relative to the focal negotiator's behavior. As we begin to delineate the different roles and functions that audiences play, we will make distinctions among these different roles.

One form of audience is *additional team members* who are present with the negotiator at the deliberations. Members of a negotiating team may take on one or more important roles: chief spokesperson, expert or resource person on a specific issue, advocate for a particular subgroup with a stake in the outcome, legal or financial counsel, statistician or cost analyst, recorder, or observer. Team members may also change into another role as the negotiation evolves. The most frequent role shift is from being a negotiator to being a more passive observer. The observer may be taking notes, listening to the discussion, preparing for comments to be introduced later on, or simply evaluating and judging the actions of those who currently hold the floor. It is important to recognize these multiple roles that team members can play because an audience can do as much to influence and shape a spokesperson's behavior as what the opposing negotiator says or does. Figure 7.4 represents a simple negotiation between two pairs of negotiators—on each side, one may be the primary spokesperson while the other assists, but they may change roles at any time.

A second type of audience is a *constituency*. A constituency is one or more parties whose interests, demands, or priorities are being represented by the focal negotiator at the table. The term *constituency* usually applies to politics; elected officials are usually accountable to their constituents who elected them. For an attorney, his constituent is his client. The social structure of this negotiation is represented in Figure 7.5. As the figure suggests, negotiators with constituencies are involved in two distinctly different relationships—and often in two separate and distinct negotiations. The first relationship is with the constituency. The negotiator and constituency decide on their collective view of what they want to achieve in the negotiation and the strategy and tactics of how to get it. The constituency then delegates some power and authority to the negotiator to pursue the goals and strategy through negotiation. Constituents expect that the negotiator will accurately and enthusiastically represent their interests in the deliberations, periodically report back as negotiations evolve, and finally report the outcomes back at the end of the process. Constituents therefore expect to directly profit (or lose) as a result of the negotiator's effectiveness, and they often select their agent based on her ability to achieve the goals.

FIGURE 7.5

Negotiators Representing Constituents

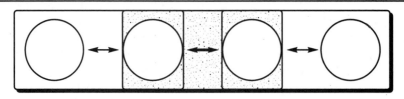

The second relationship is with the opponent—in this relationship, the negotiator and his opponent attempt to reach a viable and effective resolution of their
differences. Reaching that resolution may require the negotiator to compromise
on the goals set for him by his constituency, and then to explain and justify those
compromises back to the constituent. Therefore, representing a constituent creates unique pressures and conflicts for agents because they may be unable both to
satisfy their constituent completely and to achieve a resolution satisfactory to
their opponent.

A third type of audience is composed of *bystanders* and *observers*. In many
negotiations, there are often bystanders whose interests are not directly represented at the negotiating table, but who are affected by the outcome, can observe
the process, or have a need to comment on the process or the emerging outcome.
Figure 7.6 represents this most complex social environment for a negotiation. A
situation that includes bystanders and observers not only offers a context in which
many parties are watching and evaluating the negotiation, but also offers a number of ways for the negotiator to use the audiences to bring indirect pressure to
bear on the other negotiator. We will examine some of the most common tactics
later in this chapter.

Characteristics of Audiences and Bystanders. Audiences differ in several key
ways:[1]

• Most important, audiences can be physically *present* or *absent* from the
negotiation event. Some audiences may actually be at the negotiating table and
directly witness the events that occur; others may be physically removed and only
learn about what happens through reports of the events. Whether an audience is
present or absent will affect how a negotiator behaves because she may say one
thing with the audience present and another with the audience absent. When audiences are absent, negotiators often distort what happened at the negotiating table
in order to impress the audience.

• Audiences can be *dependent* or *nondependent* on the negotiators for the
outcomes derived from the negotiation process. The more an audience directly
depends on the negotiator for their own outcomes, the more control they will try
to exert.

FIGURE 7.6

Negotiators Representing Constituencies with Input from Audiences

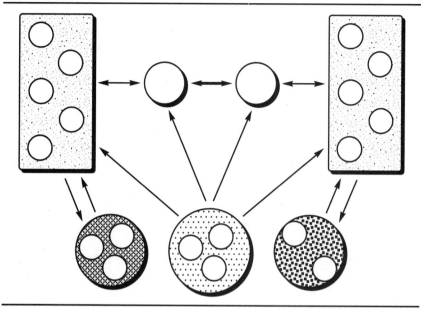

• Audiences can be *involved* or *uninvolved*. The more involved they are, the more they will attempt to influence the deliberations, directly or indirectly. For example, in international affairs, the United States has often become directly involved in other country's local disputes—the Middle East, Eastern Europe, the former Yugoslavian republics, or Somalia. United States involvement has occurred in almost every form and variation—from expressing a preference for a particular resolution, to influencing local policy, providing advice or armaments, to becoming militarily involved and keeping parties separate to help achieve a peaceful resolution.

• Audiences can differ in the amount of *feedback* they give to the negotiators, evaluating their effectiveness and letting them know how they are doing. Feedback may be written or verbal, such as notes or messages, or it may even be in nonverbal form, such as smiles and nods of affirmation or scowls and frowns of disapproval. Feedback may be directed toward the positions that a negotiator has taken, concessions she has made, agreements she has arrived at, or the manner in which she has conducted herself in the deliberations.

Having described different types of audiences and how they differ, let us summarize the most important principles about audiences and the significant ways that they influence the negotiator's choice of tactics.

Negotiators Seek a Favorable Reaction from an Audience. The mere presence of an audience, particularly one that can easily observe or exercise surveillance over the negotiator, motivates a negotiator to seek a favorable (positive) evaluation from that audience and to avoid an unfavorable (negative) evaluation. This has been demonstrated in several research studies. First, merely being aware that they are under surveillance motivates negotiators to "act tough."[2] When negotiators were observed negotiating with others, those who believed they were under surveillance were significantly more likely to conduct their negotiations in a distributive bargaining manner and to use threats, "commitment tactics," and put-downs of their opponents to gain advantage (see Chapter 2). When questioned later about their behavior, negotiators under surveillance felt that it was more important to look tough and strong than to make concessions or pursue strategies of mutual gain.[3]

The presence of a "salient" audience—one that the negotiator values for their opinions and supportive comments—affects a negotiator even more dramatically. A classic study by researcher Bert Brown reveals the power of feedback from a salient audience on a negotiator's behavior.[4] In Brown's experiment, high-school students did a bargaining simulation and received contrived feedback messages from a group of observers who they thought were their "peers." The message said that either they looked weak and foolish in the simulation, or that they looked tough and strong because they had "played fair." Students then played a second round of the simulation, during which they were given the choice of using a retaliatory strategy to "get back at" the opponent who took advantage of them. Brown summarized:

> The results were striking. Publicly humiliated subjects—those who received the derogatory feedback—were far more likely to retaliate, and with greater severity and self-sacrifice—than subjects who received the more favorable feedback. . . . Of special interest is the fact that when asked why they chose severe retaliation, 75 percent of the subjects who did so reported that they didn't want to look foolish and weak as a result of having been exploited, and that they retaliated in order to reassert their capability and strength.[5]

Brown's study has several important implications for understanding the power of an audience over a negotiator. First, the student subjects in the study did not know the specific identity of anyone in the audience—only that they were from the same high school. Second, the power of the feedback message from the audience overshadowed everything that happened in the negotiation game. Thus, audiences that are only vaguely viewed as an important group to please can nevertheless exert powerful influences over a negotiator's behavior. Finally, some students retaliated toward their opponent even when there was no audience present. This suggests that *the opposing negotiator can act as an audience.* Negotiators who believe that the opposing negotiator has caused them to look foolish or evaluated them negatively may try to punish the other. Anyone who has ever played a "friendly" game of tennis, golf, ping pong, or basketball will recognize that much of the banter, teasing, and verbal harassment that occurs is designed to undermine the opponent's self-confidence or to challenge him to play better in the future. All of this is usually done with good-natured humor, yet the banter can quickly turn serious if a comment is made too sharply or taken wrong, and it can both seriously unsettle the opponent and hurt the relationship.

Audiences Hold the Negotiator Accountable. Audiences maintain control over a negotiator by holding her accountable for her performance and by administering rewards or punishments based on that performance. This accountability will occur (*a*) when a bargainer's performance is *visible* to the audience (so that the audience is able to judge how well the bargainer performs) and (*b*) when the audience is *dependent* on the bargainer. A dependent audience will generally insist that the negotiator be tough, firm, demanding, and unyielding in her struggle to obtain the best possible outcome for her constituents. Failure to perform in this manner (in the eyes of the audience) may lead to public criticism of the negotiator, in order to pressure (embarrass) her into better performance.

Continued characterizations of a negotiator as weak, soft, or someone who sells out may lead to unfortunate but predictable outcomes. First, the bargainer may become increasingly inflexible or retaliatory to demonstrate to her constituency that she is capable of defending their interests. Second, the bargainer may try to be a more loyal, committed, and dedicated advocate of the constituency's preferred outcomes and priorities, simply to attempt to regain their good favor and evaluation. Finally, she may find herself forced to resign, judged by herself or others as incapable of representing the constituency's best interests.

Tactical Implications of Audience Dynamics: Managing the Negotiator's Dilemma. The presence of an audience—particularly an outcome-dependent audience—creates a paradox for negotiators because of two sets of pressures. One set comes from the constituency, which communicates expectations that the agent should be tough, firm, unyielding, and supportive of the constituency's demands. The other set comes from the opposing negotiator and from the definition of negotiation itself: that the negotiator should be flexible, conciliatory, and willing to engage in give and take. (Visualize these pressures as depicted in Figure 7.5, simultaneously pushing the negotiator from opposite directions.) The basic dilemma, then, is to determine how a bargainer can satisfy both the constituency's demand for firmness (and a settlement favorable to their interests), and the opponent's demand for concessions (and a settlement favorable to the opponent or to their mutual gain).

The answer is that a negotiator must build relationships with both the constituency *and* the opponent. The relationship with the constituency must be cultivated on the basis of complete support for their demands and a willingness to advocate these demands in negotiation. However, the relationship with the opponent must be developed by stressing the desirability of establishing and maintaining a productive working relationship and the similarity and commonality of their collective goals or fate. However, each of these relationships must be developed *privately, and without visibility to the other group.* This privacy assures that a negotiator can conduct deliberations with the opponent without accountability pressures. It may also require a certain degree of duplicity, with the negotiator promising utmost loyalty and dedication to both the opponent and the constituent, each out of view of the other. Typically, negotiators first meet with the constituency to define their collective interests and objectives. They then meet with opposing negotiators, in privacy, so that they can openly state their constituent's expectations while also making necessary concessions without looking weak or foolish. Finally, a negotiator returns to the constituency to sell the concessions to them, persuading them that the achieved settlement was the best possible.

Successful management of a constituency requires that the negotiator have control over the visibility or invisibility of negotiating behavior to the constituency. A negotiator who cannot control this visibility is going to be on public display all the time. Every statement, argument, concession, and mistake will be in full view of a critical audience that may pick it apart, critique it, and challenge it as possibly disloyal. A few of the most common tactics to manipulate audience visibility are as follows:

Limit Concessions by Making Negotiations Visible to the Constituency. Because negotiators who negotiate in full view of their constituencies are less likely to make concessions than negotiators who deliberate in private, negotiators can enhance their own visibility in order to limit making concessions. Negotiators go public, typically, when they want to remain firm in their positions. For example, the negotiator may insist on allowing his constituency to be present for all negotiations.

Use the Constituency to Show Militancy. A second way that a constituency can be used is to make the constituency visible and demonstrate that they are more extreme, radical, committed, and inflexible than the negotiator. Community groups that want to bring about change from public officials usually insist that the officials come to an open meeting of the community, in which community representative's confront the officials with their concerns or grievances. Those invited to speak at the meeting are often the most demanding or militant, and are the ones who communicate a tough and demanding posture to the opponent. As a result, a negotiator can look cooler, calmer, and more rational than her out-of-control constituency. If the negotiator then implies that "either you deal with me and my demands, or you work with someone else from my constituency who is far more irrational than me," the negotiator is likely to gain significant ground with an opponent. This is a variation of the classic "tough guy–nice guy" or "Mutt and Jeff" negotiating tactic.

Limit a Negotiator's Authority. The third way a negotiator can use a constituency is by showing the opponent that the constituency has limited the negotiator's authority to make concessions—particularly "unauthorized" ones. This tactic may be used as a bluff or a genuine limit on authority. As a bluff, the negotiator mis-leads the opponent to believe that all concessions must be cleared with the con-stituency. As a genuine tactic, the negotiator's constituency has actually defined limits to what the negotiator can decide on his own. In banks, for example, new loan officers may have very limited authority to approve loans on their own sig-nature, whereas the bank's senior loan officer probably has wider latitude. Yet although the senior loan officer could easily approve the loan on her own author-ity, she uses the constituency (the bank's loan committee) both for protection (to make sure that the loan is not granted foolishly) and perhaps also to pressure the borrower into meeting certain terms and conditions.

Increase the Possibility of Concessions by Cutting Off Audience Visibility. If increased audience visibility increases the likelihood that negotiators will take tougher stands, be less flexible, and make fewer concessions, then a negotiator who wishes to be more flexible and conciliatory would want negotiations to be less visible. There are two approaches to accomplishing this objective:

Establish Privacy Prior to the Beginning of Negotiations. One ground rule that should be considered is that the negotiations will be conducted in private, that no media or public interviews will be granted, and that contact with the other party's constituency (or visibility to audiences) will be strictly controlled. To enhance the privacy of the negotiations, parties may select a remote location in neutral terri-tory, where their comings and goings will not be too obvious or visible. When the time comes for announcements about negotiating progress or achievements, both parties can make them jointly, coordinating their communications.

Screen Visibility during Negotiations. If negotiators have not agreed beforehand to a location that is private and secure, there are other options for screening out unwanted observers from sensitive discussions. One of the simplest ways is to have some discussions occur informally, on a strictly unofficial basis. These dis-cussions can occur during coffee breaks, meal breaks, walks around the building, or even during a quick trip to the washroom. During such meetings, parties can speak more candidly "off the record," or they can give hints about their bottom-line position or their willingness to make certain concessions. Other kinds of information can also be privately exchanged in these informal venues. Negotiators can grumble and complain, brag about their constituency and its sup-port, or even let conversations with their own constituents be "overheard" by an opponent. All these tactics give the other side information about what is really possible without saying it directly at the table. Heads of state who negotiate major arms-and-trade agreements are frequently photographed at dinners, receptions, or walks in the garden. (The play *A Walk in the Woods* is an interesting re-creation of the way President Jimmy Carter shaped the Camp David accords between Israel and Egypt.)[6]

FIGURE 7.7

Indirect Communication through Managers (union–management example)

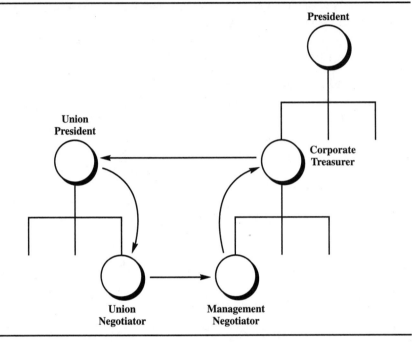

Communicating Indirectly with the Constituency or Audiences. A third technique that negotiators use in manipulating the social structure of negotiations is to communicate *indirectly*. Indirect communications are efforts by the negotiator to bring the opinions of audiences and constituents to bear on the opposing negotiator. Although the opponent may believe he is well defended against his adversary's arguments, he may not be able to defend himself against other people—his constituents, his friends, his superiors, or public opinion—when they appear to side with his opponent. This informal communication takes place in the following four ways:

Communicate through Superiors. This technique is frequently used when negotiators are representatives of two hierarchically structured organizations (e.g., a company and a union, or two companies engaged in a business deal) and when parties are dissatisfied with the progress of negotiations or the behavior of their opponent. To manage their frustration and dissatisfaction, they may go to their own superiors (who are probably not directly involved) and ask the superiors to either attend a negotiating session or, more commonly, to contact their counterpart in the opposing organization. The situation is represented in Figure 7.7.

FIGURE 7.8

Indirect Communication through a Constituency

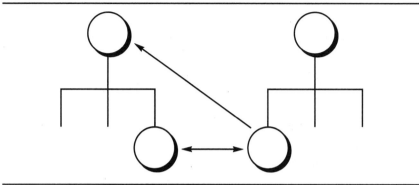

Communicate through Intermediaries and Constituency Members. This approach is used when negotiators need to make informal contact with an opposing negotiator or constituency. Here the approach is made through any external contact who can serve as an intermediary or communication conduit. Those selected are usually chosen for some valid reason—trust, past experience in working together, a personal friendship or relationship, or a personal reputation for credibility, impartiality, and integrity. The tactic is most often used under two major circumstances: when a negotiator wants to "feel out" the opposing group to possibly gain inside information, or when deliberations are deadlocked and need to be unfrozen.

Communicate Directly to an Opponent's Constituency. In a third form of indirect communication (see Figure 7.8), one agent seeks to bypass the opposing negotiator and communicate *directly* with his constituency to persuade them to change their position or the instructions they are giving their representative. The agent himself may initiate this tactic, usually when he believes that the opposing agent is not communicating effectively with her constituency—when the opposing agent is either not representing her constituency's interests clearly and effectively or not accurately reporting to his constituency. Thus, the agent attempts to eliminate the middle man and communicate directly with the opponent's constituency. In a union–management situation, for example, management representatives frequently prefer to speak or write directly to the rank and file rather than through the union leadership. However, direct communication with an opposing constituency—particularly without the sanction of the opposing negotiator—can be viewed as an inflammatory tactic. If the negotiator is not consulted and does not grant permission, the act of going around her is usually interpreted as a lack of confidence in her skills.

Communicating to Bystanders and Audiences. In this case, the agent's intent is to manipulate the opinion of bystanders (other than constituencies) and to mobilize their support. Communication through bystanders may occur (1) as an explicit and conscious tactic to exert influence on the opponent, but through circuitous channels, (2) as an effort to build alliances and support for one's own position; or (3) as a result of the natural tendency for conflict to proliferate and envelop innocent bystanders. In all cases, negotiators are public about their own (or their organization's) demands. They will tell anyone who will listen about how fair, legitimate, just, and appropriate their own side's position is, and how unfair, unjust, illegitimate, and inappropriate the opponent's position is. As a result, negotiators hope that third parties will openly side with them (hence lending strength and credence to their arguments). Communication through audiences—particularly the media—is extremely common in major interorganizational negotiations such as intergovernmental, international, or labor–management relations. This process may be designed to activate and win over *interested audiences* who will communicate directly with the opponent.

Building Relationships with Opponents

Finally, rather than undermining an opponent's support, negotiators frequently try to develop personal relationships with the opponent. The negotiator's underlying assumption is that it is easier (and definitely more pleasant) to work with and persuade a friendly opponent than an unfriendly one. In addition, the assumption is that building a personal relationship will permit the agent to get his message across to a less defensive, less antagonistic adversary. Individuals who see themselves as *similar* to one another, who are *attracted to* one another, or who are likely to experience a *common fate* are more likely to change their attitudes toward one another. Because negotiation may be viewed as a mutual effort by both parties to change the other's attitudes (e.g., objectives, opening demands), the same principles apply.

Negotiators use a variety of techniques to make this tactic work (see Chapter 3 and 5). Some negotiators meet informally to get to know each other outside of the context of negotiations. Shared cocktails, a meal, or even an informal coffee break are well-known opportunities for promoting friendliness, easy conversation, and cordiality. Second, negotiators may also stress their "common fate"—namely, the accountability pressures put on them by their constituencies. If both negotiators feel strongly pressured by their constituencies, this can serve as a basis to build the relationship. "You and I are in this together," "We both have our constituencies to deal with," or "We want to achieve the best for all of us" are all phrases that typify the opening stages of negotiation.[7] A further purpose of informal meetings is to permit each party to get a sense of each other's objectives. In many negotiations, chief negotiators meet before the formal deliberations, much like the chief executives we described earlier. The purpose of this meeting is usually twofold: to sense what the other side's major demands will be and to develop a relationship and an open channel of communication that can be used regardless of how tense the negotiations become. Some negotiators may choose to publicize the event to demonstrate a spirit of cooperation. When the president of the United States appears before the television cameras in the White House Rose Garden with some visiting foreign dignitary, the two are usually shown smiling, shaking hands, embracing, and demonstrating to their constituencies and audiences that they have developed a harmonious relationship that will lead to mutual agreement on substantive problems. The discussion between them, however, is private and we rarely know what was actually said.

Summary

Sometimes negotiation is a private affair between two parties. Up until now we have talked about negotiation in this more private context. However, at other times, there are constituencies and audiences to a negotiation, and their presence can have both a direct and a subtle impact on negotiations.

Three types of constituencies and audiences may be encountered. First, when more than two people negotiate, those who are not in the immediate conversation act as an audience to the negotiation. They may be there to support the key negotiators or they may represent other interests and be involved in the conversation. The very fact that we negotiate in front of other people changes negotiation dynamics.

A second type of audience is the constituency the negotiator represents. A wife negotiating for a new house represents her family, diplomats negotiate for their countries, and division heads on a companywide budget committee negotiate what portion of capital resources their departments will have for the coming year. These audiences have a stake in the outcome of the negotiation and benefit or suffer according to the skills of their representatives. The third type of audience is bystanders. Bystanders see or hear about the negotiations, and although they have little or no stake in the outcome, they form opinions (favorable or unfavorable) of the settlement and the parties involved.

Audiences influence negotiators through two different routes. One way is that negotiators desire positive evaluations from those who are in a position to observe what they have done. The other is that audiences can (and do) hold negotiators responsible for the outcomes of negotiations. They can reward negotiators by publicly praising them and punish negotiators by dismissing them. They can intrude and change the course of negotiations—as when the public requires mandatory arbitration or fact-finding in some disputes. They can find ways of making their preferences known—for example, talking to the press—thereby putting pressure on one or both negotiators.

In the next chapter, we will explicitly address group negotiations, when there are more than two parties at the table representing their interests, and where the dynamics of influence become more complex than the simpler bilateral process.

End Notes

1. Compare to Rubin and Brown (1975).

2. Benton and Druckman (1974).

3. Carnevale, Pruitt, and Britton (1979).

4. Brown (1968).

5. Rubin and Brown (1975, p. 45).

6. Blessing (1988).

7. Many experienced negotiators refer to these expressions of common fate as a tactical ploy to soften them up before the opposing negotiator presents tough demands. Although that allegation may be true, these comments play a critical role in negotiation. Even if the speech is ritualistic, it *does* communicate that the opposing negotiator is interested in building a personal relationship. Moreover, the absence of the speech may indicate that the parties are so adamant in their positions or so angry at one another that they cannot bring themselves to make the speech. This may be a clear sign that the negotiations will be tense and are likely to be deadlocked.

8 NEGOTIATION IN GROUPS

In the previous chapter, we described the larger social context of negotiation and the roles played by constituencies and audiences. However, we described this social context in terms of its impact on the *two* focal primary negotiators who are operating in that social context. We now move to another level of social complexity: three or more negotiators, each one representing either their own individual interests *or* acting as an agent for a constituency. We will describe this type of negotiations as *multiparty negotiations*. The general model for a multiparty negotiation is represented in Figure 8.1 (which is identical to Figure 7.3 except that each negotiator has constituents who are also part of his group). Although we have represented a multiparty negotiation in the diagram as a four-party deliberation (four agents representing four constituencies), multiparty dynamics will occur whenever there are *three or more* negotiators.

This section will be divided into several parts. First we will briefly comment on some of the different types and variations of multiparty negotiations. We will then note the factors that make multiparty negotiations more difficult to deal with than one-on-one negotiations. Additionally, we will discuss strategies that can be used to manage multiparty negotiations. As we will consistently show, multiparty negotiations are very complex and highly susceptible to breakdown, and they therefore often require a commitment to manage the negotiation process in order to assure an effective multiparty agreement.[1]

Differences between Group Negotiations and Multiparty Negotiations

Multiparty negotiations differ from two-party deliberations in a number of important ways. In every case, the differences are what make multiparty negotiations more complex, challenging, and difficult to manage.

167

FIGURE 8.1

A Multiparty Negotiation

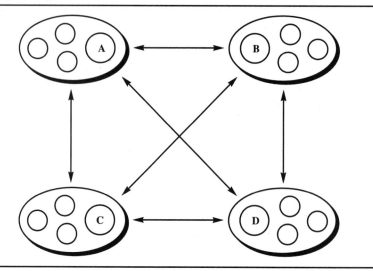

Number of Parties

The first difference is the most obvious one, as we have been discussing in this chapter: multiparty negotiations put more negotiators at the table. Thus, negotiations simply become bigger because there are more agents in the negotiation.

Informational and Computational Complexity

A second difference is that in multiparty negotiations, more issues, more perspectives on issues, and more total information (facts, figures, viewpoints, arguments, documentary support) are introduced. "One of the most fundamental consequences of increasing the number of parties is that the negotiation situation tends to become less lucid, more complex, and therefore, in some respects, more demanding. As size increases, there will be more values, interests, and perceptions to be integrated or accommodated."[2] Keeping track of all this information, the perspective of each side, and the parameters into which a solution must fit becomes a major challenge for the negotiators.

Social Complexity

A third difference is that as the number of parties increases, the social environment changes from a one-on-one dialogue to a small group. As a result, all the dynamics of small groups and group process begin to affect the way the negotiators operate. Social pressures develop and members must become cohesive, unified, and together, yet the members are in conflict with each other and cannot be cohesive unless they can find an acceptable solution. Members compare themselves to each other, evaluate themselves against each other, and begin to try to use a variety of influence tactics to persuade each other toward their point of view. Strong pressures for conformity develop as members pressure other members to adopt a common perspective or definition of the problem or to endorse a particular solution. The group may attempt to avoid or minimize conflict by downplaying their differences or by not working them through adequately to reach an effective solution. Research on policy-making and decision-making groups has shown that these efforts to minimize and avoid conflict can frequently lead to group decision-making disasters.[3] Fiascoes such as the U.S.-supported invasion of the Bay of Pigs in Cuba during the Kennedy administration or NASA's decision to launch the Challenger space shuttle were caused by dynamics in the key decision-making groups in which group members were hesitant to create conflict and express their real reservations about going ahead with the project.

Procedural Complexity

A fourth way in which multiparty negotiations are more complex is that the process they have to follow is more complicated. In one-on-one negotiations, the parties simply take turns in either presenting their issues and perspectives, challenging the other's perspectives, or moving the negotiation along from its early stages to the later ones. When more parties are involved, however, the procedural rules become far less clear. Whose turn is it to do what? How do the parties coordinate where they are in the negotiations (e.g., opening statements, presentation of viewpoints, moving toward agreement)?

There are several results of this procedural complexity. First, negotiations will definitely take longer; more time must be allowed.[4] Second, the greater the number of parties, the more complex and out of control the process can become— particularly if some parties choose to adopt a strategy of tough positional bargaining and dominate the process in an effort to railroad through their particular viewpoints.[5] Third, as a result of these two elements, negotiators will probably have to devote discussion time explicitly to how they will manage the process to arrive at the type of solution or agreement they want.

Strategic Complexity

Finally, multiparty negotiations are more strategically complex. We hinted at this strategic complexity in the previous paragraph. In a group negotiation, we must consider the strategies of *all* the other parties at the table and decide whether we are going to deal with each of them separately or as a group. The actual process of dealing with each of them usually evolves into a series of one-on-one negotiations, but conducted within the view of all of the other group members. These exchanges are thus subject to all the observability and audience dynamics that we described earlier in this chapter. In this milieu, negotiators will be sensitive to being observed and will probably feel the need to be tough in order to show their firmness and resolve (both to the specific opponent and to other negotiators who are observing). As a result, the social milieu will lead negotiators to adopt more distributive strategies and tactics—even if they did not intend to do so—simply to show their toughness and resolve to others.

There are two other ways in which multiparty negotiations increase in strategic complexity. First, negotiators who have some way to control the number of parties at the table (or even in the room) may begin to use this control. The tactic used will be determined by the strategic interests to be served by adding other parties. Additional parties may be invited to add support or credence to the negotiator's position, to provide independent support, or simply to present a show of force. A second strategic manipulation is to explicitly engage in coalition building as a way to marshal support. Parties explicitly (and sometimes implicitly) agree to support each other's positions in order to add collective weight to their combined view. These coalitions may emerge as a discussion proceeds (two or more parties begin to realize that they have compatible views and agree to help each other achieve their separate objectives as the group objective is attained), or they may be explicitly created prior to negotiations. We will say more about this when we talk about coalitions as a source of power.[6]

Managing Multiparty Negotiations

Given all the added complexity that occurs in a multiparty negotiation, what is the most effective way to cope with and manage this complexity? There are a number of things that can be done, and we will discuss only the most prominent ones here.

Understand the Costs and Consequences of No Agreement

The first thing a negotiator needs to do is to understand the costs and consequences if the group fails to agree.[7] This suggestion has been given repeatedly for negotiators in one-on-one negotiations. For example, suppose that the vice presidents in a computer company are trying to decide which models of a new line of personal computers should be built next year and the quantities of each. First, what will happen if the parties fail to agree on what to do? Will someone else (i.e., the president) step in and decide for them? How will the president feel about the group if members can't agree? Second, are the costs for nonagreement the same for every negotiator? Usually this is *not* the case—agents have different costs for nonagreement. For example, if they cannot agree, the president may mandate the model line and quantities, which may have greater costs for engineering and manufacturing (which would have to change over) than for the marketing and sales departments (which would have to design a new marketing and ad campaign regardless of what was done). The group members with the better nonagreement alternatives are likely to have more power in the negotiation, because they care less about whether the group reaches a particular solution relative to no agreement.

Understand the Decision Rule

The second element in managing a multiparty negotiation is to understand what standards will be used for making the decision. Is it possible that one member could push her entire preferences on the rest of the group, because she has significant formal status (e.g., the president) or has the ability to be persistent and argue for her own views? Could a small group push their views on everyone else—for example, could a small coalition agree and dominate a split or fractured majority? Will the group vote? If so, will a majority rule? Or is the group aiming for true consensus in the form of a solution that incorporates everyone's views and represents all interests? These are not all the possible decision rules, but they do represent the most common ones. Understanding the decision rule allows individuals to shape the negotiation strategy they will pursue. If the current rule is unsatisfactory—for example, the president may dominate and everyone will acquiesce, but the quality of the agreement may be inferior and create major problems for the company in the future—then it may be desirable (if possible) to challenge the rule early on and push for a different decision rule. We will come back to this below.

Strive for a First Agreement rather than a Final Agreement

If the objective is consensus or the best quality solution, do not strive to achieve it in one sitting. Rather, strive for a first agreement that can be revised, upgraded, and improved. As we have pointed out, the additional complexity of multiparty negotiations increases the complexity of the events, the likelihood of communication breakdown, and the likelihood that the parties will negotiate more positionally (either because of the competitive dynamics or the consequences of audience or constituency dynamics). Given these conditions, achieving true consensus among the parties may become so difficult that the parties may stop trying. Hence, it is often better to set a more modest objective for these negotiations: to reach a preliminary agreement or a tentative consensus that can then be tried out and revised later—a plateau that can be modified, reshaped, and improved upon in a follow-up negotiation effort.[8]

Manage the Group Process and Outcome

The following processes are likely to assure a high-quality group decision as the result of a multiparty negotiation.

Appoint an Appropriate Chair. Multiparty negotiations will be greatly facilitated by the presence of a neutral chairperson who can implement many of the tactics we describe below. If at all possible, appoint a chair who has no clear stake in
a specific outcome but a strong stake in the process. The chairperson functions as
a third party who has no stake in any particular outcome but has a strong interest
in assuring that the group works toward achieving the best possible outcome. If no
individual within the organization can serve as a chair, it may be useful to invite
a consultant or independent neutral to chair the meeting (see also Chapter 10).

Assure a Diversity of Information and Perspectives. A second task is to assure
that the group receives a wide variety of input from different perspectives on the
task and different sources of information that may help in accomplishing the
task. Because the nature of the information changes depending on the group's
task—for example, designing and implementing a change, finding the best possible solution to a problem, or simply finding a solution that is politically acceptable to several constituencies—it is difficult to prescribe which information is
critical and how to assure that the group is exposed to it. Group members may
bring in relevant external information, link the group to some other important
constituency (e.g., senior management or shareholders), link the group to the
constituencies they represent, or make sure that no key-information leaks occur.
Clearly, agents can play more than one role and can rotate roles in the course of
a multiparty negotiation.[9]

Create Appropriate Discussion Norms. A discussion norm is an informal rule
about how a group is going to discuss an issue. Although it would be highly desirable to do so, groups seldom actually talk about which discussion norms they are
going to follow in advance of their deliberations. In most cases, this failure is
probably due to a lack of understanding about how much deliberations can be
improved by explicitly proposing and discussing these norms and rules in
advance. Several group norms can specifically undermine an effective discussion:

   • *Unwillingness to tolerate conflicting points of view and perspectives.*
There may be many reasons for this: one or more members dislike conflict, the
group is afraid that conflict will be uncontrollable, or conflict is seen as destructive to group cohesiveness. But as we noted above, the absence of conflict can
also lead to disastrous decisions.

   • *No means for diffusing an emotionally charged discussion.* Thus, anger,
frustration, or resentment become mixed in with the issues and hamper the group's
efforts. Although a great deal of negotiation literature suggests that parties should
simply be calm and rational at all times, to do so is simply not human. The more
the parties care about a particular issue and are invested in it, the more emotions
will creep in, and vehicles must exist for the parties to vent emotions productively.

   • *Coming to a meeting unprepared.* Usually, preparation for a meeting consists of either no preparation at all or simply preparing one's own position.

Attention to the other's position or to assessing underlying interests and priorities requires more thorough preparation as well as effectively tuning in to what others want and are saying.

Several action strategies may be used for each of these three potentially destructive discussion norms. The parties must generate and exchange ideas in a manner that permits full exploration and allows everyone to have some input, yet avoids some of the destructive conflict and emotions that can creep in. Several group decision-making and brainstorming techniques are frequently used to achieve this objective.[10]

• *The Delphi technique.* Without necessarily formally meeting as a group, a moderator can structure an initial questionnaire about the issues and send it out to all parties, asking for input. Parties reply and send it back to the moderator. The moderator summarizes the input and sends it back to the parties. Parties then make further input and return it to the moderator. Over a number of rounds, through the questions and inquiries shaped by the moderator, the parties can exchange a great deal of information and share different perspectives. The advantages are that the group has little face-to-face interaction, does not get bogged down in personal hostility or inefficient communications, and can go through a number of iterations. The limitations are that the real priorities and preferences of group members may not get expressed, and the way the problem is defined and shaped early in the process will greatly determine the outcome achieved. The parties may miss opportunities to expand the pie of resources, redefine the problem in an important way, or truly evaluate important trade-offs. Delphi techniques may thus tend to generate compromise settlements rather than truly creative, integrative solutions.

• *Brainstorming.* In brainstorming, the parties are instructed to define a problem and then to uncritically generate as many solutions as they can think of. Many of the suggestions may be unrealistic or impractical, but the purpose is to suggest as many solutions as possible and to be as creative as possible in suggesting them. Brainstorming tends to generate a wider variety of solution options than might normally occur, particularly because it explicitly encourages more generation of possible solutions than normally occurs.

• *Nominal group technique.* This approach typically follows brainstorming. Once the brainstormed list of solution options is created, group members can rank, rate, or evaluate the alternatives in terms of the degree to which each alternative solves the problem. The leader collects, posts and records these ratings so all group members have an opportunity to formally evaluate the options and vote on the ones they consider to be most effective.

Manage the Group Decision Rule. In decision-making groups, the dominant view is to assume that majority rules and at some point take a vote of all members, assuming that any settlement option that receives more than 50 percent of the votes will be the one adopted. Obviously, this is not the only option. Groups can make decisions by dictatorship (one person decides), oligarchy (a small but dominant minority coalition decides), simple majority (one more person than half the group), two-thirds majority, broad consensus (most of the group agrees, and those who dissent agree not to protest or raise objections), and true unanimity (everyone agrees). Understanding what decision rule a group will use before deliberations begin will also significantly affect the group process. For example, if a simple majority will make the decision in a five-person group, then only three people need to agree. Thus, any three people can get together and form a coalition—during the meeting or even prior to the meeting. In contrast, if the rule will be consensus and unanimity, then the group must meet and work hard enough to assure that all parties' interests are raised, discussed, and incorporated into the group decision. Whether a coalition-building strategy or a complete sharing of positions and interests and problem solving will be necessary requires significantly different approaches. Table 8.1 summarizes three different negotiating strategies—pursuing mutual gain, entering into a coalition, or maximizing individual gain—and the related tactics and decision rules.

Structure and Use an Agenda. Another way to control the flow and direction of negotiation is through an agenda. Either the chair or parties to the negotiation may introduce and coordinate the agenda. An agenda is an effective decision aid for several reasons: it establishes the issues that will be discussed, it can define how each issue is discussed, it defines the order in which issues are discussed, it can be used to introduce process issues (decision rules, discussion norms, procedural questions), and it can be used to define the approximate time that is devoted to issues. The advantage of an agenda is that it adds a high degree of structure, organization, and coordination to a discussion. For low-power or disadvantaged groups, agendas provide a vehicle for getting their issues heard and addressed, assuming that they can get them on the agenda. However, the *manner* in which an agenda is built (by collective consensus at the beginning of a meeting versus by one person prior to the meeting) and *who* builds it will have a great deal of impact on the flow of negotiation. Unless group members feel comfortable challenging the person who introduces a "preemptive" agenda, the agenda will go unquestioned, and hence the implicit discussion structure and format it suggests will prevail. Another disadvantage is that the construction of an agenda may artificially partition related issues so they are discussed separately rather than coupled or traded off to assure more integrative agreements.

Manage the Process, Not the Outcome. Finally, chairpersons of multiparty negotiations must be sensitive to keeping tight control over the group process while not directly affecting the group's outcome. Particularly when the group wants to achieve a consensus or unanimous decision, the job of the chair is to be constantly attentive to group process. The following principles assume that the chair's objective is to achieve an integrative, mutual-gains solution.[11] They are presented in an order that approximates the way groups move toward solutions.

TABLE 8.1 **Tactics, Decision Rules, Goal Orientations, and Decision Aids for Mutual, Coalition, and Individual Gain**

Mutual	*Coalition*	*Individual*
Tactics		
1. Share own and elicit others' interests	1. Seek similar others and construct an alternative that meets your interests	1. Open with a high, but not outrageously high, demand
2. Consider many alternatives; be creative; look for ways to use available resources	2. Recruit just enough members to control the group's decision	2. Argue the merits of your alternative; do not reveal your interests
3. Don't just compromise; make trade-offs	3. Encourage interpersonal obligations among coalition members	3. Appear unable or unwilling to concede
4. Encourage positive relations		4. Encourage positive relations
		5. Use threats, time deadlines, and promises, if necessary
Decision Rules		
Consensus	Oligarchy	Dictator
Unanimity	Majority	
Goal Orientation		
Cooperative	Cooperative or individual	Individual
Decision Aids		
Packaging	Packaging	
Search models	Search models	

From J. Brett, "Negotiating Group Decisions," *Negotiation Journal,* July 1991, pp. 291–310.

- Introduce yourself to the group and describe the nature of the role you will take. Be clear that you are there only to manage the process and that the group will determine the outcome.
- Introduce the agenda or build one based on the group's issues, concerns, and priorities. If you introduce an agenda, make sure the group has an opportunity to discuss, modify, or challenge it before you begin.
- Introduce any necessary ground rules or let the parties suggest them:

  How long will the group meet?

  What is the expected output or final product?

  Will minutes be taken?

  Will the group take breaks?

  Where will negotiations take place?

  How and when can group members consult with their constituents?

- Review the decision rule—how will the group ultimately decide? Test for any concerns or questions.
- Assure that individual members have an opportunity to make opening statements or have other ways of laying their individual concerns and issues on the table.
- Be a gatekeeper—make sure that people have a chance to speak and that the more-vocal people do not dominate and that the less-vocal people do not become silent and drop out.
- Summarize frequently, particularly when conversation becomes mired down, confused, or tense. State where you think the group is, what has been accomplished, and what needs to be done next.
- Listen for interests and commonalities. Encourage people to express interests, mirror them back if you hear them, and encourage people to identify not only what they want but also why they want it. Listen for priorities and concerns.
- Introduce external information (studies, reports, statistics, fact finding, testimony from experts) that will shed further light on the issues and interests. Push people for data to support their assertions.
- Assure parties that once they are familiar with the issues, simultaneous discussion of several issues can take place. This will permit trade-offs among issues rather than forcing a compromise on each individual issue.
- Use a flip chart, blackboard, or overhead projector to write down issues and interests. Many negotiators have found that it is easier and produces less conflict to amass all information on a chart or blackboard "out there" rather than for group members to verbally confront each other face-to-face.
- Once issues and interests have been identified, explicitly set aside a time for inventing options. Use the brainstorming and other decision process techniques to generate options and evaluate them. Use the flip chart or blackboard to record this information, to keep it in the view of all.
- Determine standards for what parties believe will be a fair or reasonable settlement. Determine the criteria that might be used to decide on whether a particular solution is fair, reasonable, and effective. Use the criteria to evaluate the solution options that are proposed.
- Move the group toward selecting one or more of the options. Use the process rules we mentioned earlier and the techniques for achieving an integrative agreement, mentioned in Chapter 3. Listen for the emergence of a coalition of members who appear to be forming a consensus. Permit packaging, trade-offs, or modification of agreements. If the decision is particularly controversial, pursue a first agreement, with the understanding that the group can refine the agreement at a later date.
- Shape a tentative agreement. Write it down. Work on language. Test to

make sure all parties understand the agreement and its implications and consequences.

- Discuss whatever follow-up, or next steps, need to occur. Make sure individuals who have a role in this process understand what they need to do.
- Thank the group for their participation, their hard work, and their efforts. If it has been a particularly difficult discussion or required a large time commitment, a small group celebration and formal thank-yous may be in order.
- If the decision is going to be revisited or a similar issue is to be debated in the near future, conduct a post mortem. Have group members discuss the process and the outcome and evaluate what they might do better or differently next time. This will assure learning for both the group members and the chair.

Summary

Many negotiations are not one-on-one discussions. When there are more than two negotiators involved, each with his own interests and positions, the group must arrive at a collective agreement as to a plan, decision, or course of action. In this chapter, we first discussed several ways that multiparty negotiations were significantly more complex than bilateral negotiations. We then described many approaches that parties—particularly the chairperson—can use to assure a productive group negotiation. The major points include:

- Understanding the consequences of failing to agree.
- Understanding what decision rules will be used.
- Understanding that group negotiations may be sequential and involve multiple discussions.
- Most critical, understanding that productive group negotiations usually require strong and effective control by a neutral chair.

If these procedures are followed carefully, the group is likely to feel considerably better about the process and make a far more effective decision than if these factors are left to chance.

End Notes

1. The section draws heavily on the recent writings of Bazerman, Mannix, and Thompson (1988); Brett (1991); and Kramer (1991), who have done an excellent job of providing an overview of the problems and challenges of multiparty negotiations.
2. Midgaard and Underal (1977, p. 332), as quoted in Kramer (1991).
3. Janis (1982, 1989).

4. Sebenius (1983)

5. Bazerman, Mannix, and Thompson (1988)

6. In fact, some authors (e.g., Murnighan, 1986) who have studied decision-making groups from a negotiation perspective have suggested that the emergence of consensus in these groups proceeds as a "snowballing coalition." In this process, as parties share information and then deliberate possible solutions, a few people emerge with a common perspective and then tacitly or explicitly agree to support each other's views. Other individuals then negotiate with the emerging coalition to incorporate their own views, and those who may be unwilling to negotiate or modify their views are eventually "rejected" and left out of the group decision. See Murnighan (1978, 1986, and 1991) for reviews.

7. Brett (1991).

8. See Brett (1991) for further elaboration on this point.

9. See Ancona and Caldwell (1988) for further elaboration on these roles.

10. See Bazerman, Mannix, and Thompson (1988) for further elaboration on these procedures.

11. See also the description of the mediation role in Chapter 10.

9   POWER IN NEGOTIATION

In this section, we will focus on the role of power in negotiation. In negotiation, parties often attempt to exert both direct and indirect pressures on the other, in order to advocate their interests and win the conflict. We will define the sources of this pressure as *power,* and the tactics designed to apply this pressures as *influence.* This chapter will review the major sources of power and types of influence used in negotiations.

Power has multiple, often overlapping, or even contradictory meanings. It is often used interchangeably with *leadership*, *influence*, and *persuasion*. And like these concepts, power is multidimensional and complex; thus, before going further, we need to clarify what we mean by the term and how we are going to use it.

Why Is Power Important to Negotiators?

The primary reason that negotiators seek power is because power gives the negotiator some *advantage* or *leverage* over the other party. Negotiators usually use this advantage to secure a greater share of the outcomes or derive their preferred solution. Seeking power in negotiation usually arises from one of two beliefs:

- The negotiator believes she currently *has less* power than the other party. In this situation, she believes the other party already has some advantage that can and will be used in the negotiation process, so she seeks power to balance or offset the power of the other.

- The negotiator believes he *needs more* power than the other party to increase the probability of controlling the process and securing a desired outcome. In this context, one negotiator believes that added power is necessary to gain or sustain an advantage in the upcoming negotiation.

179

The types of power negotiators seek in these two situations may well be the same, but the likely impact is different. The impact varies depending on whether the negotiator seeks power to create a power balance or imbalance relative to the other, and whether she does so for offensive or defensive strategic purposes. In the first situation, the negotiator who seeks a power balance is doing so to increase the likelihood that each negotiator can achieve his goals. As an offensive strategy, balancing or equalization is likely to be more consistent with a desire to pursue an integrative strategy and achieve either a compromise or collaborative outcome. As a defensive strategy, a negotiator pursues equalization to assure that the other does not obtain an inappropriate or undeserved share of the outcome or settlement. Thus, as a general rule, power equalization is consistent with intentions either to pursue a collaborative outcome or to block the other from gaining a competitive advantage.

In contrast, the negotiator pursuing a power imbalance (enhancement) seeks to gain more power than the other. As an offensive strategy, the negotiator may pursue this option to assure greater control over the division of resources—in short, to competitively win the negotiation. As a defensive strategy, the negotiator usually pursues this end because he fears that the other is also trying to increase his or her power—in order to beat him at his own game. In both cases, negotiators pursue power enhancement for distributive, competitive purposes—to enhance the likelihood of achieving a preferred solution or to gain a disproportionate share of the negotiated outcomes.

As we discuss in this section, there are many forms of power in a negotiation context and hence many ways that negotiators can gain and use power. Moreover, as we will point out, having the potential for power does not necessarily mean that it is used, or used wisely. In general, negotiators who don't care about their power or who have matched power—equally high or low—will find that their deliberations proceed with greater ease and simplicity toward a mutually satisfying and acceptable outcome. In contrast, negotiators who *do* care about their power and who are seeking to match or exceed the other party's power may find that their efforts are highly successful in the short term but also create problematic long-term consequences.

A Definition of Power

In a broad sense, people have power when they have "the ability to bring about outcomes they desire," or "the ability to get things done the way one wants them to be done."[1] However, the same people could also be described as having influence, being persuasive, or being leaders. We need some way of separating power from other influence processes that are used in interpersonal relations.

There are many definitions of power. We prefer what may be called a relational definition of power proposed by conflict scholar Morton Deutsch:

> An actor . . . has power in a given situation (situational power) to the degree that he can satisfy the purposes (goals, desires, or wants) that he is attempting to fulfill in that

situation. Power is a relational concept; it does not reside in the individual but rather in the relationship of the person to his environment. Thus, the power of an actor in a given situation is determined by the characteristics of the situation as well as by his own characteristics.[2]

In his discussion of power, Deutsch suggests that there has been a tendency to view power as an attribute of the actor only. This view would ignore that power is derived from the situation or context in which an actor operates. Rather, as Deutsch suggests, when considering the statement "A is more powerful than B," a discussion of power should view it from three distinct perspectives (which are often interrelated):

> *Environmental power,* or 'A is usually more able to favorably influence his overall environment and/or to overcome its resistance than is B'; *relationship power,* or 'A is usually more able to influence B favorably and/or to overcome B's resistance than B is able to do with A'; and *personal power,* or 'A is usually more able to satisfy his desires than is B.'[3]

In this chapter, we organize our discussion of negotiator power into two stages: *power bases,* or sources, and *influence strategies.* We will refer to power bases as the repertoire of tools available to influence the environment, the other party, or our own desires. We will talk about a number of different bases of power, or types of tools, that are available to a negotiator. *The tools themselves are not power—power is the effective use of those tools in the right way in the appropriate situations.* In this chapter, as we consider the different bases of power, we will essentially be looking at the way each base can be used to gain some advantage or leverage over the environment or the other party.

After discussing the dominant bases of power, we will then turn to a discussion of *patterns (or strategies) of influence.* Influence strategies are the manner in which the tools are put into use, or enacted through a strategy, to accomplish a particular influence objective. We will describe several major influence strategies, each of which uses one or more of the power bases in a different way. In any given negotiation or influence situation, one or more influence strategies may be possible, depending upon the power sources available and the user's preference for using some influence strategies and not others.[4]

Sources of Power

Understanding the different ways that power can be exercised is best accomplished by looking at the various sources (or bases) of power and the ways that they are typically exercised. One well-known typology of power identified five major power bases: reward power, coercive power, legitimate power, expert power, and referent power.[5] Although many contemporary discussions of power are still grounded in this typology, we will reclassify this list somewhat and add several new sources of power. A summary list of our major sources of power is shown in Table 9.1.

TABLE 9.1   Sources of Power

Information and expert power

Resource control

Legitimate power
  Authority
  Reputation
  Performance

Location in the structure
  Centrality
  Criticality and relevance
  Flexibility
  Visibility

Personal power
  Attractiveness and friendliness
  Integrity
  Patience and tenacity
  Emotion

Information Power and Expert Power

Within the context of negotiation, information power is perhaps the most common source of power. Information power is derived from the ability to assemble information that can then be used to support the position we want to take, arguments we want to make, or outcomes we desire. This information may also be used as a tool to challenge the other's position or desired outcomes and hence undermine the effectiveness of his negotiating arguments.

Information power refers to the accumulation and presentation of information that will change the other's point of view or position on an issue. Information power and its sources are related to the *message* or *content* strategies of persuasion that we described earlier in the previous chapter. For example, information power can be related to the credibility and trustworthiness of the sender (source) of the message, the content of the message, the structure of the message (particularly in the way that the information is presented), or the style and techniques used in presenting and delivering the message.[6]

Within the context of negotiation, information is the key source of power, at the heart of the process. In even the simplest negotiation, the parties take a position and then present facts, arguments, viewpoints, and data to support that position. I want to sell a used motorcycle for $1,000; you say it is only worth $500. I proceed to tell you how much I paid for it, point out what good condition it is in, what the attractive features are, and why it is worth $1,000. You point out the fact that it is five years old, emphasize the paint chips and rust spots, and comment that the tires are worn and really should be replaced. You also tell me that you can't afford to spend $1,000. After 20 minutes of discussion about the motorcycle, we have exchanged extensive information about its original cost and age, its depreciation and current condition, the benefits and drawbacks of this particular style and model, your financial situation and my need to raise cash, and a variety of other factors.

Through the information presented by each side, a common definition of the situation emerges. By the amount and kind of information shared and the way the negotiators talk about it, both parties derive a common (and, hopefully, realistic) picture of the current condition of the motorcycle, its market worth, and the preferences of each side with regard to buying and selling that motorcycle. This information need not be 100 percent true—bluffs, exaggerations, omissions, and distortions of information may occur. I may tell you I paid $1,800 for the bike when I only paid $1,500; I may not tell you that the clutch needs to be replaced. You may not tell me that you can actually pay $1,000 but that you simply don't want to spend that much. (We return to these issues in Chapter 11, when we discuss how lying and deception are used as power tactics.) Nevertheless, the information exchanged, and the common definition of the situation that emerges, serves as a rationale for each side to modify his or her positions and eventually to accept a settlement. Both of us arrive at a mutually satisfactory price—$800, including a loan of $200 that I have given you to pay me back over six months. Our feelings of satisfaction come from deciding on the price itself and from also deciding that the price is justified because of the way the other party behaves in the negotiation.

Expert power is a special form of informational power. Expert power is accorded to those who are seen as having achieved some level of command and mastery of specific information. These individuals gain respect and credibility deference based on their expertise. You can establish yourself as an expert in a number of ways. One way is to show off your credentials, such as a university degree or a real estate license. This is why physicians hang their degrees and licenses on their walls, and accountants use the C.P.A. abbreviation after their name and always appear in conservative business dress. So, if credentials can be hung on the wall, why not have the negotiation in your office so they can see the evidence of your expertise? Or if you have written an important article on the subject, give them a copy. Another way is by providing evidence that other people have acknowledged your expertise. People commonly provide references from those who can verify their expertise. Also, you can practice name-dropping, mentioning persons whose expertise is well-known and established. Finally, you can show that you have a level of knowledge worthy of being deemed an expert by rattling off a mass of facts and figures, referencing relevant but obscure bits of critical information, or discussing the pros and cons of a strategy or argument at great length. In fact, a common negotiation technique is the snow job, in which the negotiator inundates the other party with so much information that the other cannot process it all—he thus may be more likely to accept the expert's simplification of this information in a way that promotes the expert's preferred strategy or solution.

Resource Control

The second major source of power in negotiation is control over resources.[7] People who control resources are powerful because they can allocate and dispense those resources to people who will do what they want and withhold (or take away) those resources from people who don't do what they want.

Resources can be of all types. As already discussed, the most important resources are those which matter most to the target. In an organizational context, some of the most important resources include:

- Money, in its various forms: cash, salary dollars, budget allocations, grants, bonus money, expense accounts, and so on.
- Supplies: raw materials, components, pieces, and parts.
- Time: if the other party is pressured to produce a quick settlement or meet a deadline, control over time can put extreme pressure on the other party.
- Equipment: machines, tools, technology, hardware and software, vehicles, conveyor belts, and the like.
- Critical services: repair, maintenance, upkeep, installation and delivery, technical support, transportation, and so on.
- Human capital: labor power, work teams, staff.

Resource power comes not only from being able to control and dispense resources, but also from the ability to create a resource base in an environment where resources appear to be scarce. Researcher Jeffrey Pfeffer described how political and corporate figures have built powerful empires founded on resource control.[8] Lyndon Johnson built a major power base during his early years in Congress by taking over the "Little Congress" (a speaker's bureau for clerical personnel and aides to members of Congress) and leveraging it into a major power base. Similarly, Robert Moses, beginning as Parks Commissioner of New York City, built a power empire that resulted in the successful construction of 12 bridges, 35 highways, 751 playgrounds, 13 golf courses, 18 swimming pools, and more than 2 million acres of park land in the New York metropolitan area, making him one of the major power brokers of New York from 1960 to 1990.

To use resources as a basis for negotiation power, we must develop or maintain control over some scarce commodity that the other party wants. Successful control over resources must also assure that the other party cannot get those same resources from someone else—in order to get what she wants, she must deal with you directly. Finally, in dispensing those resources, the power holder must be willing to give them out to others depending upon the other's compliance or cooperation with the power holder's request. Increasing scarcity of resources of all kinds has led to the new golden rule of organizations: "Whoever has the gold makes the rules."

Legitimate Power

There are times when people respond to directions from another, even directions they do not like, because they feel it is proper (legitimate) for the other to tell them and proper (obligatory) for them to obey, even though they do not like what they are being directed to do. This type of power is legitimate power, derived from occupying a particular job title, office, or position in an organizational hierarchy.

Most legitimate power comes from the social structure.[9] When individuals and groups organize themselves into any form of social system—a small business, a combat unit, a union, a political action committee, or a sports team—they almost immediately create some form of organizational structure and hierarchy. They elect or appoint a leader and may introduce formal rules about how decisions will be made, work divided, responsibilities allocated, and conflicts managed. Without this social ordering, chaos would prevail and group coordination would take forever. The need for a social structure to enhance efficiency and effectiveness, then, creates the basis for legitimate power.

There are several ways to acquire legitimate power. First, it may be acquired by birth. Elizabeth II, as queen of England, has the title of queen and all of the stature this title commands in the structure of the British constitution and the history of the Empire. Yet she has little actual power in terms of her ability to run the day-to-day affairs of Britain. Second, legitimate power may be acquired by election; the president of the United States has substantial legitimate power, derived from the legal structure of the American government. Third, legitimate power is derived simply by being appointed or promoted to some office, job, rank, or organizational position. Thus, by holding the office or title of director or general manager, the person is entitled to all the rights, responsibilities, and privileges that go with that position.

Finally, legitimate authority is also accorded to individuals who hold a position for which we show respect. In many societies, the young listen to and obey older people. People listen to those who occupy highly respected public offices and certain occupations, like the clergy. They do what these people say because they believe that it is proper to do so. Although these power holders also have some reward and coercive power, they seldom, if ever, use it.[10] Legitimate power cannot function without obedience, the "consent of the governed." If enough British citizens question the legitimacy of the queen and her authority—even given the hundreds of years of tradition and law on which it is founded—her continued rule will be in serious jeopardy. If enough women challenge the pope's rulings on abortion, birth control, or other social policy, the pope's authority will erode. When enough people begin to distrust formal authority or discredit its legitimacy, they will begin to defy it and undermine its potential as a power source.

As a result, it is not uncommon for those who hold legitimate power to accumulate other power sources (such as resource control and information) to buttress their power base. With the title of vice president of a company also comes privileged information and control over financial and human resources. When that vice president needs to implement an organizational decision, she may call on her title, information, and control over resources to get others to comply.

In the context of extending legitimate authority, it is also important to discuss two other derivative sources of power: *reputation* and *performance.* Reputation is the image one develops in an organization, the way people come to talk about and describe a particular individual. Reputation is shaped by what one has done before—performance. If you want to build a reputation for being powerful, then you have to use power, get things done, have an impact on others, and make sure that such accomplishments are made public so that others will know of them. In short, with the acquisition of legitimacy comes resource control and information control. These three sources of power may be used to do a job well, get performance to occur, or have impact. To the degree that you make performance sufficiently visible, others will see it and comment on it. In this way, reputations are derived and employed as a power source—so that when an individual needs to actually exercise power, she may not actually have to use information, resources, or authority but may simply invoke her reputation for using those tools.[11] For example, the reputations of Mahatma Ghandi and Martin Luther King were derived from incidents in which they were willing to undergo great personal sacrifice for their causes early in their careers, a reputation that then served them well as they sought to mobilize larger groups of people to bring about broad societal change.

Location in an Organizational Structure

Some individuals become powerful simply by virtue of being in a key position, even though that position does not have a lot of organizational authority.[12] Individuals who are exposed to a large amount of information, who are responsible for collecting vital information and passing it from one place to another, or who do jobs the organization has deemed central to its organizational mission or success can gain power through these activities. Particularly as organizations change to meet the demands of changing markets, environmental conditions, economic turbulence, and worldwide competitive pressures, individuals find themselves in tasks, duties, and functions that become critical to the organization's ability to change or be successful. The job may not have a fancy title, a big budget, or a large corner office, but it can provide significant power by virtue of the information and resource control associated with it.

From an organizational perspective, understanding power in this way is derived from conceptualizing an organization not as a hierarchy, but as a network of interrelationships.[13] Networks represent key individuals as circles or nodes, and relationships between nodes as lines of transaction. (See Figure 9.1A and B for an example of a network, as compared to an organizational hierarchy.) Individuals who need to interact with each other (or who do interact with each other) in the organization are connected by these lines.[14] In hierarchy terms, position and

FIGURE 9.1A

Formal Organizational Chart

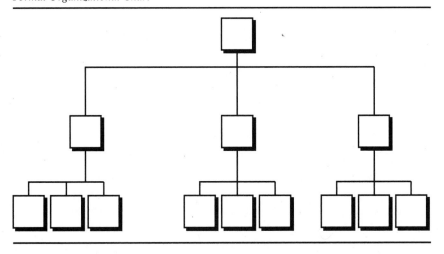

FIGURE 9.1B

Organizational Network

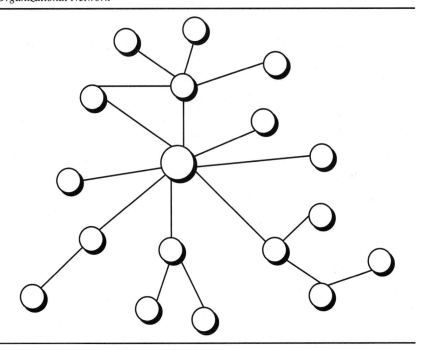

formal authority are directly related to how high up the position is in the hierarchy, and to how many people report to that individual. In network terms, in contrast, power is determined by the following alternative criteria.

Centrality. The more central a position (node) is in a network of exchanges and transactions, the more power that node occupant will have. Centrality may be determined by the amount of information that passes through a node, the number of transactions that occur through the node, or the degree to which the node is central to the flow.[15] Centrality may also simply relate to where one's office is located in the organization—in the hallway where the president walks to lunch or in some back corner where one is never seen.

Criticality and Relevance. A second source of network power is the criticality of the node. Although a great deal of information or resources may not flow through the node, what does flow through it is essential to the organization's mission, major task, or key product. In jobs that are high in criticality, the key person is charged with assembling information from many locations, which brings him or her into frequent contact with important people and requires the key person to integrate the information into a recommendation, action strategy, or decision.

Flexibility. A third source of network power lies in the position's flexibility, or the degree to which the key individual can exercise discretion in how certain decisions are made or who gains access. Flexibility is often related to criticality. A classic example of flexibility is the role of gatekeeper, the person in a network who controls the access to a key figure or group. Anyone who wants to get to the key person has to go through the gatekeeper. If you want to see the boss, for example, you have to get permission and access from the secretary.

Visibility. Finally, nodes differ in their degree of visibility—that is, how visible the task performance is to others in the organization. A negotiator who negotiates with his constituency (or team) in the room has high visibility; if the negotiator gains significant concessions from the other party while being watched, the team will give him a great deal of affirmation.

In summary, the more traditional view of legitimacy as a source of power is that it is derived from the formal title, duties, and responsibilities that accompany an organizational position. However, power can also be derived from one's location in the overall flow of information, goods and services, and personal relationships in that system. Acquisition of power requires the savvy individual to understand which jobs and duties are central, critical, flexible, and visible, since occupants may also use their position to accumulate information, resources, and personal relationships that may be leveraged into further power and influence.

Personal Sources of Power

We come to the last category of sources of power: the personal qualities that an individual brings to the negotiator role that individuals can convert into influence.

Although a large number of personal qualities may contribute to a power base, we will mention the four most important here: personal attractiveness, integrity, persistence, and emotion.

Personal Attractiveness (Friendliness). One critically important attribute that a negotiator can bring is the ability to be friendly and outgoing and to establish a personal relationship with the other parties in the negotiation. The ability to show some direct, personal interest in the other helps to soften the harder edges of some of the other power sources. Friendliness also involves a strong emotional component; warmth, empathy, and caring about others appeals to the moods and feelings of the other party as well as the intellect. Rather than immediately getting down to business, the negotiator uses friendliness to get to know the other negotiator, talks about topics that will put the other at ease, discovers things that they may have personally in common, uses empathy and sensitivity, and establishes a personal relationship with the other.

Emotion. Although emotion is clearly a component of friendliness, other emotions beside warmth, empathy, and compassion enter into negotiation. Fear, anger, or excitement can become an integral part of many negotiations—particularly over issues about which we feel strongly. Emotion combines with persistence to lead to assertiveness and determination.

Emotion is a power source because expressing it sometimes offers a dramatic contrast to our expectations—which is that negotiation should be a cool, calm, rational exchange of information and resources. As we have previously stated, most people expect negotiation to be driven by cold, logical analysis of outcome maximization and economic valuation of alternatives. Yet we also know that negotiators frequently do not behave according to the principles of logic and economic rationality. In addition, when everyone else is being rational, it is frequently the person who expresses strong feelings, gets angry, or makes an impassioned speech in favor of her proposed solution who carries the day.[16] Emotion is a power source when it can be effectively used to win over the other party's heart by appealing to her passions, values, or personal sense of what is right, fair, and just. Union organizers, politicians, and motivational speakers all understand the importance of arousing emotion as a way to persuade someone.

Integrity. A third personal quality is integrity. Integrity is character—the personal values and ethics that ground our behavior in high moral principles. Integrity is the quality that assures people we can be trusted. If people expose their vulnerabilities to us, we usually will not exploit those vulnerabilities when we are attempting to influence them. If people trust us with confidential information, we will not disclose that information to others. Finally, integrity is the quality that assures people that if we make an agreement, we can be trusted to keep that agreement, to abide by its terms and conditions and to follow through on it. If people will trust us with confidential information and expose their vulnerabilities to us, we are likely to establish stronger personal relationships with them and to make stronger deals.[17] Similarly, if people believe that we can be trusted to follow through and implement our agreements, we are more likely to be able to complete agreements that will benefit us.

Persistence and Tenacity. Finally, persistence and tenacity are also valuable personal qualities in a negotiator. Children are often called great negotiators because they are so wonderfully persistent in pursuing what they want. Saying no to a child does not mean that the child gives up asking; usually, kids find all kinds of creative ways to persist in trying to achieve their objective (the candy bar, the toy, watching the TV show). Another part of success comes from finding new, unique, and creative ways to pursue the same request. Persistent people aren't necessarily doggedly committed to pursuing their goals blindly and rigidly; instead, they also display creativity in finding new ways to pursue the same objective.

In summary, we have considered five major sources of power: information and expertise, resources, legitimacy and formal authority, location within a communication network, and personal sources such as personal attractiveness, emotion, integrity, and persistence. We will now turn to the ways negotiators implement these power sources, or "tools," through various strategies and tactics of interpersonal influence.

The Application of Power: Strategies of Influence

In this section, we examine power in action, which we will call *influence*. Researchers have not reached a consensus on either the number of specifically different influence strategies used or the most meaningful groupings of these strategies.[18] In this section, we propose 10 different influence strategies that may be used in negotiation. Each one draws on one or more sources of power, and each may be effective under specific conditions. Although we describe each one separately, they may be used in various combinations to enhance their strength and impact or to suit the needs of the situation. Let us now consider each in detail. Table 9.2 presents a summary of these influence strategies and ties them to their power bases.

Persuasion

Persuasion is used when the negotiator wants to change the target's mind through information. The agent uses rational arguments, logic, facts, analyses, statistics, scientific studies, reports, data, and any other information that is available to construct a fact-based, logical case. Information and expertise are the primary sources of power used in this influence strategy. Use of the strategy assumes that the information and facts create a compelling logical argument, that the information and facts are not subject to bias or distortion, and that the other is seeking facts and logic and will make a decision based on high-quality information. Persuasion is a very common form of influence, particularly in logical decision making and when exerting influence upward (to a boss).

TABLE 9.2 **Influence Strategies and the Power Tools They Use**

Influence Strategy	Power Sources Used
1. Persuasion	Information and expertise—information may be derived from position in structure
2. Exchange	Resources
3. Legitimacy	Position in structure—may extend resources
4. Friendliness	Friendliness, attractiveness, and emotion
Ingratiation	More explicit use of friendliness for expedient purposes
5. Praise	"Verbal" resources combined with friendliness
6. Assertiveness	Information combined with persistence and emotion
7. Inspirational appeal	Information combined with emotion
8. Consultation	Information and resources combined with solicitation of others' information and resources
9. Pressure	Information, negative resource control, and emotion
10. Coalitions	Various power tools used to build support among a coalition (information, resources, friendliness) and then use group support as leverage

Exchange

A second influence strategy is exchange, the process of explicitly or implicitly offering resources or favors (promises and assistance) to secure the other's compliance and cooperation. Some authors have said that exchange is the same as *bargaining* in that the user either directly or implicitly suggests a trade—in short, "If I do X for you, will you do Y for me?" Exchange or bargaining relies on resources as the power base, particularly resources that can be translated into rewards for the other—favors, benefits, incentives, treats, perks, and the like. Exchange frequently invokes the use of *promises* and *commitments* as persuasive tools—obligations we are willing to make in exchange for the other's cooperation, compliance, or commitment to give us what we want. These are often negotiated so that I complete my obligation now, but choose not to ask you to complete your obligation until some point in the future. By doing so, we leave a series of chits or other obligations out in our interpersonal marketplace, which we can call back in when we need them.[19] Obligations may be created in several ways— doing favors for people, recognizing and praising them for their accomplishments, helping people out, or paying them individual attention when the job demands do not require it or people do not expect it.[20]

Legitimacy

The third influence strategy is legitimacy—using the power vested in the organizational position, title, and office and exerting influence by asking people to follow directives derived from that position or title. Legitimacy is effective to the extent that the target believes that the request is derived from the agent's formal authority base, is consistent with that authority, and is also consistent with organizational rules, policies, practices, and procedures. Individuals using legitimacy styles may be more likely to give direct orders; to pull rank and refer to their higher status, title, or position; or to use the trappings of their position, such as a uniform, a title, or an office location (e.g., the big corner office on the senior-executive floor) to reinforce their authority.

As we noted, this tactic is often accompanied by other influence approaches: information that is only available to the office holder, or control of rewards and punishments for compliance or noncompliance. While the exercise of the duties and responsibilities of the office frequently requires certain behaviors, office holders who want to extend these powers sometimes abuse the privileges.[21] Power holders extend the use of legitimate power beyond the scope and boundaries for which it was meant. The academic dean may let some athletes stay in school, even when they have failing grades, as a favor to the football coach. The banker may actually take a bribe from a businessman and, in exchange, fail to take action on the bad loan. Such behavior is not defined by the role, but occurs because the power enjoyed by the office holder is now being abused. A variation on the use of legitimacy is to suggest that the target should comply because the organization and its higher authorities are really the ones making the request. In this variation, the agent suggests that "the organization would like you to do this" or "those in higher authority in the organization" desire compliance.[22]

Friendliness

A fourth influence tactic is to use the power base of attractiveness and friendliness and to create a relationship with the other person. By establishing this relationship with the other person, we hope that the friendship that develops will lead the other to comply simply because friends like each other, help each other out, and do favors for each other. Some friendliness tactics include gaining rapport with others, showing genuine concern and interest for the other person, sharing feelings, expressing liking and appreciation for the other, working hard to understand the other's perspective and preferences, emotionally supporting the other, being loyal to her, and keeping confidences. Listening to others, eliciting contributions from others, and giving them credit for work done or contributions made are also effective interpersonal tactics for building friendships and strong interpersonal relationships.

Using friendliness is a less-effective influence approach when there are time pressures or a decision is needed quickly. Developing a relationship takes time and must progress at its own pace. In fact, using friendliness as an influence tactic usually requires that the relationship between the agent and the target already exist before the request is made so the relationship can be effectively exploited. If the agent tries to cultivate a relationship very quickly and to use it simply as a vehicle in which to lodge the influence request, it is likely that the target will see the friendliness gestures as superficial and insincere, a perception that will raise the target's defensiveness rather than lower it. This use of "expedient friendliness" is often called ingratiation, or, more colloquially, "kissing up." Ingratiating behavior can be particularly irritating as the agent attempts to use flattery, emotion, and other friendliness tactics to soften up the target before making the request, yet people who are very accomplished at using ingratiation tactics are often so good at it that the target may not realize what is happening until after the deed is done.

Praise or Reinforcement

A fifth influence tactic is the use of verbal praise, encouragement, and affirmation that the other is doing well. Research shows that verbal reinforcement, approval, and praise are highly effective, perhaps as effective as tangible, economic resources, in shaping behavior.[23] This same research has also shown that managers do not use positive reinforcement and praise enough. Too often, managers assume that praise is not necessary for people who are "just doing what they are supposed to do."

It is important for the negotiator to use verbal reinforcement, praising language, and supportive words, gestures, and commentary to reward the target person for desired behaviors. If the other party expresses a view we like, show your approval of that view. If the party makes a favorable concession, express your appreciation for that concession. If he stops advocating a negotiating position that you did not like, affirm that behavior. You can use praise consistently and repeatedly throughout a negotiation, but you should particularly use it at the end, when the parties are summarizing and wrapping up their agreement. Express support and appreciation to the other party for whatever she did that was consistent with our own objectives: cooperation, sharing information, willingness to make concessions, or whatever part she took in shaping the final deal.

Assertiveness

A sixth influence strategy is assertiveness, which is to express what one wants in a strong, forceful style and manner. Assertiveness is information presented in clear, strong, compelling language—a combination of the personal quality of persistence and determination with emotional language that signals that determination. One way to express assertiveness is by making demands, clearly and emphatically stating what you want. You can also demonstrate assertiveness by making unilateral decisions—who will attend a meeting, what the agenda will be, what the issues are, who gets to speak, and what alternatives will be considered. Assertiveness may work when used selectively but is unlikely to be effective in the long term because of the resistance and resentment it engenders in the other party.[24]

Inspirational Appeal

A seventh influence tactic is to create an inspirational appeal. This tactic successfully combines information with an emotional message that appeals to the target's idealism, personal values, or hopes and aspirations for the future. In short, inspirational appeals are motivational in the best sense of the term: they inspire people to perform, energize them, and build feelings of strength and confidence that will hopefully lead to superior performance.

Inspirational appeals are often called by other names: pep talks, sales pitches, or motivational speeches. They require several things to be successful. First, the agent must be able to present ideas powerfully, especially by invoking emotions. Speeches are full of these emotional messages as well as the colorful language of symbols, metaphors, word pictures, and phrases that appeal to our values and ideals. Charismatic leaders and motivational speakers understand these language principles well and know how to use them. Second, inspirational appeals must be able to articulate a future—a future state or condition that is significantly better than the present, and a *future that the other party desires*. Finally, inspirational appeals must outline a desired course of action that will supposedly lead to the attainment of the vision or values. Although the inspirational message may be strong on values and emotional content, it must also be translated into a specific course of action that will lead to the objective.

Consultation

As an influence strategy, consultation is the process of involving others in planning a strategy, process, or outcome, or being willing to modify one's own position based on the other's ideas, suggestions, and input. Consultation is not a strategy that is frequently mentioned as an influence tactic. In fact, in many ways, it is redundant with the concept of negotiation because, by definition, negotiation is the process of give and take in order to arrive at an outcome shaped by both sides. Yet it is important to recognize that a consultative influence strategy is empowering because it explicitly solicits and invites the other's input, as opposed to the strategies of persuasion or assertion, which unilaterally direct the other toward particular behaviors and outcomes. Consultation seeks to draw on the other's information, perspective, personal integrity, and self-respect by asking her advice and input. The power of participative decision making in management is drawn directly from the power of consulting others about their preferences rather than unilaterally directing their choices. (Roger Fisher and Scott Brown develop the mnemonic ACBD—Always Consult Before Deciding—as a key way to manage and strengthen an important relationship through consultation.)[25]

Pressure

We will use the term *pressure* to broadly define the strategic use of information plus sanctions—particularly punishment—to accomplish objectives. By using pressure, an agent makes demands, suggests consequences about what will happen if the demands are not met, engages in frequent surveillance to determine whether the demands are carried out, reminds the other person frequently about what is expected, and eventually may deliver the actual punishment if the demand is not met or not met on time. A sales manager may cut her salesperson's pay for repeatedly failing to achieve sales target projections. An executive may fire her secretary for failing to improve her typing skills. A father may deny his son television privileges for a week because he didn't clean up his room. A supplier may put a late charge on an overdue bill to a customer. And, like reward power and the use of praise, coercive or punishment power can be as effective in verbal form as the withdrawal or denial of tangible resources. If the sales manager berates the salesperson for failing to make target sales quotas rather than firing him, or if the father yells at his son rather than denying him television privileges, the impact may be just as great.

The conditions for the use of pressure are similar to those for the use of exchange and praise: the other party is dependent on the power holder in some way, the agent controls some form of resources which can be denied or taken away from the other party, and the punishment can be administered in a manner that will ensure the other person's compliance. The decision to use pressure is most likely related to the power holder's perception of the willingness of the other party to comply. Sanctions, whether positive or negative, are most likely to be involved when expectations of successful influence are lowest.[26]

The few empirical studies of power use in negotiation have tended to find that parties with higher power tend to use more pressure tactics, such as threats, and make fewer concessions. Interestingly, when the power distribution between the parties is relatively small, the low-power party also displayed a high level of threat use and power tactics, creating an escalation between the parties that usually destroyed the negotiation.[27] At best, pressure tactics produce short-term compliance with requests, but they also are likely to produce high resistance from the other party. As a result, frequent use of pressure tactics leads to very high resistance, in which the agent must consistently escalate the severity of consequences for non-compliance and the willingness to invoke them. It should be clear, therefore, that frequent use of pressure strategies alienates the other party and requires a great deal of coercive pressure to sustain compliance. If possible, therefore, pressure strategies should be used sparingly and selectively because any use is likely to corrode the relationship between the parties, and any frequent use is likely to destroy it.

Coalitions

The last influence tactic is the use of coalitions. In a coalition strategy, the agent enlists the aid or endorsement of a number of other people (who the agent knows, likes, or respects). The agent then either asks these other people to make direct requests to the other party or suggests to the other party that many people have already endorsed or supported the desired behavioral objective. Coalitions can be used in upward and lateral influence. In upward influence, the subordinate attempts to influence the boss and suggests that a number of other subordinates endorse the action. In lateral influence, the agent suggests that a number of the other party's peers already endorse the desired action and asks the other person to "get on board and be a team player." The agents can use these supporters by simply suggesting that they support the desired action or as go-betweens to approach the other party directly. In the latter case, go-betweens are usually selected because of already-strong friendship relationships with the other party that may now be exploited to change the other party's view or willingness to comply.[28]

Summary

A great deal has been written on power and its use in organizations, and this literature has been significantly enriched in the past 10 years. However, few of these works have been specifically directed at understanding power in negotiations. We began by stating that power is important to negotiators for different reasons, depending on their intentions. If their intent is to gain some competitive advantage over the other party, then they will seek ways to enhance and use their power to achieve that objective. Thus, negotiators may use power to pursue a competitive objective. In contrast, they may also use power to pursue an integrative or cooperative objective; in this case, power will be sought to balance the power between the parties so they may pursue collaboration on an equal footing. We then discussed the different ways that power could be defined and the implications of these different definitions for a complete understanding of power use in negotiation. Finally, we explored a number of influence strategies that combine various power sources into more explicit strategies in order to exert leverage on the other.

We encourage more research in how these tactics draw on power, when they are used, and under what conditions they are effective so we might enrich this discussion in the future.

End Notes

1. Salancik and Pfeffer (1977).
2. As defined by Deutsch (1973, pp. 84–85).
3. Ibid., p. 85, italics in original.
4. A great deal has been written on power, and we have drawn extensively from some of the best major sources on this subject: Boulding (1989); Cialdini (1993); Cohen and Bradford (1990); French and Raven (1959); Kipnis (1976); Kipnis, Schmidt, and Wilkinson (1980); Kotter (1977, 1985); Mintzberg (1983); Pfeffer (1992;) Steward (1989); and Zucker (1991).

5. French and Raven (1959).

6. Scarcity of information can often be a source of power. Cialdini (1993) points out that banning certain types of information, as when information is censored, actually increases the demand for that information.

7. Pfeffer and Salancik (1974), among others, stress that the ability to control and dispense resources is one of the major power sources in organizations.

8. See Pfeffer (1992).

9. See Barnard (1938).

10. See Cialdini (1993) for an excellent discussion on the "illusions of authority."

11. See Tsui (1983, 1984) for a discussion of reputational effectiveness.

12. See Kaplan (1985) for one discussion.

13. See Kotter (1985).

14. Primarily information and resources are transacted, although personal relationships and authority may also be currencies transacted across the network lines.

15. Research by Brass (1984) indicates that being in the center of information flows—the work-flow network, the informal-communication network, and the friendship network—was particularly important to being promoted in an organization.

16. Henderson (1973).

17. Shapiro, Sheppard, and Cheraskin (1992); Lewicki and Bunker (1995).

18. There has been a boom in research and writing on the strategy and tactics of influence in the past 8 to 10 years. Several researchers have performed exhaustive surveys and inventories of the influence tactics managers use (e.g., Kipnis, Schmidt, and Wilkinson, 1980; Keys and Case, 1990; Yukl and Tracey, 1992), and others have written normative treatises on how and when to use these tactics (Cohen and Bradford, 1990; Falbe and Yukl, 1992; Zucker, 1991).

19. In his studies of successful managers and their use of power in organizations, Kotter (1977) emphasizes that a manager must recognize, create, and cultivate dependence among those around her—subordinates, peers, and even superiors—and to convert these dependencies into obligations.

20. Pfeffer and Salancik (1974) stress that one of the major hallmarks of power in organizations is the ability to control and dispense desired resources. Cohen and Bradford (1990) advocate exchange as the medium by which we most successfully get things done in organizations, particularly when we lack formal position authority and titles, and they describe a wealth of other currencies that may be used in effective exchange transactions.

21. See Kipnis (1976).

22. See Kipnis, Schmidt, and Wilkinson (1980).

23. Luthans and Kreitner (1985).

24. See Taetzsch and Benson (1978) for one approach to the effective use of assertiveness.

25. Fisher and Brown (1988).

26. Kipnis (1976) notes that "*praise and rewards* appear to be preferred when the power holder wishes to retain the goodwill of the target person, or when the power holder anticipates that compliance is likely to drop off in the future. *Criticism and*

sanctions appear to be preferred when the goodwill of the target is less involved, and the influence attempts are directed at changing some behavior rather than maintaining it" (p. 104, emphasis his).

27. Hornstein (1965); Michener, Vaske, Schleiffer, Plazewski, and Chapman (1975); see also Vitz and Kite (1970).

28. Several researchers (Kipnis, Schmidt, and Wilkinson, 1980; Yukl and Tracey, 1992) have noted that coalitions are an especially popular strategy for use with superiors and peers, over whom a manager may have no specific, direct authority.

10 THIRD-PARTY INTERVENTIONS

In Chapter 5, we reviewed a number of techniques that negotiators themselves can use to break deadlocks, reduce unproductive tension and hostility, and return negotiations to a productive pace. However, frequently the parties cannot effectively implement these techniques by themselves. As we will explain, when the "heat of battle" overwhelms negotiators, when mistrust and suspicion are high, or when the parties cannot take actions toward defusing conflict without those actions being misinterpreted and mistrusted by others, third-party involvement may become necessary. This chapter will describe the typical roles that third parties play and how those roles contribute to conflict resolution.

Adding Third Parties to the Negotiation Process

The essence of negotiation entails parties working face-to-face, without the direct involvement of others. It is exactly this sort of direct, personal involvement that creates the understanding of the issues and the personal commitment necessary to manage conflict constructively. As long as this direct form of negotiation proves to be productive, it is best to allow it to proceed without the involvement of other parties. As we say throughout this book, however, negotiations are often tense, difficult, and generate more heat than light. Negotiation over critical issues may also reach an impasse free of anger and resentment, but an impasse, nevertheless; the parties are unable to move the process beyond a particular sticking point. At these points, third-party intervention may be a productive (if not the only) way to break deadlocks and get the negotiations back on track.

Advantages and Disadvantages of Third-Party Intervention

At a minimum, third parties can provide (or even enforce) the stability, civility, and forward momentum necessary for the negotiators to readdress the problems at hand—problems central to the negotiation, and problems that have stalled or derailed it. Depending on the nature of the third party and the type of intervention involved, third-party interventions can provide a number of advantages:

- Breathing space, or a cooling-off period.
- Reestablished or enhanced communications.
- Refocus on the substantive issues.
- Remedy or repair for strained relationships.
- Establishment of, or recommitment to, time limits.
- Salvaging the "sunk cost" of stalled negotiations.
- Increased levels of negotiator satisfaction with, and commitment to, the conflict resolution process and its outcomes.

Even if the relationship between the parties is so damaged that future exchanges would be highly problematic, third parties may provide vehicles and processes that enable some degree of hostility abatement and closure on the issues at hand.

However, third-party interventions may also present certain disadvantages:

- Evidence of a failure of the negotiation process, even if only temporarily.
- Failure to grow, to build relationships, or to become more adept in managing their own lives and conflicts.

Third-Party Interventions: When and What Kind?

When Is Third-Party Involvement Appropriate? Serious negotiators must make a realistic effort to resolve their own disputes. In general, though, negotiators initiate third-party interventions when they believe they can no longer handle the dispute on their own. When one negotiator requests intervention, it must be acceptable to all the disputing parties. If only one party recognizes a need for third-party intervention, he must usually persuade the other party to go along. However, interventions may also be *imposed* by someone with power or authority over the negotiators when a failure to resolve the dispute threatens to lead to significant costs for the affected organization or for individuals affected by (but unable to act on) the dispute being negotiated. Negotiators might seek third-party involvement if they experience or observe:

- Intense emotions that appear to be preventing a settlement.
- Poor quality or quantity of communication, beyond the ability of the negotiators to fix (see Chapter 6).
- Misperceptions or stereotypes that hinder productive exchanges.

FIGURE 10.1

Categories of Third-Party Intervention

		Level of negotiator control over outcome	
		Low	**High**
	Low	Autocracy	Mediation
Level of negotiator control over procedure			
	High	Arbitration	Negotiation

Adapted from B.H. Sheppard, "Third Party Conflict Intervention: A Procedural Framework," in *Research in Organizational Behavior,* Vol. 6, ed. B. M. Staw and L. L. Cummings, (Greenwich, CT: JAI Publishing, 1984), pp. 141–90, and from J. Thibaut and L. Walker, *Procedural Justice: A Psychological Analysis* (Hillsdale, NJ: Lawrence Erlbaum Associates, 1975).

- Repeated negative behaviors (e.g., anger, name-calling, blaming others) creating barriers between the parties.
- Serious disagreement over the importance, collection, or evaluation of data.
- Disagreement as to the number, order, and combinations of issues under dispute.
- Actual or perceived incompatible interests that the parties are unable to reconcile.
- Unnecessary (but perceived-as-necessary) value differences that divide the parties.
- Absence of a clear, common negotiation procedure or protocol, or not using established procedures (such as caucuses or cooling-off periods) to their best advantage.
- Severe difficulties initiating negotiations or "bargaining through" an impasse.[1]

What Kind of Intervention Is Appropriate? In third-party processes, typically, negotiators give up their control over either the dispute process (the *how* of negotiation) or the dispute outcome (the *what*) of negotiation. Sometimes they give up control over both of these, and sometimes they surrender control over neither one (see Figure 10.1).

Surrender of neither process nor outcome control constitutes the negotiation process, as addressed by most of this book; surrender of both constitutes a complete withdrawal from negotiation and dependence on the peremptory involvement of an otherwise uninvolved person. Of the two mixed situations (arbitration and mediation, both discussed in detail later in this chapter), mediation is third-party involvement that controls the process but not the outcome. Mediation, then, is *less intrusive* to the negotiations in that negotiators surrender control over the process, but they can still control the outcome (the actual agreement). If the primary rule of third-party intervention is "Don't involve third parties unless necessary," then the first corollary of the rule is "If involvement is necessary, use a minimally intrusive intervention" such as mediation.

As for invited interventions, they support the needs of negotiators who desire guidance or procedural assistance but who wish to maintain control over the choice and implementation of the ultimate outcome. Battle-weary negotiators may feel they just want an end to the dispute, but abdicating control completely to a third party will likely have a number of detrimental effects. Choice of invited intervention may also be a function of what is available—what a community or organization offers, as well as what the negotiating parties know how to seek (and use). Failure to use third-party intervention when appropriate is just as wasteful and as damaging to the ultimate negotiation process as using the wrong intervention method (e.g., arbitration rather than mediation, when negotiator commitment to outcomes is critical for a lasting resolution), or even using the right method at the wrong time (e.g., before negotiators have exhausted unassisted methods, or after expressed anger and personal attacks have soured one or both parties on the entire process).

The same measures of propriety and timeliness apply to *uninvited* interventions, as when a manager chooses to intervene in a dispute between two of her subordinates. The chooser (who, in this case, is usually the intervening third party) has the advantage of being potentially more objective than the disputants about the choices of whether and how to intervene. The chooser must also keep in mind, however, the likely effect of the intervention on the negotiators—specifically, on their ability to address and manage disputes more effectively in the future. Again, the rule should be one of moderation: "Intervene and control only as deeply as appropriate," and—to borrow a medical dictum—"First, do no harm" to the negotiators or their willingness and ability to negotiate. This advice assumes that the most important principle is to permit and encourage the negotiators to constructively interact with each other as much as possible without injuring each other; it also assumes that the resolution of a particular dispute does not have to occur in a short time period. To the extent that the disputants will have little or no interaction in the future and that a timely resolution is critical, relatively more invasive (i.e., controlling) interventions may be acceptable—even necessary. We discuss some of the factors that drive the choice of intervention in more detail later in this chapter.

An Overview of Formal Intervention Methods

Third-party interventions can be described as formal or informal. By formal, we refer to roles and activities that are intentionally designed and recognized as third parties in a traditional sense, such as those taken by judges, labor arbitrators, divorce mediators, or process consultants such as psychologists or organization development (OD) practitioners. By informal, we mean roles and behaviors that are incidental to other primary roles and behaviors, such as those of managers, supervisors, or concerned friends. In this section, we describe three formal styles of third-party behavior: arbitration, mediation, and process consultation. In the next section we will address informal intervention techniques. We will review the objectives, style, and procedural impact of each approach and describe their impact on negotiation outcomes.

Arbitration

Arbitration, typically, involves low levels of *negotiator* control (high third-party control) over outcomes, but high levels of negotiator control over process (see Figure 10.1). Even though arbitration represents loss of outcome control by negotiating parties, it is probably the most common and well-known form of third-party dispute resolution. The process is clear-cut: parties in dispute, after having reached a deadlock or a time deadline without successful resolution of their differences, present their positions to a third party. The third party listens to both sides and then makes a ruling in regard to the outcome of the dispute. Arbitration is used widely in disputes between businesses, and between business and their union-organized workers.

Arbitration has come under increasing scrutiny and criticism as a dispute resolution mechanism, even in the labor relations area. While arbitration initially appears to have two distinct advantages as a resolution procedure (it imposes a clear-cut resolution to the dispute, and thereby the costs of prolonged, unresolved disputes can be avoided), it appears to have several negative consequences as well.

- *The chilling effect.* If the parties in negotiation anticipate that their own failure to agree will lead to a binding arbitrator's intervention, it may cool their incentive to work seriously for a negotiated settlement. This chilling effect occurs as they avoid making compromises they might be otherwise willing to make, because they fear that the fact finder or arbitrator will split the difference between the last offers the negotiators have on the table. If negotiators anticipate that the arbitrator will split the difference, then it is in their best interest to maintain an extreme, hard-line position because difference-splitting is more likely to result in the hard-liner's favor.

- *The narcotic effect.* When arbitration is anticipated as a result of the failure of parties to agree, negotiators may also lose interest in the process of negotiating.

Because hard bargaining is costly in time and effort, because there is no guarantee that agreement will be reached, and because an imposed settlement is a guarantee under arbitration, negotiators may take the easy way out. Negotiator passivity, loss of initiative, and dependence on the third party are common results of recurring dispute arbitration.

• *The half-life effect.* Parents are often aware that as the demand for arbitration increases, the sheer number of decisions required also increases and it becomes more likely that decisions will not please one or both sides. This is known as the half-life effect. As the frequency of arbitration increases, disenchantment with the adequacy and fairness of the process develops, and the parties may resort to other means to resolve their disputes.[2]

• *The biasing effect.* Arbitrators must be careful that their decisions do not systematically favor one side or the other and that they maintain an image of fairness and impartiality. Even if each decision, taken separately, appears to be a fair settlement of the current conflict issue, perceived patterns of partiality toward one side may jeopardize the arbitrator's acceptability in future disputes.

• *The decision-acceptance effect.* Arbitrated disputes may engender less commitment to the settlement than alternative forms of dispute resolution. Lasting dispute resolution requires timely and effective implementation, and the key to effective implementation is often the commitment to a decision derived from prior participation in making it. For this reason, arbitration (as a procedure that minimizes disputants' choice of resolution or outcome) is likely to lead to situations in which disputants are less than fully committed to following through, especially if they feel dissatisfied with the arbitrator's decision.

Mediation

In contrast to arbitration—and as a way to alleviate some of the problems with arbitration mentioned above—mediation has developed increasing support. Although the ultimate objective of mediation is the same as arbitration—to resolve the dispute—the major difference is that mediation seeks to achieve the objective by having the parties themselves create the agreement. It is important to note that formal or contractual mediation is based on established and accepted rules and procedures; later in this chapter, when examining informal interventions, we will discuss informal mediation, which is less well defined. Mediators, typically, have no formal power over outcomes, and they cannot resolve the dispute on their own or impose a solution. Instead, their effectiveness comes from their ability to meet with the parties individually, secure an understanding of the issues in dispute, identify areas of potential compromise in the positions of each side, and encourage the parties to make concessions toward agreement.

Mediator Behaviors. Mediation generally proceeds in several stages. In the early stages of a dispute, a mediator will assume a reasonably passive role; she is most concerned with securing acceptance by the parties and with understanding the nature of the dispute. Mediator strategies may include separating the parties, questioning them about the issues, and actively listening to each side. The mediator must be able to separate rhetoric from true interest and to identify each side's priorities. Once this has been accomplished, the mediator will then begin managing the exchange of proposals and counterproposals, testing each side for areas where concessions may be possible.

As mediation progresses, mediators often become more active and take a more aggressive role. They may bring the parties together for face-to-face deliberations, or they may keep them separate; press one or both sides to make concessions that the mediator judges to be essential; invent proposals and solutions that they think will be acceptable, testing them with each side or even announcing them publicly; or try to get the parties to agree in private. If the mediation effort has been successful, the mediator will ultimately bring the parties together to endorse a final agreement or to publicly announce their settlement. It has been suggested that mediators facilitate concession making without loss of face by the parties, and thereby promote more rapid and effective conflict resolution than would otherwise occur.[3]

Several elements of the mediation process are integral to its success. The first is *timing the mediation efforts* based on the readiness of the parties. Because mediation, typically, is a voluntary process—the parties usually are not forced to enter into mediation except by their willingness to do so—mediation cannot be effective if the parties do not choose to cooperate. If they believe that they have more to gain by holding out or protracting the dispute, then mediation cannot work.

Second, *the mediator must be acceptable* to the parties. The traditional view of the mediator is as a neutral individual whom the parties recognize as impartial, experienced, and potentially helpful. An exception to this might be a friend, peer, or supervisor who chooses to intervene as a mediator. A variety of qualities such as integrity, impartiality, and experience in comparable disputes may be required for a potential mediator to be viewed as acceptable by both sides. At times, however, the only (or most appropriate) mediator available is not without bias to some degree. Such mediator bias has two forms: that of general alignment or affiliation with one side *prior* to mediation, and that of greater support for one side than the other *during* mediation.[4] Disputants may overlook bias of the first sort if they are convinced that the mediator in question shows no bias of the second sort (i.e., actually mediates evenhandedly).

Is Mediation Effective?

Mediation has been judged effective in from 20 percent to 80 percent of the cases in which it is used; its greatest effectiveness occurred in situations marked by only moderate conflict.[5] By moderate, we mean situations in which tension is apparent and tempers are beginning to fray, but in which negotiations have not deteriorated to physical violence and irrevocably damaging threats and actions.

Disputes beyond the moderate stage are often characterized by drastic actions and reactions and by the "burning of bridges" (relational and perhaps other) by one or both parties.

When the resistance points of both sides don't overlap (see Chapter 2), mediators may have to exert greater direct and indirect pressure on the negotiators in order to create a "positive contract zone," an overlap of resistance points. Direct pressure occurs if the mediator uses tactics to encourage the parties to soften their positions; indirect pressure comes, typically, through the passage of time, wearing the parties down and increasing the cost of holding out. Mediation is less effective in more intense conflicts, as when the conflict is large, many issues are at stake, or the parties disagree on major priorities. Under such conditions, mediation tactics may be insufficient to move the parties toward mutual agreement.

Mediation tends to be most effective when:

- Conflict is moderate rather than intense.
- The parties are highly motivated to settle.
- Parties are committed to mediation.
- The issues do not concern allocation of severely limited resources.
- The issues do not involve broad, general principles.
- The parties are essentially equal in power.
- Greater intrusion (i.e., arbitration) is threatened as a next step.[6]

Mediation effectiveness can be viewed from a variety of perspectives, including the issues, the disputing parties, and the mediator's behaviors. Relating to the issues, effective behaviors include:

- Identifying the issues.
- Uncovering underlying interests and concerns.
- Setting agendas.
- Packaging, sequencing, and prioritizing agenda items.
- Interpreting and shaping proposals.
- Making suggestions for possible settlements.[7]

Relating to the parties, mediation tended to be more effective if mediators assisted them in one or more of four ways:

- Helping them to save face when making concessions.
- Helping them to resolve internal disagreements.
- Helping them to deal with constituents.
- Applying positive incentives for agreement or concession making (or negative sanctions for noncooperation).[8]

Certain mediator behaviors, in particular, seem to lead to more effective mediation. These include:

FIGURE 10.2

A Strategic Choice Model of Mediator Behavior

Mediator's perception of "common ground"

		Low	High
	High	Compensation	Problem solving
Mediator's concern for parties' aspirations			
	Low	Pressure	Inaction

Adapted from P.J.D. Carnevale, "Strategic Choice in Negotiation," *Negotiation Journal* 2 (1986), pp. 41–56.

- Creating and controlling the agenda.
- Assisting the parties in establishing priorities.
- Maintaining calm, friendly, but firm control over the mediation process.

Mediators deal with a variety of situations and may choose their behaviors based on what they feel a given situation warrants. This suggests a "strategic choice model" of mediator behavior (see Figure 10.2).

Mixing high or low levels of two variables—concern for the disputing parties' aspirations and perception of parties' common ground (i.e., areas of agreement)—produces four basic mediation strategies:

- Problem solving (assisting the parties to engage in integrative exchange).
- Compensation (mediator application of rewards and inducements to entice the parties into making concessions and agreements).
- Pressure (trying to force the parties to reduce their levels of aspiration in the absence of perceived potential for an integrative, or win–win, resolution).
- Inaction (standing back from the dispute, leaving the parties to work things out on their own).[9]

Mediator-applied pressure seems to interact with the type of situation being mediated. Success in mediations marked by intensity (e.g., major conflicts involving many issues and disagreement over major priorities) and high levels of interparty hostility tend to respond better to more forceful, proactive mediation behaviors. Low-hostility situations tend to respond better to a less-active, more facilitative approach.[10] When high hostility was accompanied by high levels of problem-solving behavior by the negotiators, mediators assisted best by posing problems, challenging negotiators to solve them, and suggesting new ideas and soliciting negotiator responses to them.[11]

Liabilities of Arbitration and Mediation

It should be clear from the above that both mediation and arbitration have their liabilities. The liabilities of *arbitration* are these:

- Negative consequences for negotiator behaviors in anticipation of third-party decisions (e.g., chilling and narcotic effects).
- Removal of outcome control from negotiators.
- Possible lack of disputant commitment to implementing the imposed outcome.

In contrast, the liabilities of *mediation* include:

- Lack of impetus or initiative to adhere to any particular settlement or to settle at all.
- Possible perpetuation of the dispute, perhaps indefinitely (lack of incentive to negotiate).
- Possible extension or escalation of the dispute into more damaging, more costly forms and forums.

Process Consultation

A third formal approach to the resolution of disputes is process consultation, "a set of activities on the part of the consultant that helps the client to perceive, understand, and act upon the process events which occur in the client's environment."[12] The objective of process consultation is to defuse the emotional aspect of conflict and to improve communication between the parties, leaving them with renewed or enhanced abilities to manage future disputes. The difference between mediation and process consultation is that mediators are at least somewhat concerned with the issues in dispute, whereas process consultants focus only on procedures. Process consultants assume that if they can teach the parties how to manage conflict more productively and effectively, these improved procedures will lead to productive outcomes. The purpose of the third party's intervention is to create the foundation for more productive dialogue over substantive issues and to teach the parties how to prevent conflicts from escalating destructively in the future.

Process Consultation Behaviors. Process consultants usually employ a variety of tactics.[13] Their first step is often to separate the parties and interview them individually in order to determine each side's view of the other side, position, and a history of the relationship and its conflicts. Following this diagnostic phase, the consultant uses this information to structure a series of dialogues or confrontations between the parties. These meetings are designed specifically to address the causes of past conflicts and each side's perceptions of the other. Meetings are held on neutral turf, and the questions of who should attend and what issues should be discussed are planned ahead of time.

The purpose of the third party is to encourage the parties to confront their differences and the reasons for them. The process consultant is referee, timekeeper, and gatekeeper of the process, working to keep the parties on track while also ensuring that the conflict does not escalate. Finally, the third party directs all sides toward some type of problem solving and integration, assuming that by confronting and airing their differences, the parties can create a format for working on their substantive differences in the future and can pursue this agenda without a recurrence of unproductive escalation. Thus, changing the climate for conflict management, promoting constructive dialogue around differences of opinion, and creating the capacity for other people to act as their own third parties are major parts of the process consultant's agenda.

The description of successful process consultation suggests that process consultants should possess many of the same attributes that we have ascribed to other third parties:

- They should be perceived as experts in the technique, knowledgeable about conflict and its dynamics, able to be emotionally supportive while confronting the parties, and able to diagnose the dispute.
- They should be perceived as clearly neutral, without bias toward one side or the other.
- They should be authoritative—that is, able to establish power over the process that the conflicting parties are pursuing, thereby intervening and controlling it.

Although they do not attempt to impose a particular solution or outcome, process consultants must be able to shape the manner in which the parties interact, separating them or bringing them together, and to control the agenda that they follow when interaction occurs. Without such control, the parties will resort to their earlier pattern of destructive hostility. Process consultation goes the farthest of the techniques discussed here in putting the issues under dispute back in the hands of the disputing parties. To make process consultation work, however, the parties must put aside these substantive differences, something that is hard for them to do. Process consultation is not likely to be effective when:

- The parties are deeply locked in a dispute over one or more major unresolved issues.

- The disputants are involved in a short-term relationship and will not be working together very long.
- The substantive issues in dispute are distributive (i.e., zero-sum).
- The level of conflict is so high that the parties are more intent on revenge or retribution than reconciliation.

In effect, process consultation may work only when sustained conflict has worn the parties out, making them want resolution more than continued warfare, or when the parties sincerely want to coexist but do not have the skills to do so. If the parties do not have sufficient incentive to work together, efforts at process consultation will be undermined. One side will exploit trust, cooperation, and honesty, and the dispute will quickly escalate.

Other Third-Party Styles: Informal Interventions

We have reviewed several major approaches used by third parties to resolve disputes. These approaches—arbitration, mediation, and process consultation—represent formal, or "textbook," approaches to the resolution of disputes, and they are the three most commonly described in the research on third-party behavior. However, a variety of other, *informal* third-party approaches are possible, as in the case of a manager intervening in a dispute between two subordinates. Considering that such informal third parties can exert either high or low amounts of process or decision control, the possibilities appear in Figure 10.3:

A recent study (asking practicing managers to describe the last time they intervened in a dispute between their subordinates) concluded that managers tend to use one of three of these four styles (*not* mediation).

1. **Inquisitorial Intervention.** This was the most common style. A manager who uses this style:

   - Exerts high control over both the process and the decision.
   - Tells both sides to present their cases.
   - Asks lots of questions to probe into each side's position.
   - Frequently controls who is allowed to speak and what they say.
   - Then invents a solution that she thinks will meet both parties' needs and usually enforces that solution on both parties.

2. **Adversarial Intervention.** A manager who uses this style:

   - Exerts high control over the decision, but not the process.
   - Does not control the process in that he does not ask questions to try to "get the whole story" or to control the destructive aspects of the conflict between the parties.
   - Passively listens to what each side chooses to tell him.

FIGURE 10.3

Informal Third-Party Intervention Styles

		Degree of managerial outcome control	
		High	Low
Degree of managerial process control	High	Inquisitorial Intervention	(Mediational Intervention?)
	Low	Adversarial Intervention	Providing Impetus

Adapted from B.H. Sheppard, "Managers as Inquisitors: Some Lessons from the Law," in *Negotiating in Organizations,* ed. M. Bazerman and R.J. Lewicki (Beverly Hills: Sage Publications, 1983).

- Then makes a decision (tells the parties how to solve the conflict) based exclusively on the presentations.

3. **Providing Impetus.** Managers who use this style, typically:

- Do not exert control over the decision.
- Exert only a small amount of control over the process.
- Try to make a quick diagnosis of what the conflict is about.
- Tell the parties that if they don't find a solution, one will be imposed on them.[14]

Which Approach Is More Effective?

Managers spontaneously tend to use styles that resemble acting like arbitrators or judges, or that provide a common enemy by threatening to settle the dispute for the parties in an undesirable way if they can't settle it themselves. Note that the remaining cell in Figure 10.3, which we have labeled "Mediational Intervention," is *not* a style commonly used by managers. Although managers claim to prefer mediation as a third-party style, it is not clear that managers really understand how to mediate without being trained to do so.[15] When handling a conflict, managers seem prone to assume responsibility for having a major impact on the outcome of the conflict, that is, the specific decision or outcome arrived at by the disputing parties.[16] Therefore, managers may be very uncomfortable using a mediation strategy, which requires that they control the process of conflict but leave the solution in the hands of the disputants.

We believe that mediation should be used more often for informal third-party interventions than it is. However, more attention needs to be focused on determining how managers can better identify mediational opportunities, and on how they can learn to mediate more effectively.

Summary

If negotiators are unable to manage disputes effectively, third-party intervention may be a way to help. In this chapter, we reviewed three prototypical styles of third-party intervention: arbitration, mediation, and process consultation. Each of these styles has its strengths and weakness as an intervention and dispute-resolution approach. The styles differ as to whether the disputants surrender control over the way they interact with the other negotiator, or over deciding what the actual outcome of the negotiation will be, to the third party. Arbitrators, typically, specify a structured process in which disputing parties have relative freedom to present their side and perspective on the issues; then the third party decides the outcome, often imposing a resolution of the disputants. Mediators exert a great deal of control over how the parties interact, both physically and communicationally; typically, they do *not* choose the actual solution for the disputants, although they may offer guidance and suggestions. Finally, process consultants are less involved in the disputed issues than arbitrators or mediators, but they are heavily involved in helping the parties to establish or enhance their communication and dispute-resolution skills, which the parties can then apply to specific problems as they deal with each other in the future.

In addition, there are other third-party roles and styles in common use (including informal versions of the three formal approaches we addressed). A great deal remains to be done in this area, both in determining the mastery and propriety of particular informal third-party styles and techniques for various types of conflict, as well as in achieving a better understanding of the kinds of conflicts that third parties can effectively assist in resolving, and the ways third parties go about deciding when and how to intervene in disputes.

End Notes

1. See Moore (1986, pp. 11–12).
2. See Anderson and Kochan (1977).
3. See Rubin (1980).
4. See Carnevale and Conlon (1990).
5. See Kressel and Pruitt (1989).
6. See Carnevale and Pruitt (1992).

7. Ibid.

8. Ibid.

9. See Carnevale (1986).

10. See Donohue (1989), Hiltrop (1989), and Lim and Carnevale (1990).

11. See Zubek, Pruitt, Pierce, and Iocolano (1989).

12. See Schein (1987, p. 34).

13. See Beckhard, (1967) and Walton (1987).

14. See Sheppard (1983).

15. See Lewicki and Sheppard (1985).

16. See Sheppard, Blumenfeld-Jones, Minton, and Hyder (1994).

11 ETHICS IN NEGOTIATION

In this chapter, we shall explore a subject not often addressed in writing on negotiation (particularly in management and business negotiations): the question of whether there are, or should be, ethical standards for negotiations. As we will indicate, the topic has received increased attention and research in recent years. It is our view that fundamental questions of ethical conduct arise *whenever* we negotiate. The effective negotiator must recognize when the questions are relevant and what factors must be considered to answer them.

Why Do Negotiators Need to Know About Ethics?

Consider the following situations:

Situation 1. You are a manager badly in need of more clerical assistance for your office. Although work is getting done, a large and often unpredictable volume of work is creating periodic delays. Some of your staff members are complaining that the work flow could be managed much more effectively if another clerk were added. However, you also know that your boss is not sympathetic; she thinks that the problem could be solved if all the current clerks simply agreed to work a bit harder or volunteer a few hours of overtime. Moreover, your department's budget is very tight, and to get a new clerical position approved, you will clearly have to demonstrate to senior management (particularly your boss) that you need additional personnel. You have to make a case to your boss. This is a negotiation. You see the following options open to you:

1. Document the amount of work that each of your clerks is doing and the amount of work that is being delayed or is not being done properly, and make a complete report to your boss.

2. Give each of your clerks a lot of extra jobs to do now, particularly ones that could really be deferred for a few months (such as cleaning out and completely reorganizing the files). Thus, you will create an artificial backlog of incomplete work that can be used to support your argument for adding more staff.

3. Talk to your clerks and stress that the most important standard by which they should do their jobs is to follow procedures exactly and to focus on high-quality work rather than getting all the work done. This will probably create a slowdown and a backlog that you can then use to support your argument.

4. You've been watching the operation of the payroll office down the hall. Many of those clerks are standing around drinking coffee half the time. Talk to your boss about your observation and ask to have one of these clerks transferred to your department.

Question: Are some of these approaches more ethical than others? Which ones? Which ones would you try?

Situation 2. You are an entrepreneur interested in acquiring a business that is currently owned by a competitor. The competitor, however, has not shown any interest in either selling the company or merging with your business. To gain inside knowledge of his firm, you instructed a consultant you know to call contacts in that company to determine if the company is having any serious problems that might threaten the viability of the business. If you can find out about these problems, you might be able to use the information to either hire away their employees or find a way to get the competitor to sell.

Question: Is this ethical? Would you be likely to do it if you were the entrepreneur?

Situation 3. You are a vice president of personnel, negotiating with a union representative for a new labor contract. The union has insisted that it will not sign a new contract until the company agrees to raise the number of paid holidays from four to six. Management has calculated that it will cost approximately $150,000 for each paid holiday and has argued to the union that the company cannot afford to meet the demand. However, you know that, in reality, money is not the issue—the company simply doesn't think that the union's demand is justified. To convince the union that they should withdraw their demand, you have been considering the following alternatives:

1. Tell the union that their request is simply unacceptable to you because they haven't justified why they need six paid holidays.

2. Tell the union that the company simply can't afford it (without explanation).

3. Prepare some erroneous financial statements that show that it will cost about $300,000 per paid holiday, which you simply can't afford.

4. Offer the union leadership an all-expenses-paid trip to a Florida resort if they will simply drop the demand entirely.

   Question: Do any of the strategies raise ethical concerns? Which ones? Why?

The scenarios described are hypothetical; however, the problems they present are real ones for negotiators. Managers are frequently confronted with important decisions about the strategies and tactics that they will use to achieve important objectives, particularly when many influence-tactics are open to them. In this chapter, we will turn our attention to the major ethical questions that arise in negotiation. We will consider several questions:

1. What are ethics and how do they apply to negotiation?
2. What motivates ethically marginal behavior?
3. What major types of ethical and unethical tactics are likely to occur in negotiation?
4. What external factors shape a negotiator's decision to use unethical tactics?

What Are Ethics and Why Do They Apply to Negotiation?

We want to be clear that it is *not* our intention to advocate a specific ethical position for all negotiators or for the conduct of all negotiations. Many works on business ethics take a strongly prescriptive or normative position, advocating what a person *should* do. Instead, we intend to take a more descriptive stance, illustrating how a person *might* think about choices and options when confronted with strategies and tactics that are potentially unethical. We will identify several factors which motivate unethical conduct and we will suggest how those dimensions affect a negotiator's choice of strategies and tactics. Second, we will provide negotiators with a framework for making more-informed decisions about the strategies and tactics available to them. In doing so, we will be working in an area in which there has been considerably less systematic research than in other topics in this book, so many of our assertions will be speculative.

Judging What Is Appropriate in Negotiations. In determining what is ethically appropriate in negotiation, we wish to distinguish among different criteria for judging and evaluating a manager's actions, particularly when questions of ethics might be involved. There are at least three standards for evaluating strategies and tactics in business and negotiation: ethics, prudence, and practicality.[1] *Ethical* judgments evaluate strategies and tactics based on some standards of moral behavior, or of what is right and wrong. *Prudent* judgments are based on what is most effective—for example, what is beneficial or harmful for the people who perform those actions. Finally, *practical* judgments are based on what is the easiest, cheapest, or fastest way of getting something done to achieve an objective. For example, a salesperson preparing a presentation on a new product could use one or more of these standards in determining her strategy. The ethical salesperson would ask, "What is the truth about this new product?" or, "How can I compare this product fairly to its competitors on the market?" The prudent salesperson would ask, "How can I best present this product?" or, "What can I say about it that will make it attractive to the buyer?" Finally, the practical salesperson will ask very pragmatic questions: "How should we lay out the advertisements? How quickly can I do this? What is the cheapest or most cost-effective way to sell this product?"

Discussions of business ethics frequently confuse the ethical, prudent, and practical criteria for judging conduct—they try to determine what is wise or practical as distinct from what is ethical. In earlier chapters, we have extensively evaluated negotiation strategies and tactics by the prudence and practicality criteria; in this chapter, we turn to ways by which we can judge negotiation strategies and tactics by ethical criteria.

A Simple Model of Ethical Decision Making

Why do some negotiators choose to use tactics that may be unethical? The first answer that occurs to many of us is that these people are corrupt, degenerate, or immoral. In fact, that answer is much too simplistic. In addition, the answer reflects a more systematic bias in the way we tend to perceive other people and explain the reasons why they do what they do. Simply put, this bias encourages us to attribute the causes of other people's behavior to their personalities, whereas we attribute the causes of our own behavior to factors in the social environment around us.[2] Thus, in attempting to explain why another negotiator used one or more ethically questionable negotiating tactics, we would probably say that this individual was unprincipled and willing to use any tactic to get what she wanted. In contrast, when attempting to explain why we might use the same tactic, we would tend to say that we are highly principled and had very good reasons for deviating from those principles just this one time. We propose a relatively simple model of decision making to help us understand the decision to employ ethically marginal tactics. This decision has three major components: the motivation to behave unethically, the functions served by this unethical conduct, and the consequences resulting from this decision.

The Motivation to Behave Unethically

There are three primary motivations that may lead to unethical conduct: profit making, competition, and the restoration of justice. We will say a little about each.

Profit. The pursuit of profit is fundamental to a capitalistic economic system. Whether it is the company president who is striving to maximize the profitability of the corporation, the stockholders who are looking for bigger dividends, or the salesperson who is pushing the customer to buy that new refrigerator so she can get a bigger commission, all are concerned both about profitability and its impact on them personally. Profit is clearly a motive in negotiating. By its very nature, negotiating is a process by which individuals strive to maximize their outcomes, to get an advantageous gain or return. In addition, profit is the motive that often pushes individuals toward negotiation as a strategy for maximizing objectives— we frequently use negotiating strategies and tactics because they are recognized as techniques for improving the outcome: the other would give us less if we did *not* negotiate. In short, the profit motive and the pursuit of negotiation as one strategy to improve profitability often go hand in hand.[3]

Competition. The pursuit of profit often occurs in a social context in which others also want to achieve that profit. The total amount of resources available in any situation is usually insufficient to satisfy everyone's desires; therefore, competition occurs. As one writer points out, "As one embarks on one's journey to become a millionaire, one must face a salient and perhaps disturbing fact: Others also want to become millionaires, and in the resulting competition, not everyone will be successful."[4] On the tangibles, bargainers are motivated to gain a favorable outcome and even to maximize that outcome. Sometimes the pressure to achieve the best outcome on the tangibles leads negotiators to use either deception or dirty tricks to achieve their objective (we discussed this in depth in Chapters 2 and 6). In addition, a strongly competitive orientation can lead negotiators to value specific intangibles (such as winning at any price) that cause them to use strategies and tactics that allow them to beat the other and even harm the other's ability to compete in the future. For example, if there is a history of acrimonious relations between a supplier and a purchaser, or a personal antagonism and vendetta between them, it may not take long for any given act of essential competition to quickly escalate and turn destructive.

Justice. The third major dimension of human conduct that motivates parties toward unethical action is a reaction against perceived injustice. Questions about fairness often are raised concerning the outcomes being derived through a negotiation, the processes being used to lead to those outcomes, or the larger system (and its rules) in which a negotiation is taking place.[5] Questions of *outcome* justice relate to how we decide on a fair distribution of a negotiated outcome. This is a problem that often occurs when we need to divide up a scarce resource, such as a pool of money. According to David Lax and Jim Sebenius, this is the problem of "distributive fairness," and they see it as a key ethical issue in negotiation.[6] For ex-ample, suppose that three of us have worked hard at some joint project— let's say a new business—that has become very successful. Now we are negotiating over how to divide up the first year's profits. You believe that the profit should be divided equally—we were all in this together and should all get a one-third cut of the profit. I believe that I should get more than one-third because the business was basically my idea and I should get some financial reward for that. Our third partner believes that she should get more than one-third because she is a poor, young, struggling student and really needs the money badly to pay off educational debts. Our negotiation, therefore, is over which common principle of outcome fairness—*equality* (we all get the same), *equity* (the person who contributes more gets more), or *need* (the person who needs more gets more)—should be used to divide the money. Second, we could also debate the fairest procedure (*process*) for making that decision, or turn to some dispute resolution *system* to help us out—a mediator, an arbitrator, a grievance system, or some other existing mechanism. How these issues are raised and resolved in negotiation are problems that have not been well researched. Although negotiators are often advised to use "objective criteria" to determine when outcomes and procedures are fair, we know very little about how the parties negotiate the criteria and processes used to decide what's fair.[7] Interestingly enough, the pursuit of justice or fairness—which is, in itself, a strong ethical value—may lead negotiators to be unethical (dishonest) in the pursuit of a just end. When a negotiator believes that she has been treated unfairly—exploited, tricked, or taken advantage of by another party—the negotiator is likely to feel angry or duped or experience a loss of face, and she may be likely to seek revenge for the behavior.[8]

The Function of Unethical Conduct

The purpose of using unethical negotiating tactics is to increase the negotiator's power in the bargaining environment. Most unethical tactics in negotiation are violations of standards for telling the truth. As we pointed out when we discussed interdependence (Chapter 1), negotiation is based on "information dependence"— the exchange of information to learn the true preferences and priorities of the other negotiator.[9] Information is one of the major sources of power in negotiation (Chapter 9). In most exchanges, we assume that the information presented is accurate and truthful. To assume otherwise—that it is not truthful—is to question the very premises on which daily social communication is based. So when violations of the truth—lies—are introduced into this social exchange, they manipulate information in favor of the dispenser of that misinformation. A lie enhances the power of the liar by changing the balance of "accurate" information in the negotiating relationship. This can occur in several ways.[10]

1. Misrepresentation of one's position to another party. In misrepresentation, the negotiator lies about the preferred settlement point or resistance point. Negotiators may tell the other party that they want to settle for more than they really expect or threaten to walk away from a deal when they are actually ready to make further concessions and believe that the parties are close to agreement. Misrepresentation is the most common form of deceit in negotiation.

2. Bluffing. Bluffing is also a common deceptive tactic. The negotiators state that they will commit some action that they don't actually intend to fulfill. The best examples of bluffs are false threats or promises. A false threat might be a negotiator's statement that she will walk out if her terms and conditions are not met (when she really doesn't intend to take that action); a false promise might be a negotiator's commitment to perform some personal favor for the opposing negotiator later on, when in fact she has no intention of ever performing that favor.

3. Falsification. Falsification is the introduction of factually erroneous information into a negotiation. Falsified financial information, false documents, or false statements of what other parties are doing, will do, or have done before are common examples.

4. Deception. The negotiator constructs a collection of true or untrue arguments that leads the other party to the wrong conclusion. For example, a negotiator may describe in detail what actions were taken in a similar circumstance in the past and lead the other party to believe he intends to take the same actions again in this context.

5. Selective disclosure or misrepresentation to constituencies. The negotiator does not accurately tell her constituency what has transpired in negotiation, does not tell the other party the true wishes, desires, or position of her constituency, or both. She may therefore play both sides (the constituency and the other party) against each other to engineer the agreement she wants most.

In summary, negotiators use unethical tactics to gain power. They derive power either by manipulating the information (through some form of truth distortion), gaining some form of tactical advantage over a competitor, or undermining the other party's negotiating position. Using these tactics frequently leads to consequences for the negotiator, the other party, and the observers.

The Consequences of Unethical Conduct

As a result of employing an unethical tactic, the negotiator will experience positive or negative consequences. First, consequences will occur depending on whether the tactic worked or not—that is, whether the negotiator got what she wanted as a result of using the tactic. A second set of consequences may result from the judgments and evaluations that may come from the other negotiator, constituencies, or audiences that can observe the tactic (Chapter 7). Depending on whether these parties recognize the tactic and whether they evaluate it as proper or improper to use, the negotiator may receive a great deal of feedback. Finally, a third set of consequences will occur depending on how the negotiator evaluates his own use of the tactic—whether using the tactic creates any discomfort, personal stress, or even guilt—or, in contrast, whether the actor sees no problem in using the tactic again and even begins to consider how to use it more effectively.

FIGURE 11.1

A Simple Model of Ethical Decision Making

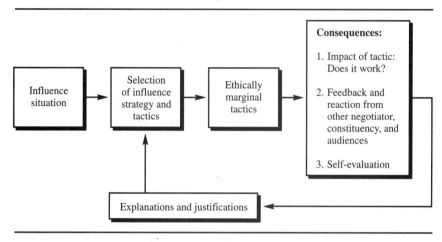

Figure 11.1 presents a simple model of this process—the decision to use an unethical tactic and its consequences. Let us first consider the consequences that occur based on whether the tactic is successful or not. It should be fairly clear that whether the tactic works—that is, leads to the outcome the negotiator hoped to achieve—should have some impact on whether the tactic is more likely or less likely to be used in the future (essentially, a simple learning and reinforcement process). If using the tactic (*a*) allows a negotiator to attain rewarding outcomes that would be otherwise unavailable to him, and (*b*) if the unethical conduct is not punished by others, we would expect the frequency of unethical conduct to increase because the negotiator believes he can get away with it. Thus, real consequences— rewards and punishments that arise from using a tactic or not using it—should not only motivate a negotiator's present behavior, but also affect the negotiator's predisposition to use similar strategies in similar circumstances in the future.[11]

A second set of consequences occurs when the negotiator experiences the reaction of the target person. If the target person is unaware that a deceptive tactic has been used, then there is no reaction—other than the target being disappointed in having lost the negotiation. However, if the target discovers that deception has occurred, the reaction is likely to be far stronger. People who discover that they have been deceived or exploited, typically, become angry. As a result of both the actual loss they may have suffered in negotiations and the embarrassment they feel from having been deceived, most victims are likely to seek retaliation and revenge. Thus, although the use of unethical tactics may lead to short-term success for the negotiator, it may also create an adversary who is bent on revenge and retribution.[12]

The third set of consequences results from the way the negotiator evaluates the tactic. When a negotiator has used a tactic that may produce a reaction—such as the consequences we described above—the negotiator must prepare to defend the tactic's use. These defenses explain or justify the tactic's use—to one's self (e.g., "I see myself as a person of integrity, and yet I have decided to do something that might be viewed as unethical"), to the victim, or to constituencies and audiences who may express their concerns. The primary purpose of these explanations and justifications is to rationalize, explain, or excuse the behavior—there is some good, reasonable, legitimate reason why this tactic was necessary.

Those who employ unethical tactics are prone to use a number of explanations and justifications in accounting for undesirable social behavior:[13]

• **The tactic was unavoidable.** The negotiator was not in full control of her actions, and hence should not be held responsible. Perhaps she never intended to hurt anyone, her words were misinterpreted, it was a mistake, or she was pressured into using the tactic by someone else.

• **The tactic was harmless.** What the negotiator did was really trivial and not very significant. We tell white lies all the time. For example, we greet our neighbor with a cheery "Good morning, nice to see you"; in fact, it may not be a good morning, we are in a bad mood, and we wish we hadn't even run into our neighbor at all. Exaggerations, bluffs, or peeking at the other party's private notes during negotiations can all be easily explained away as harmless actions.

• **The tactic will help to avoid negative consequences**. When using this justification, we are arguing that the ends justify the means. In this case, the justification is that the tactic helped to avoid greater harm. In a holdup, it is okay to lie to a gunman about where you have hidden your money because the consequences of telling the truth are that you will get robbed. Similarly, lying (or other similar means–ends tactics) may be seen as justifiable in negotiation if it protects the negotiator against even more undesirable consequences should the truth be known.

• **The tactic will produce good consequences, or the tactic is altruistically motivated.** Again, the end justifies the means, but in a positive sense. As we stated earlier, a negotiator who judges a tactic on the basis of its consequences is making judgments according to the tenets of utilitarianism—that the quality of any given action is judged by its consequences.[14]

• **"They had it coming" or "they deserve it" or "I'm just getting my due."** All these justifications are variations on the theme of using lying and deception against an individual who may have taken advantage of us in the past, against "the system," or against some generalized source of authority. The pollster Daniel Yankelovich noted the problem of a national erosion of honesty in the United States.[15] Increasingly, he found people believe that it is appropriate to take advantage of "the system" in various ways—through tax evasion, petty theft, shoplifting, improper declaration of bankruptcy, journalistic excesses, and distortion in advertising. A decade later, newer statistical surveys show that the problem has increased dramatically on almost every front.[16]

- **The tactic is fair or appropriate to the situation.** This approach uses situational relativism as the rationale and justification. Negotiators frequently justify their actions by claiming that the situation made it necessary for them to act the way they did. Most social situations, including negotiations, are governed by a set of generally well understood rules of proper conduct and behavior. These rules are sometimes suspended for two reasons: because it is believed that others have already violated the rules (therefore legitimizing the negotiator's right to violate them as well), and because it is anticipated that someone else will violate the rules (and therefore the other's actions should be preempted). The first case is an example of using unethical tactics in a tit-for-tat manner, to restore balance and to give others their due. Justifications such as "An eye for an eye," or "He started it and I'm going to finish it!" are commonly heard as a defense for resorting to unethical tactics in these cases. Anticipatory justification leading to preemptive behavior (the second case), usually occurs as a result of how you perceive the other party, and usually turns out to be a self-fulfilling prophecy. For example, negotiators use an unethical tactic because they believe that the other party is likely to use one; the other party retaliates with an unethical tactic of his own (because the first negotiator used one), which only goes to justify to the first negotiator that the other party was likely to behave unethically anyway.

Explanations and justifications, therefore, are self-serving rationalizations for our own conduct.[17] They allow the negotiator to convince others—particularly the victim—that conduct that would ordinarily be wrong in this situation is acceptable. Explanations and justifications also help us to rationalize the behavior to ourselves as well. We propose that the more frequently a negotiator engages in this self-serving justification process, the more her judgments about ethical standards and values will become biased, leading to a lessened ability to make accurate judgments about the truth. Moreover, although the tactics are initially used to *gain* power in a negotiation, we propose that the negotiator who uses them frequently will experience a *loss* of power over time, but through a different source of power (Chapter 9). The negotiator is less likely to be trusted, will be seen as having less credibility and integrity, and deals with this person either will not occur or will probably need to be bound by formal contracts and legal agreements.

In summary, we propose that the successful use of unethical tactics and their successful justification will help the negotiator to achieve her short-term goals, but they are also likely to distort the negotiator's perception of what is fair, necessary, and appropriate. Negotiators who use these tactics are likely to use them again in the future, but in using them, they will damage both their reputations and the long-term relationship with the other party.

The Perception of Ethical Tactics

To determine how negotiators judged the ethicality of the truth-telling and means-ends negotiation tactics, researchers[18] have asked large groups of MBA students[19] to rate 18 tactics on two 7-point scales: how appropriate each tactic would be to use in a negotiation situation, and how likely the negotiator would be to use the tactics. The collection of tactics was based on the truth-telling and means–ends principles that were described earlier.

Table 11.1 presents the 18 tactics, listed in descending order of perceived likelihood. Several observations can be made from examining this list. First, although it would be inappropriate to infer any one person's individual attitudes from a statistical summary of the data, it does appear that tactics like these can be scaled—some are clearly appropriate, some are clearly inappropriate, and some are in a middle range of questionable appropriateness. Second, some tactics are seen as definitely appropriate: four tactics, on average, received a rating of 5 or above, which we judge to be in the appropriate range. These include gaining information about the other party by asking around among friends and associates, hiding your real bottom line, making an opening demand greater than what you really want to achieve, and stalling. Third, a large number of the tactics were judged as inappropriate: 12 of the 18 tactics received average ratings of 3 or below. Finally, the researchers found that ratings of appropriateness and likelihood of using the tactic are very strongly correlated, which suggests that seeing a tactic as appropriate to use and the likelihood of using it are very closely related (although it is not at all clear whether the perception of appropriateness makes us more likely to use it, or vice versa).[20]

Thus, the research reported here indicates that there are tacitly agreed-upon norms of what is ethically appropriate in negotiation. Perceptions of these norms suggest that some minor forms of untruth—misrepresentation of one's true position to the other party and bluffs—may be seen as ethically acceptable and within the norms, whereas deception and falsification are generally seen as outside of the norms.

However, we use some caution in generalizing from these findings. First, these statements are based on ratings given by large groups of MBAs; in no way can they predict how any one individual negotiator will perceive the tactics and use them, or how any one target who experiences them will rate them. (We will discuss reactions from the victim's perspective later in this chapter.) Second, we are suggesting these conclusions on the basis of rating scales, not live negotiating experiences. Perceptions and reactions may be different when the parties are actually making decisions in a real negotiation rather than ranking the tactics on a questionnaire removed from any direct experience with another person in a meaningful social context. Third, we do not mean to suggest that it is appropriate or acceptable to draw the line where it is now drawn—that misrepresentation and bluffing are acceptable and deception and falsehoods are not. Our objective is to focus debate among negotiators on exactly these issues rather than to suggest that this is where the line should be drawn.

TABLE 11.1   Mean Ratings of Appropriateness and Likelihood of Tactics, Ordered by Mean Likelihood

Tactic Number	Variables	Mean Appropriateness Ratings	Standard Deviation	Mean Likelihood Ratings	Standard Deviation
(6)	Gain information about an opponent's negotiating position and strategy by "asking around" in a network of your own friends, associates, and contacts.	6.00	1.62	5.73	1.90
(4)	Hide your real bottom line from your opponent.	5.78	1.69	5.71	1.71
(5)	Make an opening demand that is far greater than what you really hope to settle for.	5.51	1.72	5.07	1.89
(13)	Convey a false impression that you are in absolutely no hurry to come to a negotiation agreement, thereby putting more time pressure on your opponent to concede quickly.	5.10	2.20	4.80	2.37
(10)	Make an opening offer or demand so high (or low) that it seriously undermines your opponent's confidence in her own ability to negotiate a satisfactory settlement.	4.38	2.11	4.01	2.10
(3)	Lead negotiators on the other side to believe that they can only get what they want by negotiating with you, when in fact they could go elsewhere and get what they want cheaper or faster.	4.33	1.79	4.22	1.71
(16)	Intentionally misrepresent the nature of negotiations to the press or your constituency to protect delicate discussions that have occurred.	3.20	1.97	3.15	2.03
(7)	Gain information about an opponent's negotiating position by paying friends, associates, and contacts to get this information for you.	3.17	1.94	2.79	1.82
(18)	Intentionally misrepresent factual information to your opponent when you know that he has already done this to you.	2.75	2.05	2.90	2.06

TABLE 11.1 Mean Ratings of Appropriateness and Likelihood of Tactics, Ordered by Mean Likelihood *(concluded)*

(12)	Talk directly to the people who your opponent reports to or is accountable to, and try to encourage them to defect to your side.	2.91	1.84	2.72	1.75
(9)	Gain information about an opponent's negotiating position by cultivating her friendship through expensive gifts, entertaining, or "personal favors."	2.70	1.67	2.64	1.76
(2)	Promise that good things will happen to your opponent if he gives you what you want, even if you know that you can't (or won't) deliver those good things when you have obtained the other's cooperation.	2.58	1.69	2.58	1.69
(1)	Threaten to harm your opponent if she doesn't give you what you want, even if you know you will never follow through with that threat.	2.56	2.37	2.57	2.23
(14)	Threaten to make your opponent look weak or foolish in front of a boss or others to whom she is accountable.	2.50	1.66	2.44	1.63
(17)	Intentionally misrepresent the progress of negotiations to the press or your constituency to make your own position or point of view look better.	2.49	1.75	2.55	1.84
(11)	Talk directly to the people your opponent reports to or is accountable to and tell them things that will undermine their confidence in your opponent as a negotiator.	2.22	1.49	2.14	1.47
(15)	Intentionally misrepresent factual information to your opponent to support your negotiating position.	2.11	1.49	2.29	1.61
(8)	Gain information about an opponent's negotiating position by trying to recruit or hire one of your opponents' key subordinates (on the condition that the key subordinate bring confidential information with him).	2.16	1.59	2.03	1.57

Mean correlation between individual appropriateness and likelihood ratings: .81, standard deviation = .13.

Other Factors that Create a Predisposition to Choose Unethical Tactics

Thus far, we have talked about the use of ethically questionable tactics in terms of the simple model presented in Figure 11.1. This model describes a rational calculation process in which the negotiator selects a tactic, uses the tactic, evaluates the consequences, and attempts to manage the consequences (if the tactic is detected) through explanations and justifications.

However, a number of other factors can affect the choice processes described in the model. We will briefly mention how each of these factors might influence the predisposition to use ethically questionable tactics.

Demographic Factors

Several survey-oriented research studies on ethical behavior have attempted to relate ethical conduct to differences in individual background, religious orientation, age, gender, nationality, and education. In general, women, individuals who are older, and those who are educated in parochial schools or whose professional code of ethics may be stronger (e.g., clergy) would be more likely to see certain tactics as unethical.[21]

Personality Characteristics

Researchers have sought to identify personality dimensions that would successfully predict the predisposition to behave unethically. For example, those who rate themselves as *aggressive* tend to see the tactics as more appropriate than those who rate themselves as *cooperative.* In addition, those who have a *Machiavellian* personality adhere to a very pragmatic and expedient view of human nature—i.e., "The best way to handle people is to tell them what they want to hear" or "It is hard to get ahead without cutting corners here and there." A number of researchers have shown that individuals who are strongly Machiavellian are more willing and able con artists, more likely to lie when they need to, are better able to tell bigger lies without feeling anxious about it, and are more persuasive and effective in their lies.[22] Similarly, other researchers have noted that individuals differ in their locus of control—that is, the degree to which they believe that the outcomes they obtain are largely a result of their own ability and effort (internal control) versus fate or chance (external control). Researchers have generally predicted that individuals who are high in internal control are more likely to do what they think is right (i.e., they have a stronger personal value system or ethical code), and that they had more control over producing the outcomes they wanted to achieve in a situation in which there were temptations to be less ethical.[23]

Moral Development

Individuals differ in their personal level of moral development, and this is also related to ethical decision making. The higher a stage people achieve, the more complex their moral reasoning should be and the more ethical their decisions should be. The results have indicated that higher levels of moral development are associated with more ethical decisions, less cheating behavior, more helping behavior, and more resistance to authority figures who are attempting to dictate unethical conduct.[24]

Situational Influences on Unethical Conduct

Situational factors are the last set of factors that should have an impact on a negotiator's willingness to act unethically. We will briefly examine several elements from this group.

Relationship between the Negotiator and the Other Party. Two aspects of the negotiator's relationship with the other party affect the disposition to use certain tactics: what the relationship has been like in the past and what the parties would like it to be in the future. The negotiator's past relationship will affect current behavior if the parties have been previously competitive or cooperative, are friends or enemies, feel indebted to one another, or hold grudges toward one another.[25] The more people are cooperative, are friends, and feel indebted to each other, the more ethical they will be. A second factor in the relationship that can balance this self-fulfilling dynamics is whether the negotiator expects the relationship to be short-term or long-term. Respondents who expected to be in a short-term relationship were more likely to see the ethically marginal tactics as appropriate than those expecting a long-term relationship, regardless of their own and the other party's motivations.[26]

Relative Power between the Negotiators. A second situational factor is relative power—how much power one negotiator has relative to the other party. In general, negotiators with more power are more likely to abuse that power by using less ethical tactics.[27] This result may seem paradoxical—why should negotiators with more power, who can presumably get what they want by using their power legitimately, use unethical tactics that increase their power even more? The results seem to support the "intoxication" theories of power—that power corrupts the thinking of the powerful (see Chapter 9).

Acting as an Agent versus Representing Our Own Views. As we pointed out in Chapter 7, negotiators frequently find themselves representing others' views in negotiation rather than negotiating for their own personal goals and interests. A number of authors have suggested that when we act as an agent for someone else— particularly when the goals for that agent are to get the best possible agreement—

agents may be more willing to violate personal ethical standards.[28] In essence, acting as an agent may release a person from his own personal ethical standards and code and allow him to create his own standards of legitimacy—that it is appropriate to do whatever is necessary to maximize the results for the constituent.[29]

Group and Organizational Norms and Pressures

Finally, many negotiators look to the social norms of the particular situation to decide how to behave. Norms are the informal social rules—the "do's and don'ts"—that govern social behavior. In negotiation, the rules are defined in two ways: by what people believe is appropriate in negotiation, and by what other people say is appropriate in that situation. As an example of the first case, some negotiators may define negotiation as a game, and thus they feel that "gaming rules" apply to negotiation. For example, if negotiating is a game like poker, then it is very appropriate to play negotiation as we would play poker—to bluff, fake, or bet in order to try to drive others out of the game. Is it appropriate to do these things in negotiation? Do all people agree? What happens when some people believe these tactics are appropriate and proceed to use bluffing tactics, while others don't believe they are? Recent research suggests that group and organizational norms and pressures may play a key role in legitimizing inappropriate behavior (although, again, this research has not been directly performed on negotiating situations).[30]

Summary

In this chapter, we have discussed some of the primary factors that affect how a negotiator evaluates and decides to use negotiating strategies and tactics that may be ethically marginal. We began by considering several negotiation cases, showing how they were indicative of the ways that ethical questions can be critical to the selection of particular strategic and tactical options. We then reviewed some of the primary motivational factors that lead negotiators to consider using unethical tactics: the pursuit of profit, the desire to beat the other party in a competitive environment, and the need to ensure or restore some standard of justice that may have been violated. Any of these motives may be sufficient to prompt a negotiator to move toward the use of marginally ethical and questionable behavior to accomplish his objectives.

We have included this chapter because we believe that the negotiation process raises a host of ethical issues, more so than most other interpersonal transactions. Much of what has been written on negotiating behavior has been strongly normative about ethics and has prescribed "do's and don'ts." We do not believe that this approach facilitates the understanding of how negotiators actually decide to act unethically. In contrast, we argue that this process can best be presented within a decision-making framework. We proposed that a negotiator who chooses to use an unethical tactic usually decides to do so to increase her negotiating power. Power is gained by manipulating the perceived base of accurate information in the negotiation, getting better information about an opponent's plan, or by undermining an opponent's ability to achieve his objectives. Using these tactics leads to two kinds of consequences: first, attainment of the desired goals; and second, evaluation and criticism of the tactics—by the negotiator herself, by the opponent, and by observers. As a result of the consequences and the evaluation, negotiators usually feel compelled to justify their actions—they know they have done something wrong and need to establish a good reason. The purpose of this justification is both to rationalize the action to themselves and to others and possibly to lead the negotiator to try it again in the future.

In the context of this framework, we reported the results of research designed to understand how a collection of ethically marginal tactics is perceived and judged. The results of this research indicate that although several of these tactics are less than completely honest and truthful, they are considered ethically appropriate in negotiation to achieve a negotiator's objective. However, a large number of other tactics are also considered ethically inappropriate and outside the boundaries of acceptable practice. Finally, we suggested that the decision to use ethical or unethical tactics may be influenced by factors such as differences in individual backgrounds, personality, past rewards or punishments associated with ethical or unethical actions, the anticipated relationship with the other party, and the social and cultural norms that dictate what is appropriate or inappropriate in a given environment.

End Notes

1. Missner (1980).
2. Miller and Ross (1975).
3. Businesspeople frequently defend profit and the profit motive as ethically neutral, inherently neither bad nor good. In contrast, however, many ethical philosophers and political theorists have argued that *profit* is a "six-letter dirty word." Critics of the profit motive and its tendency to make businesspeople unethical—in particular, to be dishonest—have had more evidence than they could possibly use during the last decade. To take only the financial and investment sector as an illustration, incidents of fraud, deception, malfeasance, and other illegal and unethical practices have been chronicled in the front pages of major newspapers and in such best-selling books as *Barbarians at the Gate* (Burrough and Helyar, 1990), *Liar's Poker* (Lewis, 1990), and *Den of Thieves* (Stewart, 1992).
4. Missner (1980, p. 69).
5. See Sheppard, Lewicki, and Minton (1992) for a complete discussion of justice criteria.
6. Lax and Sebenius (1986).
7. Fisher, Ury, and Patton (1991).
8. People can react to perceived injustice in a variety of ways. Among the options for redressing unfair outcomes or unfair treatment is to get back at the person, process,

or system that created the unfairness by seeking revenge, a redivision of wealth, or a restoration of what is rightfully yours. For example, employees who believe that they may have been unfairly treated by their companies may be more predisposed to pilferage, theft, work slowdowns, or other ways of getting even (Greenberg, 1990; Robinson, 1992). Although there is not much research on this type of conduct in negotiation, it seems reasonable to speculate that a negotiator who believes she was unfairly treated in a previous negotiation—because the other party lied, withheld information, or used dirty tricks—might be more willing to use the same tactics to recover lost outcomes or to save face through the current negotiation.

9. Kelley and Thibaut (1969).

10. Lewicki (1983); the scheme was also validated in research by Anton (1990).

11. These propositions have not been tested directly in negotiating situations, but they have been extensively tested in other research studies on ethical decision making. For example, research by Hegarty and Sims (1978) appears to support both of these assertions. In their study, when research participants expected to be rewarded for making an unethical decision by participating in a laboratory-simulated kickback scheme, they not only participated, but also were willing to participate again when a second opportunity arose. Moreover, when there were also strong pressures on the research subjects to compete with others, the frequency of unethical conduct increased even further.

12. See research by McCornack and Levine (1990), Miller and Vidmar (1981), Bies and Moag (1986), and Werth and Flannery (1986).

13. Although we could attempt to split linguistic hairs to make a distinction between an explanation and a justification, they are so similar and used so interchangeably that we will not attempt it. Some research has tended to focus on explanations and some has focused on justifications, and we shall simply review both here. Most of these examples were adapted from Bok (1978).

14. See Boatright (1993) for one overview of utilitarianism.

15. Yankelovich (1982).

16. See also Patterson and Kim (1991).

17. Shapiro (1991) has conducted some important research on the role these explanations and justifications play in mitigating a victim's reactions to having been deceived. Her findings indicate that the more a subject felt that the partner's explanation (for a prior deceptive behavior) was adequate to explain the deception, the less subjects expressed feelings of injustice, disapproval, punitiveness, and unforgiveness toward the partner. If subjects were mildly upset, the explanations had more impact than if the subjects were strongly upset. Explanations had the most impact when the partner stated that the deception was unintentional, less impact when the deception was altruistic, and the least impact when the deception was selfishly motivated.

18. Lewicki and Spencer (1990); Lewicki and Robinson (1996); Lewicki and Stark (1996); Robinson, Lewicki and Donahue (1996).

19. Through early 1996, more than 2,000 MBAs have been evaluated with this instrument.

20. Anton's study (1990), reported earlier, revealed a comparable scaling of negotiating tactics.

21. See studies by Hassett (June, 1981; November, 1981; 1982), Maier and Lavrakas (1976), Anton (1990), Lewicki and Robinson (1996).

22. Lewicki and Robinson (1996); Braginsky (1970); Christie and Geis (1970); Exline, Thibaut, Hickey, and Gumpert (1970); Geis and Moon (1981).

23. Research evidence from several different studies of cheating and ethical decision making has confirmed this prediction (Lefcourt, 1982; Trevino and Youngblood, 1990), although it is important to note that locus of control seems most important when individuals can also exert control over outcomes.

24. Kohlberg (1969), Gilligan (1982); see also Trevino (1986), and Trevino and Youngblood (1990) for two reviews.

25. For example, research by Gruder (1971) showed that negotiators were more likely to make more deceptive arguments, negotiate for a longer period of time, and make fewer concessions to the counterpart they previously experienced as exploitative compared to one who had been cooperative. A similar argument can be made for a negotiator's expectations about how the counterpart will behave in the present or future. If you view the other party with suspicion—as exploitative, competitive, dishonest—you can then justify a relativistic approach to strategy and claim that anticipatory self-defense legitimizes your actions. Lewicki and Spencer (1991) reported that when negotiators expected the other party to have a competitive motivational orientation, this expectation legitimized the use of more ethically marginal tactics.

26. See Lewicki and Spencer (1991) and Anton (1990).

27. For example, in one research study, Crott, Kayser, and Lamm (1980) reported that negotiators with more power bluffed more often and communicated less with their counterpart than those with less power.

28. Lax and Sebenius (1986).

29. Bowie and Freeman (1992).

30. See Carr (1968) and McDonald (1963).

12 GLOBAL NEGOTIATION

The frequency of global negotiations is increasing rapidly as people travel more frequently and farther, and as business becomes more international in scope and extent. Global negotiations have become the norm for many people and organizations rather than being an exotic activity that occurs only occasionally. Numerous books and articles, from both academic and practitioner perspectives, have been written about the complexities of negotiating across borders, be it with a person from a different country, culture, or region. Although culture has many aspects, we will use the term to refer to the shared values and beliefs of a group of people. Culture describes group-level characteristics, which may or may not be good descriptors of any given individual within the group. (For instance, countries can have more than one culture, and cultures can span national borders.) With this caveat in mind, we will use the terms *culture* and *country* loosely in this chapter to refer to negotiation across borders (legal or cultural). As we discussed in Chapters 1 and 7, negotiating is a social process that is imbedded in a much larger context. This context becomes more complex when negotiations involve more than one culture; thus, negotiation itself is a much more complicated process when it occurs across borders. Far too much has been written on this topic to summarize in one chapter.[1] Our goal is simply to highlight and discuss some of the most recent and interesting work that has been written on this topic.

It is important to recognize that this book has been written from a North American perspective, and that this cultural filter has influenced how we think about negotiation, what we consider to be important aspects of negotiation, and our advice about how to become better negotiators. This chapter will also reflect our own cultural filter, both in our choices about what we discuss and because we will use Americans as the base from which to make comparisons to other cultures. That is not to say that all Americans reflect the same culture. In fact, there is evidence that people from countries as similar as the United States and Canada negotiate differently,[2] and that within the United States and Canada, there are systematic regional and cultural differences—for example, English and French Canada; Hispanics, African-Americans, the South, the Southwest, and other areas and populations in the United States. At some level, however, Americans do share a (more or less) common culture that is different from other cultures and countries. While recognizing the differences within America, we will use the common aspects of American culture to discuss the effects of culture on negotiating with people from other countries and cultures.

This chapter is organized as follows. First we will present the results of a program of research that has demonstrated that negotiators in different countries use different negotiation processes to reach the same negotiation outcomes. Then we will discuss some of the factors that make negotiations across borders more difficult, including political, economic, legal, and cultural considerations. We will then turn to a discussion of perhaps the most critical issue that negotiators face when they negotiate across borders: the effect of culture, be it national, regional, or organizational. We will discuss how culture can be conceptualized in cross-border negotiations, how academics and practitioners use the concept of culture, and how culture can influence negotiations. The chapter concludes with a discussion of the options available to the global negotiator for managing these negotiations. Throughout the chapter you will find boxed-text examples of factors to think about when negotiating in other cultures.[3]

Not Everyone Negotiates like Americans!

John Graham and his colleagues have conducted a series of experiments comparing negotiators from the United States and 15 other countries, including Japan, China, Canada, Brazil, and Mexico.[4] These studies each used the same research materials—a version of the buyer/seller negotiation simulation developed by Kelley, in which negotiators have to decide on the prices of three products (televisions, typewriters, and air conditioners).[5] The participants in the studies were businesspeople who were either attending management seminars or graduate business courses. Participants in all these studies negotiated with people from their own countries (these were intracultural negotiations, not cross-cultural negotiations). The major dependent measures in these studies were (1) the individual profit level made by the two negotiators in the simulation and (2) the level of satisfaction that the negotiators had with the negotiation outcomes.

The results of this research have been quite consistent across studies. Graham and his colleagues found no differences in the profit levels obtained by negotiators in the simulation from the United States and the other countries studied, including: Japan,[6] China,[7] Canada,[8] Brazil,[9] and Mexico.[10] Taken as a whole, these results suggest that negotiators from the different countries studied were equally effective in obtaining negotiation outcomes. One conclusion from this research, then, is that business negotiators from different countries appear to obtain similar negotiation outcomes when they negotiate with other people from their own country.

Graham and Adler did find, however, that there were significant differences in the negotiation *process* in the countries that they studied. In other words, although negotiators from different countries obtained the same outcome, *the way that they negotiated* to obtain that outcome was quite different. For instance, Graham concludes that "in American negotiations, higher profits are achieved by making opponents feel *un*comfortable, while in Japanese negotiations, higher profits are associated with making opponents feel comfortable."[11] In addition, Graham reports that Brazilian negotiators who used powerful and deceptive strategies were more likely to receive higher outcomes; these strategies were not related to the outcomes attained by the American negotiators.[12] Further, Adler, Graham, and Schwartz report that representational strategies (gathering information) were negatively related to profits attained by Mexican and French-Canadian negotiators, whereas these strategies were unrelated to the profits that American negotiators received.[13] Finally, although Adler, Brahm, and Graham found that Chinese and American negotiators used similar negotiation strategies when they negotiated, their communication patterns were quite different—the Chinese asked more questions, said no less frequently, and interrupted each other more frequently than did American negotiators.[14]

Adler and Graham also conducted a study in which they compared intracultural and cross-cultural negotiation outcomes and processes.[15] They found that Japanese and English-Canadian negotiators received lower profit levels when they negotiated cross-culturally than when they negotiated intraculturally; American and French-Canadian negotiators negotiated the same average outcomes in cross-cultural and intracultural negotiations. These results support Adler and Graham's hypothesis that cross-cultural negotiations will result in poorer outcomes, at least some of the time. In addition, Adler and Graham found some differences in the cross-cultural negotiation process. For instance, French-Canadian negotiators used more cooperative strategies in cross-cultural negotiations than in intracultural negotiations, and American negotiators reported higher levels of satisfaction with their cross-cultural negotiations (versus intracultural negotiations).

In summary, this program of research suggests that negotiators from different cultures (countries) use different negotiation strategies and communication patterns when they negotiate with other people from their own culture. Importantly, however, there was *no* difference in the negotiation outcomes attained by the negotiators across these studies. This suggests that there are many different ways to negotiate agreements that are, on average, worth the same value, and that a negotiator must employ the process that fits the culture they are in. Further, the culture of the negotiator appears to be an important predictor of the negotiation process that will occur and of how negotiation strategies will influence negotiation outcomes in different cultures. In addition, this research suggests that cross-cultural negotiations may yield poorer outcomes than intracultural negotiations, at least on some occasions.

What Makes Cross-Border Negotiations Different?

Jeswald Salacuse has suggested six factors that make cross-border negotiations more challenging than domestic negotiations.[16] These factors can act to limit or constrain organizations that operate in the international arena, and it is important that negotiators who bargain across borders understand and appreciate their effects.

Political and Legal Pluralism

When organizations make business deals that cross a national border, they come into contact with the legal and political system of another country. There may be implications for the taxes that the organization pays, the labor codes or standards that they must meet, and for the different codes of contract law and standards of enforcement (e.g., case law versus common law versus no functioning legal system). In addition, political considerations may enhance or detract from the conduct of business negotiations in various countries at different times (compare the open business environment in the former Soviet bloc in the 1990s with the closed environment of the 1960s).

International Economic Factors

The values of international currencies fluctuate, and this factor must be considered when making deals across borders. Which currencies will the deal be made in? According to Salacuse, the risk is greater, typically, for the party who must pay in the other country's currency. The less stable the currency, the greater the risk for both parties. In addition, any change in the value of a currency (upwards or downwards) can significantly affect the value of the deal for both parties, changing a mutually valuable deal into a windfall profit for one and a large loss for the other. Many countries also control the currency flowing across their borders. Frequently, purchases within these countries may be made only with hard currencies that are brought into the country by foreign parties, and domestic organizations are unable to purchase foreign products or negotiate outcomes that require payment in foreign currencies.

Foreign Governments and Bureaucracies

Countries differ in the extent to which the government regulates industries and organizations. Organizations in the United States are relatively free from government intervention, although some industries are more heavily regulated (e.g., power generation, defense) and some states have tougher environmental regulations than others. Generally, however, business negotiations in the United States occur without government approval, and the parties to a negotiation decide whether to engage in a deal based on business reasons alone. Contrast this with the situation in many developing and (former) communist countries. Imports into these countries are closely supervised by the government, and frequently an agency of the government has a monopoly in dealing with foreign organizations.[17] In addition, political considerations, such as the effect of the negotiations on the government treasury, the general economy of the country, and other social conditions, may influence the negotiations more heavily than what Western businesspeople would consider to be legitimate business reasons.

Instability

Although the world continues to change at a rapid pace, businesspeople negotiating domestically in the United States are accustomed to a degree of stability that has not been present in many areas of the world. Instability may take many forms, including a lack of resources that Americans commonly expect during business negotiations (paper, electricity, computers), shortages of personal-care products (food, reliable transportation, potable water), and political instability (coups, sudden shifts in government policy, major currency revaluations). The challenge for negotiators in these situations is to predict these changes accurately, and with enough lead time to adjust for their consequences if they occur. Salacuse suggests that negotiators faced with unstable circumstances should include clauses in their contracts that allow for easy cancellation or neutral arbitration, and they should investigate purchasing insurance policies to guarantee contract provisions. This advice presumes that contracts will be honored and that specific contract clauses like these are culturally acceptable to the other party.

Ideology

Negotiators within the United States generally share a common ideology of individualism and capitalism. According to Salacuse, this includes a strong belief in individual rights, the superiority of private investment, and the importance of making a profit in business. Negotiators from other countries do not always share this ideology. The ideology in many other countries stresses group rights as more important than individual rights and public investment as a better allocation of resources than private investment, and it has different prescriptions for earning and sharing profit. Clashing ideologies increase the communication challenges in cross-border negotiations in the broadest sense, because the parties may disagree on the most fundamental levels about what is being negotiated.

Culture

People from different cultures appear to negotiate differently. In addition to behavioral differences in negotiation across borders, different cultures may also interpret the fundamental processes of negotiations differently (such as what factors are negotiable and the purpose of the negotiations). According to Salacuse, people in some cultures approach negotiations deductively (they move from the general to the specific) whereas people from other cultures are more inductive (they settle on a series of specific issues that become the area of general agreement). On a more fundamental level, cultures appear to differ on what is actually being negotiated. In some cultures, negotiation occurs over the content of what is discussed, and the relationship between the parties is incidental. In other cultures, the relationship between the parties is the main focus of the negotiation, and the content of the deal itself is incidental. One does not have to leave the United States to see the influence of culture on negotiations. Contrast the negotiation described in Box 12.1 with the stereotypical business negotiator from Wall Street. Clearly there is a large challenge negotiating across borders when the fundamental beliefs about what negotiation is and how it occurs can be very different. We will spend most of the remainder of this chapter exploring different aspects of this issue in more detail.

Hofstede's Dimensions Of Culture

The most frequently mentioned construct invoked to explain differences in negotiation across borders is culture. Although the term *culture* has taken on many different meanings, we use it, again, to refer to the shared values and beliefs held by the members of a group. Cultures are considered to be stable over time. Perhaps the most comprehensive and extensive program of research identifying and exploring different cultural dimensions in international business was conducted by Geert Hofstede.[18] Hofstede examined data on values that had been gathered from over 100,000 IBM employees from around the world (to date, over 53 cultures and countries have been included in his study). Statistical analysis of this data suggests that four dimensions could describe the important differences among the cultures in the study. Table 12.1 lists the countries included in the study and their ranking on the four dimensions.

Power Distance

This dimension describes "the extent to which the less powerful members of organizations and institutions (like the family) accept and expect that power is distributed unequally."[19] According to Hofstede, cultures with greater power distance will be more likely to have decision making concentrated at the top, and all of the important decisions will have to be finalized by the leader. The consequences for international negotiations are that negotiators from large-power-distance cultures may need to seek approval from their supervisors more frequently, and for more issues, leading to a slower negotiation process.

Individualism/Collectivism

This dimension describes the extent to which the society is organized around individuals or the group. Individualistic societies encourage their young to be

---

Box 12.1

Cross-Cultural Negotiations within the United States

I had a client in West Virginia who bought from me for several years. He had a family business that he'd started in a small town with his grandfather, and it had now grown to be the major employer in the town. We had developed quite a close relationship. Every few months, I would make a trip up from North Carolina to see him, knowing after a while that he would need to place an order with me as long as I spaced our visits out every few months. When we got together, at first we would talk about everything but business, catching up with each other. I would ask him about his life, the business, his family, the town, and so on, and he would ask me about my work and the company and life in the big city in North Carolina where I lived and worked. Once we'd caught up with each other, we would get down to some business, and this was often after lunch. Each and every time, it would take a few hours of this and that, but I'd always leave with an order, and it was always a pleasant break, at least for me, from my usual hectic pace.

One day I phoned in preparation for my next trip, to see if he would be in, to arrange a convenient day, and he told me that he'd like me to meet a friend of his next time I was up there to visit him. His friend, he said, was interested in some of the things my company was selling, and he thought I should meet him. Of course I was delighted, and we arranged a convenient day for the three of us to meet.

When I arrived at my client's office, his friend, Carl, was already there. We were very casually introduced, and my client began explaining Carl's work, and how he thought what my company sold could be useful to him. Carl then took over and spoke a little about what he did, and I thought for a moment that we were going to go straight into business talk. However, in just a few moments, the conversation between the three of us quickly turned back to discussions of life in town, North Carolina, our respective families, and personal interests. It turned out that Carl liked to hunt, and he and my client began regaling me with stories of their hunting adventures. I'd hunted a little, and shared my stories with them. One thing led to another, and soon we were talking about vacations, the economy, baseball—you name it.

Occasionally, we would make a brief journey back to the business at hand, but it always seemed to be in conjunction with the small talk, like how the tools we manufactured were or were not as precise as the mechanisms on the guns we used for hunting, things like that. I realized that quite a lot of information, about our mutual work, my company, their needs, and their work, was being exchanged in all this, even though business was never directly addressed. I remember the first few meetings my client and I had had with each other many years ago—how we learned about each other this way then, too. I was struck with how quaint it felt now, how different it was from the way I usually had to sell, and yet how much I enjoyed working like this!

Continued on page 240

Concluded from page 239

Well, our discussions went on this way through the rest of the morning, weaving some business back and forth through the larger context of informal chit-chat about each other and our lives. Just before lunch, my client leaned back and began what seemed to be a kind of informal summary of who I was and what I did, and how what I did seemed to him to be just the thing that Carl and his company could use. Carl agreed, and my client asked him, almost on my behalf, how much he wanted to order, and Carl thought for a moment and gave me the biggest order I ever got from West Virginia. "Now that that's done," my client said, "how about some lunch?" We all went to the same place we always go to when I'm in West Virginia, talking about life and things and some business. By midafternoon I said I had to be heading home. We all agreed to stay in touch. We've been in touch ever since, and now I've got two clients to visit whenever I'm in West Virginia.

Source: D. A. Foster, *Bargaining across Borders: How to Negotiate Business Successfully Anywhere in the World* (New York: McGraw-Hill, 1992), pp. 108–9. Reproduced with the permission of McGraw-Hill.

---

independent and to look after themselves. Collectivistic cultures, on the other hand, integrate individuals into very cohesive groups that take responsibility for the welfare of each individual. Hofstede suggests that the focus on relationships in collectivist societies plays a critical role in negotiations—negotiations with the same party can continue for years, and changing a negotiator changes the relationship, which may take a long time to rebuild. Contrast this with more individualistic societies, in which negotiators are considered more interchangeable, and competency, rather than relationship, is a more important consideration when choosing negotiators. The consequences are that negotiators from collectivist cultures will strongly depend on cultivating and sustaining a long-term relationship, whereas negotiators from individualistic cultures may be more likely to "swap" negotiators, using whatever short-term criteria seem appropriate.

Masculinity/Femininity

Hofstede found that cultures differed in the extent to which they held values that were traditionally perceived as masculine, such as "assertiveness, the acquisition of money and things, and *not* caring for others, the quality of life, or people."[20] According to Hofstede, this dimension influences negotiating by increasing the competitiveness when negotiators from masculine cultures meet; negotiators from feminine cultures are more likely to have empathy for the other party and to seek compromise.[21]

TABLE 12.1   **Ranking of Countries/Cultures on Cultural Dimensions Reported by Hofstede (1991)**

	Rank Order On			
Country	*Power Distance*	*Individualism/ Collectivism*	*Masculinity/ Femininity*	*Uncertainty Avoidance*
Arab Countries	7	26/27	23	27
Argentina	35/36	22/23	20/21	10/15
Australia	41	2	16	37
Austria	53	18	2	24/25
Belgium	20	8	22	5/6
Brazil	14	26/27	27	21/22
Canada	39	4/5	24	41/42
Chile	24/25	38	46	10/15
Columbia	17	49	11/12	20
Costa Rica	42/44	46	48/49	10/15
Denmark	51	9	50	51
East Africa	21/23	33/35	39	36
Ecuador	8/9	52	13/14	28
Finland	46	17	47	31/32
France	15/16	10/11	35/36	10/15
Germany	42/44	15	9/10	29
Great Britain	42/44	3	9/10	47/48
Greece	27/28	30	18/19	1
Guatemala	2/3	53	43	3
Hong Kong	15/16	37	18/19	49/50
India	10/11	21	20/21	45
Indonesia	8/9	47/48	30/31	41/42
Iran	29/30	24	35/36	31/32
Ireland (Rep.)	49	12	7/8	47/48
Israel	52	19	29	19
Italy	34	7	4/5	23
Jamaica	37	25	7/8	52
Japan	33	22/23	1	7
Malaysia	1	36	25/26	46
Mexico	5/6	32	6	18
Netherlands	40	4/5	51	35
New Zealand	50	6	17	39/40
Norway	47/48	13	52	38
Pakistan	32	47/48	25/26	24/25
Panama	2/3	51	34	10/15
Peru	21/23	45	37/38	9
Philippines	4	31	11/12	44
Portugal	24/25	33/35	45	2
Salvador	18/19	42	40	5/6
Singapore	13	39/41	28	53
South Africa	35/36	16	13/14	39/40
South Korea	27/28	43	41	16/17
Spain	31	20	37/38	10/15

TABLE 12.1 **Ranking of Countries/Cultures on Cultural Dimensions Reported by Hofstede (1991)** *(concluded)*

	Rank Order On			
Country	*Power Distance*	*Individualism/ Collectivism*	*Masculinity/ Femininity*	*Uncertainty Avoidance*
Sweden	47/48	10/11	53	49/50
Switzerland	45	14	4/5	33
Taiwan	29/30	44	32/33	26
Thailand	21/23	39/41	44	30
Turkey	18/19	28	32/33	16/17
Uruguay	26	29	42	4
United States	38	1	15	43
Venezuela	5/6	50	3	21/22
West Africa	10/11	39/41	30/31	34
Yugoslavia	12	33/35	48/49	8

Based on G. Hofstede, *Culture and Organizations: Software of the Mind* (London, England: McGraw Hill, 1991).

Uncertainty Avoidance

The fourth dimension identified by Hofstede "indicates to what extent a culture programs its members to feel either uncomfortable or comfortable in unstructured situations."[22] Unstructured situations are characterized by rapid change and novelty, whereas structured situations are stable, secure, and more absolute. Negotiators from uncertainty-avoidance cultures are uncomfortable with ambiguous situations and are more likely to seek stable rules and procedures when they negotiate. Negotiators from cultures more comfortable with unstructured situations are more likely to adapt to quickly changing situations and will be less uncomfortable when the rules of the negotiation are ambiguous or shifting.

Hofstede's dimensions have received a great deal of attention in cross-cultural research and international business. Although the model is not without criticism, it is fair to say that it has become a dominating force in cross-cultural research in international business.[23] Little research exploring the effects of Hofstede's dimensions on negotiation has been conducted, however, and the extent to which these dimensions influence cross-cultural and intracultural negotiations needs to be further explored.[24] At this point in time, our interpretations of the effects of these dimensions on negotiations should be considered tentative.

How Do Cultural Differences Influence Negotiations?

Given that these cultural differences exist, can be measured, and operate on different levels, the issue becomes how they influence negotiations. Adopting work by Weiss and Stripp, Foster suggests that culture can influence negotiations across borders in at least eight different ways.[25]

1. Definition of Negotiation. The fundamental definition of what negotiation is or of what occurs when we negotiate can differ greatly across cultures. For instance, "Americans tend to view negotiating as a competitive process of offers and counteroffers, while the Japanese tend to view the negotiation as an opportunity for information sharing."[26]

2. Selection of Negotiators. The criteria used to select who will participate in the negotiations varies across cultures. These criteria can include knowledge of the subject matter being negotiated, seniority, family connections, gender, age, experience, and status. Different cultures weigh these criteria differently, leading to varying expectations about what is appropriate in different types of negotiations.

3. Protocol. Cultures differ in the degree to which protocol, or the formality of the relations between the two negotiating parties, is important. American culture is among the least formal cultures in the world. The use of first names, ignoring titles, and a generally familiar communication style are quite common. Contrast this with the situation in other cultures. Many European countries (e.g., France, Germany, England) are very formal, and not using the proper title when addressing someone (e.g., Mr., Dr., Professor, Lord) is considered highly insulting.[27] Formal calling cards or business cards are always used in many countries in the Pacific Rim (e.g., China, Japan), and they are essential for introductions there. Negotiators who forget to bring business cards or who write messages on them are often considered to be breaching protocol and insulting their counterpart.[28] Even the way that business cards are presented, hands are shaken, or people dress are subject to interpretation by negotiators and can be the foundation of attributions about a person's background and personality.

4. Communication. Cultures influence the way that people communicate, both verbally and nonverbally. There are also differences in body language across cultures; the same behavior may be highly insulting in one culture and completely innocuous in another.[29] To avoid insulting the other party in negotiations across borders, the international negotiator needs to observe cultural rules of communication carefully. For example, the truly international negotiator needs to heed the advice in Box 12.2. Clearly, an international negotiator must remember a lot of information about how to communicate in order to avoid insulting, angering, or embarrassing the other party during negotiations. Many culture-specific books and articles have been written. These provide considerable advice to international negotiators about how to communicate in various cultures, and becoming familiar with such works is an essential aspect of planning for negotiations that cross borders.[30]

5. Time. Cultures have a large effect on defining what time means and how it affects negotiations. In the United States, people tend to respect time. This is shown by appearing for meetings on time, being sensitive to not wasting the time of other people, and a general belief that faster is better than slower because it symbolizes high productivity. Other cultures have quite different views about time. In more traditional societies, especially in hot climates, the pace is slower than in the United States. This tends to reduce the focus on time, at least in the short term. Americans are perceived by other cultures as enslaved by their clocks, because time is watched carefully and guarded as a valuable resource. In some cultures, such as China and Latin America, time per se is not important. The focus of negotiations is on the task, regardless of the amount of time that it takes. The opportunity for misunderstandings because of different perceptions of time is great during cross-cultural negotiations. Americans may be perceived as always being in a hurry and as flitting from one task to another. Chinese or Latin American negotiators, on the other hand, may appear to the American to be doing nothing and wasting the American's time.

6. Risk Propensity. Cultures vary in the extent to which they are willing to take risks. Some cultures produce quite bureaucratic, conservative decision makers who want a great deal of information before making decisions. Other cultures produce negotiators who are more entrepreneurial and who are willing to act and take risks when they have incomplete information (e.g., "Nothing ventured, nothing gained"). According to Foster, Americans fall on the risk-taking end of the continuum, some Asians may be even more risk oriented, and some European cultures are quite conservative (such as Greece). The orientation of a culture toward risk will have a large effect on what is negotiated and on the content of the negotiated outcome. Risk-oriented cultures will be more willing to move early on a deal and will generally take more chances. Risk-avoiding cultures will seek further information and will be more likely to take a wait-and-see stance.

7. Groups versus Individuals. Cultures differ according to whether they emphasize the individual or the group. The United States is very much an individual-oriented culture, where being independent and assertive is valued and praised. Group-oriented cultures, on the other hand, favor the superiority of the group, and the individual comes second to the group's needs. Group-oriented cultures value fitting in, and reward loyal team players; those who dare to be different are socially ostracized, a large price to pay in a group-oriented society. This cultural difference can have a variety of effects on negotiation. Americans are more likely to have one individual who is responsible for the final decision, whereas group-oriented cultures like the Chinese are more likely to have a group responsible for the decision. Decision making in the group-oriented cultures involves consensus making and may take considerably more time than American negotiators are used to. In addition, because so many people can be involved in the negotiations in group-oriented cultures, and because their participation may be sequential rather than simultaneous, American negotiators may be faced with a series of discussions over the same issues and materials with many different people. In a negotiation in China, one of the authors of this book met with more than six different people on successive days, going over the same ground with different negotiators and interpreters, until the negotiation was concluded.

Box 12.2

Example Communication Rules for Global Negotiators

Never touch a Malay on the top of the head, for that is where the soul resides. Never show the sole of your shoe to an Arab, for it is dirty and represents the bottom of the body, and never use your left hand in Muslim culture, for it is reserved for physical hygiene. Touch the side of your nose in Italy and it is a sign of distrust. Always look directly and intently into your French associate's eye when making an important point. Direct eye contact in Southeast Asia, however, should be avoided until the relationship is firmly established. If your Japanese associate has just sucked air in deeply through his teeth, that's a sign you've got real problems. Your Mexican associate will want to embrace you at the end of a long and successful negotiation; so will your Central and Eastern European associates, who may give you a bear hug *and* kiss you three times on alternating cheeks. Americans often stand farther apart than their Latin and Arab associates but closer than their Asian associates. In the United States people shake hands forcefully and enduringly; in Europe a handshake is usually quick and to the point; in Asia, it is often rather limp. Laughter and giggling in the West Indies indicates humor; in Asia, it more often indicates embarrassment and humility. Additionally, the public expression of deep emotion is considered ill-mannered in most countries of the Pacific Rim; there is an extreme separation between one's personal and public selves. The withholding of emotion in Latin America, however, is often cause for mistrust.

Source: D. A. Foster, *Bargaining across Borders: How to Negotiate Business Successfully Anywhere in the World* (New York: McGraw-Hill, 1992, p. 281). Reproduced with the permission of McGraw-Hill.

---

8. Nature of Agreements. Culture also has an important effect both on concluding agreements and on what form the negotiated agreement takes. In the United States, typically, agreements are based on logic (e.g., the low-cost producer gets the deal), are often formalized, and are enforced through the legal system if such standards are not honored. In other cultures, however, obtaining the deal may be based on who you are (e.g., your family or political connections) rather than on what you can do. In addition, agreements do not mean the same thing in all cultures. Foster notes that the Chinese frequently use memorandums of agreement to formalize a relationship and to signal the *start* of negotiations (mutual favors and compromise). Frequently, however, Americans will interpret the *same* memorandum of agreement as the *completion* of the negotiations that is enforceable in a court of law. Again, cultural differences in how to close an agreement and in what exactly that agreement means can lead to confusion and misunderstandings when we negotiate across borders.

In summary, a great deal has been written about the importance of culture in cross-border negotiations. Hofstede suggests that four important dimensions can be used to describe cultural differences: power distance, individualism/collectivism, masculinity/femininity, and uncertainty avoidance. Academics and practitioners may use the term *culture* to mean different things, but they agree that it is a critical aspect of international negotiation that can have a broad influence on many aspects of the process and outcome of negotiations across borders.

Culturally Responsive Negotiation Strategies

Although a great deal has been written about international negotiation and the extra challenges that occur when negotiating across borders, cultures, or nationalities, far less attention has been paid to what the individual negotiator should specifically *do* when negotiating with someone from another culture. The advice given by many theorists in this area, either explicitly or implicitly, has been, "when in Rome, do as the Romans do."[31] In other words, negotiators are advised to be aware of the effects of cultural differences on negotiation and to take them into account when they negotiate. Much of the material discussed in this chapter reflects this tendency. Many theorists appear to assume implicitly that the best way to manage cross-border negotiations is to be sensitive to the cultural norms of the person with whom you are negotiating and to modify your strategy to be consistent with behaviors that occur in that culture (contrast this with the less culturally sensitive views that "business is business everywhere in the world" and that the other party can adapt to "my style of negotiating," that style is unimportant, or, more arrogantly, that "my style" should dictate what the other does). Although it is important to avoid cultural gaffes when negotiating, it is *not* clear that the best approach is to modify your strategy to match the other person's approach.

Several factors indicate that negotiators should *not* make large modifications to their approach when they negotiate across borders.

1. Negotiators may not be able to modify their approach *effectively*. It takes years to understand another culture deeply, and you may not have the time necessary to gain this understanding before beginning negotiations. Although a little understanding of another culture is clearly better than total ignorance, it may not be enough to make effective adjustments to your negotiation strategy. Attempting to match the strategies and tactics used by negotiators in another culture is a daunting task that requires fluency in their language as a precondition.

2. Even if negotiators can modify their approach effectively, it does not mean that this will translate automatically into a better negotiation outcome for their side. It is quite possible that the other side will modify their approach too. The results in this situation can be disaster, with each side trying to act like the other "should" be acting, and both sides not really understanding what the other party is doing. Consider the following example contrasting typical American and

Japanese negotiation styles (also see Box 12.3). Americans are more likely to start negotiations with an extreme offer in order to leave room for concessions. Japanese are more likely to start negotiations with gathering information in order to understand the party whom they are dealing with and what the relationship will be. Assume that both parties understand their own and the other party's cultural tendencies (this is a large assumption that frequently is not met). Now assume that each party, acting out of respect for the other, decides to "do as the Romans do" and to adopt the approach of the other party. The possibilities for confusion are endless. When the Americans gather information about the Japanese, are they truly interested or are they playing a role? It will be clear that they are not acting like Americans, but the strategy that they are using may not be readily identified. How will the Americans interpret the Japanese behavior? The Americans have prepared well for their negotiations and understand that the Japanese do not present extreme positions early in negotiations. When the Japanese *do* present an extreme position early in negotiations (in order to adapt to the American negotiation style), how should the Americans interpret this behavior? The Americans likely will think "that must be what they *really* want because they don't usually open with extreme offers." Adopting the other party's approach does not guarantee success, and in fact may lead to more confusion than acting like yourself (where at least your behavior is understood within your own cultural context).

3. Research suggests that when they are with people from their own culture, negotiators may naturally negotiate differently from the way they do when they are with people from other cultures.[32] The implications of this research are that a deep understanding of how people in other cultures negotiate, such as two Japanese people negotiating with each other, may not help an American negotiating with a Japanese.

4. Research by Francis suggests that moderate adaptation may be more effective than "doing as the Romans do."[33] In a simulation study of Americans' responses to negotiators from other countries, Francis found that negotiators from a familiar culture (Japan) who made moderate adaptations to American ways were perceived more positively than negotiators who made no changes or those that made large adaptations. Although these findings did not replicate for negotiators from a less-familiar culture (Korea), more research needs to be conducted to understand why. At the very least, the results of this study suggest that large adaptations by international negotiators will not always be effective.

Recent theoretical work by Stephen Weiss has advanced our understanding of the options that people have when negotiating with someone from another culture.[34] Weiss observes that a negotiator may be able to choose among up to eight different culturally responsive strategies. These strategies may be used individually or sequentially, and the strategies can be switched as the negotiations progress. According to Weiss, when choosing a strategy, the negotiators should be aware of their own and the other party's culture in general, understand the specific factors in the current relationship, and predict or try to influence the other

Box 12.3

A Simple "Hai" Won't Do

When a TV announcer here reported Bill Clinton's comment to Boris Yeltsin that when the Japanese say yes they often mean no, he gave the news with an expression of mild disbelief.

Having spent my life between East and West, I can sympathize with those who find the Japanese yes unfathomable. However, the fact that it sometimes fails to correspond precisely with the Occidental yes does not necessarily signal intended deception. This was probably why the announcer looked bewildered, and it marks a cultural gap that can have serious repercussions.

I once knew an American who worked in Tokyo. He was a very nice man, but he suffered a nervous breakdown and went back to the United States tearing his hair and exclaiming, "All Japanese businessmen are liars." I hope this is not true. If it were, all Japanese businessmen would be driving each other mad, which does not seem to be the case. Nevertheless, since tragedies often arise from misunderstandings, an attempt at some explanation might not be amiss.

A Japanese yes in its primary context simply means the other person has heard you and is contemplating a reply. This is because it would be rude to keep someone waiting for an answer without supplying him with an immediate response.

For example: A feudal warlord marries his sister to another warlord. (I am back to TV.) Then he decides to destroy his newly acquired brother-in-law and besieges the castle. Being human, though, the attacking warlord worries about his sister and sends a spy to look around. The spy returns and the lord inquires eagerly, "Well, is she safe?" The spy bows and answers, "*Hai*," which means yes. We sigh with relief, thinking, "Ah, the fair lady is still alive!" But then the spy continues, "To my regret she has fallen on her sword together with her husband."

Hai is also an expression of our willingness to comply with your intent even if your request is worded in the negative. This can cause complications. When I was at school, our English teacher, a British nun, would say, "Now children, you won't forget to do your homework, will you?" And we would all dutifully chorus, "Yes, mother," much to her consternation.

A variation of hai may mean, "I understand your wish and would like to make you happy but unfortunately . . ." Japanese being a language of implication, the latter part of this estimable thought is often left unsaid.

Is there, then, a Japanese yes that corresponds to the Western one? I think so, particularly when it is accompanied by phrases such as "*sodesu*" (it is so) and "*soshimasu*" (I will do so).

A word of caution against the statement "I will think about it." Though in Tokyo this can mean a willingness to give one's proposal serious thought, in Osaka, another business center, it means a definite no. This attitude probably stems from the belief that a straightforward no would sound too brusque.

When talking to a Japanese person, it is perhaps best to remember that although he may be speaking English, he is reasoning in Japanese. And if he says, "I will think about it," you should inquire as to which district of Japan he hails from before going on with your negotiations.

party's approach. Weiss's culturally responsive strategies may be arranged into three groups, based on the familiarity that a negotiator has with the other party's culture. Within each group there are some strategies that the negotiator may use individually (unilateral strategies) and others that involve the participation of the other party (joint strategies).

Low Familiarity with the Other's Culture

1. Employ Agents or Advisors. (Unilateral strategy.) One approach for negotiators who have very low familiarity with the other party's culture is to hire an agent or advisor who is familiar with the cultures of both parties. This relationship may range from having the other party conduct the negotiations under your supervision (agent) to receiving regular or occasional advice during the negotiations (advisor). Although using an agent or advisor may create other problems (such as tensions between that person and yourself), they may be quite useful for negotiators who have little awareness of the other's culture and little time to become aware.

2. Bring in a Mediator. (Joint strategy.) Many types of mediators may be used in cross-cultural negotiations, ranging from someone who conducts introductions and then withdraws, to someone who is present throughout the negotiation and takes responsibility for orchestrating the negotiation process.[35] Interpreters will often play this role, providing both parties with more information than the mere translation of words during negotiations. Mediators may encourage one side or the other to adopt one of the culture's approaches or a third cultural approach (the mediator's home culture).

3. Induce the Other Party to Use Your Approach. (Joint strategy.) The third option available to you as a negotiator with low familiarity with the other party's culture is to persuade the other party to use your approach. There are many ways to do this, ranging from a polite request to asserting rudely that your way is best. It can also be done with more subtlety by continuing to respond in your own language to their requests because you "cannot express yourself well enough in their language." Although this strategy has many advantages for you (the negotiator with low familiarity), there are also some disadvantages. For instance, the other party may become irritated or insulted at having to make the extra effort to deal with you on your own cultural terms. In addition, the other party may also have a strategic advantage because she may now attempt more extreme tactics, and if they don't work, excuse them on the basis of "cultural ignorance" (after all, one can't expect *them* to understand everything about how one conducts business).

Moderate Familiarity with the Other's Culture

4. Adapt to the Other Party's Approach. (Unilateral strategy.) This strategy involves making conscious changes to your approach so that it is more appealing to the other party. Rather than trying to act like the other party, negotiators using this strategy maintain a firm grasp on their own approach but make modifications to help relations with the other person. These modifications may include acting in a less-extreme manner, eliminating some behaviors, and including some of the other party's behaviors. The challenge in using this strategy is to know which behaviors to modify, eliminate, or adopt. In addition, it is not clear that the other party will interpret your modifications in the way that you have intended.

   5. Coordinate Adjustment. (Joint strategy.) This strategy involves both parties' making mutual adjustments to find a common process for negotiation. Although this can be done implicitly, it is more likely to occur explicitly ("How would you like to proceed?"), and it can be thought of as a special instance of negotiating the *process* of negotiation. This strategy requires a moderate amount of knowledge about the other party's culture and at least some facility with their language (comprehension of their language, if not the ability to speak). Coordinate adjustment occurs on a daily basis in Montreal, the most bilingual city in North America (85 percent of Montrealers understand both English and French). It is standard practice for business people in Montreal to negotiate the process of negotiation before the substantive discussion begins. The outcomes of this discussion are variations on the theme of whether the negotiations will occur in English or French, with a typical outcome being that either party may speak either language. Negotiations often occur in both languages, and frequently the person with the superior second-language skills will switch languages to facilitate the discussion. Another outcome that occasionally occurs has both parties speaking in their second language (i.e., the French speaker will negotiate in English while the English speaker will negotiate in French) to demonstrate respect for the other party. Another type of coordinating adjustment occurs when the two negotiating parties adopt aspects of a third culture to facilitate their negotiations. For instance, during a recent trip to Latin America, one of the authors of this book conducted discussions in French with a Latin American colleague who spoke Spanish and French, but not English. On a subsequent trip to China, negotiations were conducted in French, English, and Chinese where each of the six participants spoke two of the three languages.

High Familiarity with the Other's Culture

   6. Embrace the Other Party's Approach. (Unilateral strategy.) This strategy involves adopting completely the approach of the other party. To be used successfully, the negotiator needs to be completely bilingual and bicultural. In essence, the negotiator using this strategy doesn't "do as the Romans do," he or she *is* "a Roman." This is a costly strategy to use (in preparation time and expense) and places the negotiator using it under considerable stress (it is difficult to switch back and forth rapidly between cultures). On the other hand, there is much to gain by using this strategy because the other party can be approached and understood completely on their own terms.

7. Improvise an Approach. (Joint strategy.) This strategy involves crafting an approach that is specifically tailored to the negotiation situation, other party, and circumstances. Both parties to the negotiation need to have high familiarity with the other party's culture and a strong understanding of the individual characteristics of the other party to use this approach. The negotiation that emerges with this approach can be crafted with aspects from both cultures, and adopted when they will be useful. This approach is the most flexible of the eight strategies, which is both its strength and weakness. Flexibility is a strength because it allows the approach to be crafted to the circumstances at hand, but it is a weakness because there are few general prescriptive statements that can be made about how to use this strategy.

8. Effect Symphony. (Joint strategy.) This strategy works to "transcend exclusive use of either home culture" by the negotiation parties and instead has them create a new approach that may include aspects of either home culture or adopt practices from a third culture.[36] Professional diplomats use such an approach when the customs, norms, and language that they use transcend national borders and form their own culture (diplomacy). Use of this strategy is complex and involves a great deal of time and effort. It works best when the parties are very familiar with each other, familiar with both home cultures, and have a common structure (like that of professional diplomats) for the negotiation. Risks of using this strategy include costs due to confusion, time lost, and the overall effort required to make it work.

Summary

This chapter has examined various aspects of a growing field of negotiations that explores the complexities of negotiating across borders. We began the chapter with a discussion of a research program by John Graham and his colleagues that compared American negotiators with negotiators from 15 other countries. Graham and his colleagues found that regardless of where negotiators were from, they negotiated the same level of outcomes on a standard negotiation task. The process of negotiation differed across countries, however, suggesting that there is more than one way to attain the same negotiation outcome. Finally, this research program also suggested that negotiators seem to use different strategies when negotiating with people domestically and internationally.

We then examined some of the factors that make cross-border negotiations different. Salacuse suggested six factors that increase the challenge of conducting negotiations across borders: (1) political and legal pluralism, (2) international economic factors, (3) foreign governments and bureaucracies, (4) instability, (5) ideology, and (6) culture. Each of these factors acts to make cross-border negotiations more difficult, and effective international negotiators need to understand how to manage these factors.

Next, we turned to a discussion of Hofstede's work on culture, the factor that has been most frequently used to explain differences in negotiations across borders. We use the term culture to refer to the shared values and beliefs that are held by members of a group. Hofstede concludes that four dimensions can summarize cultural differences: (1) power distance, (2) individualism/collectivism, (3) masculinity/femininity, and (4) uncertainty avoidance.

The chapter concluded with a discussion of how to manage cultural differences when negotiating across borders. Weiss presents eight different culturally responsive strategies that negotiators can use with a negotiator from a different culture. Some of these strategies may be used individually, whereas others are used jointly with the other negotiator. Weiss indicates that one critical aspect of choosing the correct strategy for a given negotiation is the degree of familiarity that a negotiator has with the other culture. However, even those with high familiarity with another culture are faced with a daunting task if they want to modify their strategy completely when they deal with the other culture.

End Notes

1. For recent examples see Binnendijk (1987), Foster (1992), Habeeb (1988), Hendon and Hendon (1990), Kremenyuk (1991), Lukov (1985), and Mautner-Markhof (1989). For earlier work, see Fayerweather and Kapoor (1976), Hall (1960), and Van Zandt (1970).
2. See Adler and Graham (1987) and Adler, Graham, and Schwarz (1987).
3. For more discussion of these and other cultures, see Acuff (1993), Hendon and Hendon (1990), and Kennedy (1985).
4. For a review, see Graham (1993).
5. Kelley (1966).
6. Graham (1983, 1984).
7. Adler, Brahm, and Graham (1992).
8. Adler and Graham (1987) and Adler, Graham, and Schwarz (1987).
9. Graham (1983).
10. Adler, Graham, and Schwarz (1987).
11. Graham (1983, p. 63).
12. Graham (1983).
13. Adler, Graham, and Schwarz (1987).
14. Adler, Brahm, and Graham (1992).
15. Adler and Graham (1989).
16. Salacuse (1988).
17. Ibid.
18. Hofstede (1980a, 1980b, 1989, 1991).
19. Hofstede (1989, p. 195).
20. Hofstede (1980a, p. 46).

21. Hofstede (1989).
22. Hofstede (1989, p. 196).
23. See Kale and Barnes (1992) and Triandis (1982).
24. See Foster (1992).
25. Weiss and Stripp (1985).
26. Foster (1992, p. 272).
27. See Braganti and Devine (1992).
28. Foster (1992).
29. Axtell (1991).
30. Binnendijk (1987), Graham and Sano (1989), Pye (1992), and Tung (1991).
31. For reviews of the oversimplicity of this advice, see Francis (1991) and Weiss (1994a, 1994b).
32. Adler and Graham (1989).
33. Francis (1991).
34. Weiss (1994b).
35. See Kolb (1983a).
36. Weiss (1994a , p. 58).

Aaronson, K. (1989). *Selling on the fast track.* New York: Putnam.

Acuff, F.L. (1993). *How to negotiate anything with anyone anywhere around the world.* New York: AMACOM.

Adler, N. J., Brahm, R., and Graham, J.L. (1992). Strategy implementation: A comparison of face-to-face negotiations in the People's Republic of China and the United States. *Strategic Management Journal, 13,* 449–466.

Adler, N.J., and Graham, J.L. (1987). Business negotiations: Canadians are not just like Americans. *Canadian Journal of Administrative Sciences, 4,* 211–238.

Adler, N.J., and Graham, J.L. (1989). Cross-cultural interaction: The international comparison fallacy? *Journal of International Business Studies, 20,* 515–537.

Adler, N.J., Graham, J.L., and Schwarz, T. (1987). Business negotiations in Canada, Mexico, and the United States. *Journal of Business Research, 15,* 411–429.

Ancona, D., and Caldwell, D.F. (1988). Beyond task and maintenance: External roles in groups. *Group and Organizational Studies, 13,* 468–491.

Anderson, J.C., and Kochan, T. (1977). Impasse procedures in the Canadian Federal Service. *Industrial and Labor Relations Review, 30,* 283–301.

Anton, R.J. (1990). Drawing the line: An exploratory test of ethical behavior in negotiations. *The International Journal of Conflict Management, 1,* 265–280.

Asherman, I.G., and Asherman, S.V. (1990). *The negotiation sourcebook.* Amherst, MA: Human Resource Development Press.

Athos, A.G., and Gabarro, J.J. (1978). *Interpersonal behavior: Communication and understanding in relationships.* Englewood Cliffs, NJ: Prentice Hall.

Axtell, R.E. (1991). *Gestures: The do's and taboos of body language around the world.* New York: John Wiley and Sons.

Baranowski, T.A., and Summers, D.A. (1972). Perceptions of response alternatives in a prisoner's dilemma game. *Journal of Personality and Social Psychology, 21,* 35–40.

Barnard, C. (1938). *The functions of the executive.* Cambridge, MA: Harvard University Press.

Bazerman, M.H., Magliozzi, T., and Neale, M A. (1985). Integrative bargaining in a competitive market. *Organizational Behavior and Human Decision Processes, 35,* 294–313.

255

Bazerman, M.H., Mannix, E.A., and Thompson, L.L. (1988). Groups as mixed motive negotiations. In E.J. Lawler and B. Markovsky (Eds.), *Advances in Group Processes* (Vol. 5, 195–216). Greenwich, CT: JAI Press.

Bazerman, M.H., and Neale, M.A. (1992). *Negotiating rationally.* New York: Free Press.

Beckhard, R. (1978, July–September). The dependency dilemma. *Consultants' Communique, 6,* 1–3.

Beisecker, T., Walker, G., and Bart, J. (1989). Knowledge versus ignorance in bargaining strategies: The impact of knowledge about other's information level. *The Social Science Journal, 26,* 161–172.

Benton, A.A., and Druckman, D. (1974). Constituent's bargaining orientation and intergroup negotiations. *Journal of Applied Social Psychology, 4,* 141–150.

Bernstein, D. (1995). Negotiator Pro. Negotiator Pro Company, Beacon Expert Systems, 35 Gardner Road, Brookline, MA 02146.

Bies, R., and Moag, J. (1986). Interactional justice: Communication criteria of fairness. In R.J. Lewicki, B.H. Sheppard, and M.H. Bazerman, (Eds), *Research on Negotiation in Organizations* (Vol. 1, pp. 43–55). Greenwich, CT: JAI Press.

Bies, R., and Shapiro, D. (1987). Interactional fairness judgments: The influence of causal accounts. *Social Justice Research, 1,* 199–218.

Bies, R., Shapiro, D., and Cummings, L. (1988). Causal accounts and managing organizational conflict: Is it enough to say it's not my fault? *Communication Research, 15,* 381–399.

Binnendijk, H. (1987). *National negotiating styles.* Washington, DC: Foreign Service Institute, Department of State.

Blessing, L. (1988). *A walk in the woods.* New York: New American Library, Dutton.

Boatright, J. (1993). *Ethics and the conduct of business.* Englewood Cliffs, NJ: Prentice Hall.

Bok, S. (1978). *Lying: Moral choice in public and private life.* New York: Pantheon.

Bonoma, T., Horai, J., Lindskold, S., Gahagan, J. P., and Tedeschi, J. T. (1969). Compliance to contingent threats. *Proceedings of the 77th Annual Convention of the American Psychological Association, 4,* 395–396.

Boulding, K. (1989). *The three faces of power.* Beverly Hills, CA: Sage Publications.

Bowie, N., and Freeman, R.E. (1992). *Ethics and agency theory.* New York: Oxford University Press.

Braganti, N.L., and Devine, E. (1992). *European customs and manners: How to make friends and do business in Europe* (rev. ed.). New York: Meadowbrook Press.

Braginsky, D.D. (1970). Machiavellianism and manipulative interpersonal behavior in children. *Journal of Experimental Social Psychology, 6,* 77–99.

Bramson, R. (1981). *Coping with difficult people.* New York: Anchor Books.

Bramson, R. (1992). *Coping with difficult bosses.* New York: Carol Publishing Group.

Brass, D.J. (1984). Being in the right place: A structural analysis of individual influence in an organization. *Administrative Science Quarterly, 29,* 518–539.

Brett, J. (1991). Negotiating group decisions. *Negotiation Journal, 7,* 291–310.

Brooks, E., and Odiorne, G.S. (1984). *Managing by negotiations.* New York: Van Nostrand.

Brown, B.R. (1968). The effects of need to maintain face on interpersonal bargaining. *Journal of Experimental Social Psychology, 4,* 107–122.

Bruner, J.S., and Tagiuri, R. (1954). The perception of people. In G. Lindzey (Ed.), *The handbook of social psychology* (Vol. 2, pp. 634–654). Cambridge, MA: Addison-Wesley.

Burrough, B.A., and Helyar, J. (1990). *Barbarians at the gate.* New York: Harper & Row.

Burton, J. (1984). *Global conflict.* Center for International Development, University of Maryland, College Park, MD.

Carnevale, P.J.D. (1986). Strategic choice in negotiation. *Negotiation Journal, 2,* 41–56.

Carnevale, P.J.D., and Conlon, D.E. (1990, June). *Effects of two forms of bias in mediation of disputes.* Paper presented at the third International Conference of the International Association for Conflict Management, Vancouver, BC.

Carnevale, P.J.D., and Pruitt, D.G. (1992). Negotiation and mediation. In M. Rosenberg & L. Porter (Eds.), *Annual Review of Psychology* (Vol. 43, pp. 531–582). Palo Alto, CA: Annual Reviews, Inc.

Carnevale, P.J.D., Pruitt, D.G., and Britton, S. D. (1979). Looking tough: The negotiator under constituent surveillance. *Personality and Social Psychology Bulletin, 5,* 118–121.

Carr, A.Z. (1968, January–February). Is business bluffing ethical? *Harvard Business Review, 46,* 143–153.

Chertkoff, J.M., and Conley, M. (1967). Opening offer and frequency of concessions as bargaining strategies. *Journal of Personality and Social Psychology, 7,* 181–185.

Christie, R., and Geis, F.L. (Eds.). (1970). *Studies in machiavellianism.* New York: Academic Press.

Cialdini, R.B. (1993). *Influence: Science and practice* (3rd ed.). New York: Harper-Collins.

Cohen, A., and Bradford, D. (1990). *Influence without authority.* New York: John Wiley and Sons.

Cohen, H. (1980). *You can negotiate anything.* Secaucus, NJ: Lyle Stuart.

Cooper, W. (1981). Ubiquitous halo. *Psychological Bulletin, 90,* 218–244.

Coser, L. (1956). *The functions of social conflict.* New York: Free Press.

Crott, H., Kayser, E., and Lamm, H. (1980). The effects of information exchange and communication in an asymmetrical negotiation situation. *European Journal of Social Psychology, 10,* 149–163.

Crumbaugh, C.M., and Evans, G.W. (1967). Presentation format, other persons' strategies and cooperative behavior in the prisoner's dilemma. *Psychological Reports, 20,* 895–902.

Deep, S., and Sussman, L. (1993). *What to ask when you don't know what to say: 555 powerful questions to use for getting your way at work.* Englewood Cliffs, NJ: Prentice Hall.

Deutsch, M. (1958). Trust and suspicion. *Journal of Conflict Resolution, 2,* 265–279.

Deutsch, M. (1962). Cooperation and trust: Some theoretical notes. In M. R. Jones (Ed.), *Nebraska symposium on motivation* (pp. 275–318). Lincoln, NE: University of Nebraska Press.

Deutsch, M. (1973). *The resolution of conflict.* New Haven: Yale University Press.

Donaldson, T., and Werhane, P. (1993). *Ethical issues in business: A philosophical approach.* (4th ed.). Englewood Cliffs, NJ: Prentice Hall.

Donohue, W.A. (1981). Analyzing negotiation tactics: Development of a negotiation interact system. *Human Communication Research, 7,* 273–287.

Donohue, W.A. (1989). Communicative competence in mediators. In K. Kressel & D. Pruitt (Eds.), *Mediation research* (pp. 322–343). San Francisco, CA: Jossey-Bass.

Douglas, A. (1957). The peaceful settlement of industrial and intergroup disputes. *Journal of Conflict Resolution, 1,* 69–81.

Douglas, A. (1962). *Industrial peacemaking.* New York: Columbia University Press.

Einhorn, H., and Hogarth, R. (1986). Judging probable cause. *Psychological Bulletin, 99,* 3–19.

Eiseman, J.W. (1978). Reconciling incompatible positions. *Journal of Applied Behavioral Science, 14,* 133–150.

Exline, R., Thibaut J., Hickey, C., and Gumpert, P. (1970). Visual interaction in relation to machiavellianism and an unethical act. In R. Christie & F. Geis (Eds.), *Studies in Machiavellianism* (pp. 53–75). New York: Academic Press.

Falbe, C., and Yukl, G. (1992). Consequences for managers of using single-influence tactics and combinations of tactics. *Academy of Management Journal, 36,* 638–652.

Fayerweather, J., and Kapoor, A. (1976). *Strategy and negotiation for the international corporation.* Cambridge, MA: Ballinger.

Filley, A.C. (1975). *Interpersonal conflict resolution.* Glenview, IL: Scott, Foresman.

Fisher, R. (1964). Fractionating conflict. In R. Fisher (Ed.), *International conflict and behavioral science: The Craigville papers.* New York: Basic Books.

Fisher, R., and Brown, S. (1988). *Getting together: Building a relationship that gets to yes.* Boston: Houghton Mifflin.

Fisher, R., and Ury, W.(1981). *Getting to yes: Negotiating agreement without giving in.* Boston: Houghton Mifflin.

Fisher, R., Ury, W., and Patton, B. (1991). *Getting to yes: Negotiating agreement without giving in* (2nd ed.). New York: Penguin Books.

Fisher, R., and Ertel, D. (1995). *Getting ready to negotiate: The getting to yes workbook.* New York: Penguin Books.

Folger, J.P., Poole, M.S., and Stutman, R.K. (1993). *Working through conflict: Strategies for relationships, groups and organizations* (2nd ed.). New York: Harper Collins.

Follett, M.P. (1940). Constructive conflict. In H.C. Metcalf & L. Urwick (Eds.), *Dynamic Administration: The collected papers of Mary Parker Follett.* New York: Harper.

Foster, D.A. (1992). *Bargaining across borders: How to negotiate business successfully anywhere in the world.* New York: McGraw-Hill.

Francis, J.N.P. (1991). When in Rome? The effects of cultural adaptation on intercultural business negotiations. *Journal of International Business Studies, 22,* 403–428.

French, J. R.P., and Raven, B. (1959). The bases of social power. In D. Cartwright (Ed.), *Studies in social power.* Ann Arbor, MI: Institute for Social Research.

Froman, L.A., and Cohen, M.D. (1970). Compromise and logrolling: Comparing the efficiency of two bargaining processes. *Behavioral Sciences, 15,* 180–183.

Fry, W.R., Firestone, I.J., and Williams, D. (1979, April). *Bargaining process in mixed-singles dyads: Loving and losing.* Paper presented at the Eastern Psychological Association meetings, Philadelphia, PA.

Gahagan, J.P., Long, H., and Horai, J. (1969). Race of experimenter and reactions to black preadolescents. *Proceedings of the 77th Annual Meeting of the American Psychological Association, 4,* 397–398.

Geis, F.L., and Moon, T.H. (1981). Machiavellianism and deception. *Journal of Personality and Social Psychology, 41,* 766–775.

Gibb, J. (1961). Defensive communication. *Journal of Communication, 3,* 141–148.

Gilligan, C. (1982). *In a different voice.* Cambridge, MA: Harvard University Press.

Goffman, E. (1969). *Strategic interaction.* Philadelphia: University of Philadelphia Press.

Gordon, T. (1977). *Leader effectiveness training.* New York: Wyden Books.

Graham, J.L. (1983). Brazilian, Japanese, and American business negotiations. *Journal of International Business Studies, 14,* 47–61.

Graham, J.L. (1984). A comparison of Japanese and American business negotiations. *International Journal of Research in Marketing, 1,* 50–68.

Graham, J.L. (1993). The Japanese negotiation style: Characteristics of a distinct approach. *Negotiation Journal, 9,* 123–140.

Graham, J.L., and Sano, Y. (1989). *Smart bargaining.* New York: Harper Business.

Gray, B., and Donnellon, A. (1989). *An interactive theory of reframing in negotiation.* Unpublished manuscript.

Greenberg, J. (1990). Employee theft as a reaction to underpayment inequity. The hidden cost of pay cuts. *Journal of Applied Psychology. 75,* 561–568.

Greenhalgh, L. (1986). Managing conflict. *Sloan Management Review, 27,* 45–51.

Gruder, C.L. (1971). Relationships with opponent and partner in bargaining. *Journal of Conflict Resolution, 15,* 403–416.

Gruder, C.L., and Duslak, R.J. (1973). Elicitation of cooperation by retaliatory and nonretaliatory strategies in a mixed-motive game. *Journal of Conflict Resolution, 17,* 162–174.

Habeeb, W.M. (1988). *Power and tactics in international negotiation.* Baltimore: Johns Hopkins University Press.

Hall, E.T. (1960 May–June). The silent language of overseas business. *Harvard Business Review, 38,* 87–96.

Hall, J. (1969). *Conflict management survey: A survey of one's characteristic reaction to and handling conflict between himself and others.* Conroe, TX: Teleometrics International.

Hassett, J. (1981, June). Is it right? An inquiry into everyday ethics. *Psychology Today,* 49–53.

Hassett, J. (1981, November). But that would be wrong. . . . *Psychology Today,* 34–53.

Hassett, J. (1982, August). *Correlates of moral values and behavior.* Paper presented at the annual meeting of the Academy of Management, New York, NY.

Hegarty, W., and Sims, H.P. (1978). Some determinants of unethical decision behavior: An experiment. *Journal of Applied Psychology, 63,* 451–457.

Heller, J.R. (1967). The effects of racial prejudice, feedback, strategy, and race on cooperative–competitive behavior. *Dissertation Abstracts International, 27,* 2507–2508b.

Henderson, B. (1973). *The nonlogical strategy.* Boston: Boston Consulting Group.

Hendon, D.W., and Hendon, R.A. (1990). *World-class negotiating: Dealmaking in the global marketplace.* New York: John Wiley and Sons.

Hiltrop, J. (1989). Factors associated with successful labor mediation. In K. Kressel & D. Pruitt (Eds.), *Mediation research* (pp. 241–262). San Francisco: Jossey-Bass.

Hinton, B.L., Hamner, W.C., and Pohlan, N.F. (1974). Influence and award of magnitude, opening bid and concession rate on profit earned in a managerial negotiating game. *Behavioral Science, 19,* 197–203.

Hocker, J.L., and Wilmot, W.W. (1985). *Interpersonal conflict* (2nd ed.). Dubuque, IA: Wm. C. Brown Publishers.

Hofstede, G. (1980a). Motivation, leadership, and organization: Do American theories apply abroad? *Organizational Dynamics, 9,* 42–63.

Hofstede, G. (1980b). *Culture's consequences: International differences in work related values.* Beverly Hills, CA: Sage.

Hofstede, G. (1989). Cultural predictors of national negotiation styles. In. F. Mautner-Markhof (Ed.), *Processes of international negotiations* (pp. 193–201). Boulder, CO: Westview Press.

Hofstede, G. (1991). *Culture and organizations: Software of the mind.* London, UK: McGraw Hill.

Holmes, M., and Poole, M.S. (1991). Longitudinal analysis of interaction. In S. Duck & B. Montgomery (Eds.), *Studying interpersonal interaction* (pp. 286–302). New York: Guilford.

Hornstein, H. (1965). Effects of different magnitudes of threat upon interpersonal bargaining. *Journal of Experimental Social Psychology, 1,* 282–293.

Jacobs, A.T. (1951). *Some significant factors influencing the range of indeterminateness in collective bargaining negotiations.* Unpublished doctoral dissertation, University of Michigan, Ann Arbor, MI.

Janis, I. (1982). *Groupthink: Psychological studies of policy decisions and fiascoes.* Boston: Houghton Mifflin.

Janis, I. (1989). *Crucial decisions: Leadership in policymaking and crisis management.* New York: Free Press.

Johnson, D.W. (1971). Role reversal: A summary and review of the research. *International Journal of Group Tensions, 1,* 318–334.

Johnston, R.W. (1982, March–April). Negotiation strategies: Different strokes for different folks. *Personnel, 59,* 36–45.

Kale, S.H., and Barnes, J.W. (1992). Understanding the domain of cross-national buyer–seller interactions. *Journal of International Business Studies, 23,* 101–132.

Kaplan, R. (1984, Spring). Trade routes: The manager's network of relationships. *Organizational Dynamics, 12,* 37–52.

Karrass, C. (1974). *Give and take.* New York: Thomas Y. Crowell.

Karrass, G. (1985). *Negotiate to close: How to make more successful deals.* New York: Simon & Schuster.

Kelley, H.H. (1966). A classroom study of the dilemmas in interpersonal negotiation. In K. Archibald (Ed.), *Strategic interaction and conflict: Original papers and discussion* (pp. 49–73). Berkeley, CA: Institute of International Studies.

Kelley, H.H., and Stahelski, A.J. (1970). Social interaction basis of cooperators' and competitors' beliefs about others. *Journal of Personality and Social Psychology, 16,* 66–91.

Kelley, H.H., and Schenitzki, D.P. (1972). Bargaining. In C. G. McClintock (Ed.), *Experimental social psychology* (pp. 298–337). New York: Holt, Rinehart & Winston.

Kelley, H.H., and Thibaut, J. (1969). Group problem solving. In G. Lindzey & E. Aronson (Eds.), *Handbook of social psychology* (2nd ed.), (Vol. 4, pp. 1–101). Reading, MA: Addison-Wesley.

Kennedy, G. (1985). *Doing business abroad.* New York: Simon & Schuster.

Keys, B., and Case, T. (1990). How to become an influential manager. *Academy of Management Executive, 4* (4), 38–51.

Kimmel, M.J., Pruitt, D. G., Magenau, J.M., Konar-Goldband, E., and Carnevale, P.J.D. (1980). Effects of trust aspiration and gender on negotiation tactics. *Journal of Personality and Social Psychology, 38,* 9–23.

Kipnis, D. (1976). *The powerholders.* Chicago: University of Chicago Press.

Kipnis, D., Schmidt, S.M., and Wilkinson, I. (1980). Intraorganizational influence tactics: Explorations in getting one's way. *Journal of Applied Psychology, 65,* 440–452.

Kleinke, C.L., and Pohlan, P.D. (1971). Effective and emotional responses as a function of other person's gaze and cooperativeness in two person games. *Journal of Personality and Social Psychology, 17,* 308–313.

Kohlberg, L. (1969). Stage and sequence: The cognitive development approach to socialization. In D. Goslin (Ed.), *Handbook of socialization theory and research* (pp. 347–380). Chicago: Rand McNally.

Kolb, D. (1983a). *The mediators.* Cambridge, MA: MIT Press.

Komorita, S.S., and Brenner, A.R. (1968). Bargaining and concessions under bilateral monopoly. *Journal of Personality and Social Psychology, 9,* 15–20.

Komorita, S.S., and Mechling, J. (1967). Betrayal and reconciliation in a two person game. *Journal of Personality and Social Psychology, 6,* 349–353.

Kotter, J. (1977, July–August). Power, dependence and effective management. *Harvard Business Review, 55,* 125–136.

Kotter, J. (1979). *Power in management.* New York: AMACOM.

Kotter, J. (1985). *Power and influence: Beyond formal authority.* New York: Free Press.

Kramer, R.M. (1991). The more the merrier? Social psychological aspects of multiparty negotiations in organizations. In M. Bazerman, R. Lewicki, & B.H. Sheppard, *Research on Negotiation in Organizations* (Vol. 3, pp. 307–332). Greenwich, CT: JAI Press.

Kremenyuk, V.A. (Ed.) (1991). *International negotiation: Analysis, approaches, issues.* San Francisco: Jossey-Bass.

Kressel, K., and Pruitt, D. (Eds.) (1989). *Mediation research.* San Francisco: Jossey-Bass.

Lax, D., and Sebenius, J. (1986). *The manager as negotiator: Bargaining for cooperation and competitive gain.* New York: Free Press.

Lefcourt, H.M. (1982). *Locus of control: Current trends in theory and research* (2nd ed.). Hillsdale, NJ: Lawrence Erlbaum Associates.

Lewicki, R.J. (1983). Lying and deception: A behavioral model. In M.H. Bazerman & R.J. Lewicki (Eds.), *Negotiating in organizations* (pp. 68–90). Beverly Hills, CA: Sage Publications.

Lewicki, R.J. (1992). Negotiating strategically. In A. Cohen, (Ed.), *The portable MBA in management* (pp. 147–189). New York: John Wiley and Sons.

Lewicki, R.J., and Bunker, B.B. (1995a). Trust in relationships: A model of trust development and decline. In Bunker, B.B. and Rubin, J.Z. (Eds). *Conflict, Cooperation and Justice: A Tribute Volume to Morton Deutsch.* San Francisco: Jossey-Bass.

Lewicki, R.J., and Bunker, B.B. (1995b). "Developing, maintaining and repairing trust in work relationships." In Kramer, R. and Tyler, T. *Trust In Organizations.* Thousand Oaks, CA: Sage Publications.

Lewicki, R.J., and Sheppard, B.H. (1985). Choosing how to intervene: Factors affecting the use of process and outcome control in third-party dispute resolution. *Journal of Occupational Behavior, 6,* 49–64.

Lewicki, R.J., and Spencer, G. (1990, June). *Lies and dirty tricks.* Paper presented at the meeting of the International Association for Conflict Management, Vancouver, BC.

Lewicki, R.J., and Spencer, G. (1991, August). *Ethical relativism and negotiating tactics: Factors affecting their perceived ethicality.* Paper presented at the meeting of the Academy of Management, Miami FL.

Lewicki, R.J., Weiss, S., and Lewin, D. (1992). Models of conflict, negotiation and third-party intervention: A review and synthesis. *Journal of Organizational Behavior, 13,* 209–252.

Lewicki, R.J., and Stark, N. (1996). "What's ethically appropriate in negotiations: An empirical examination of bargaining tactics." *Social Justice Research,* Vol 9, No 1, 69–95.

Lewicki, R.J., and Robinson, R. (1996). "A Factor Analytic Study of Negotiator Ethics" *Journal of Business Ethics,* in press.

Lewis, J. D. and Weigert, A. (1985). Trust as a social reality. *Social Forces, 63, 4,* 967–985.

Lewis, M. (1990). *Liar's Poker.* New York: Penguin Books.

Liebert, R.M., Smith, W.P., and Hill, J.H. (1968). The effects of information and magnitude of initial offer on interpersonal negotiation. *Journal of Experimental Social Psychology, 4,* 431–441.

Lim, R., and Carnevale, P.J.D. (1990). Contingencies in the mediation of disputes. *Journal of Personality & Social Psychology, 58,* 259–272.

Lukov, V. (1985). International negotiations of the 1980s: Features, problems and prospects. *Negotiation Journal, 1,* 139–148.

Luthans, F., and Kreitner, R. (1985). *Organizational behavior modification and beyond.* Glenview, IL: Scott, Foresman.

McCornack, S.A., and Levine, T.R. (1990). When lies are uncovered: Emotional and relational outcomes of discovered deception. *Communication Monographs, 57,* 119–138.

McDonald, J. (1963). *Strategy in poker, business & war.* New York: William Norton.

Maier, R.A., and Lavrakas, P.J. (1976). Lying behavior and the evaluation of lies. *Perceptual and Motor Skills, 42,* 575–581.

Mautner-Markhof, F. (Ed.). (1989). *Processes of international negotiations.* Boulder, CO: Westview Press.

Michelini, R.L. (1971). Effects of prior interaction, contact, strategy, and expectation of meeting on gain behavior and sentiment. *Journal of Conflict Resolution, 15,* 97–103.

Michener, H.A., Vaske, J.J., Schleiffer, S.L., Plazewski, J.G., and Chapman, L.J. (1975). Factors affecting concession rate and threat usage in bilateral conflict. *Sociometry, 38,* 62–80.

Midgaard, K., and Underal, A. (1977). Multiparty conferences. In D. Druckman (Ed.), *Negotiations: Social psychological perspectives* (pp. 329–345). Beverly Hills, CA: Sage Publications.

Miller, D.T., and Ross, M. (1975). Self-serving bias in the attribution of causality: Fact of fiction? *Psychological Bulletin, 82,* 213–225.

Miller, D.T., and Vidmar, N. (1981). The social psychology of punishment reactions. In M.J. Lerner (Ed.), *The justice motive in social behavior* (pp. 145–172). New York: Plenum Press.

Mintzberg, H. (1983). *Power in and around organizations.* Englewood Cliffs, NJ: Prentice Hall.

Mintzberg, H. (1991). Five Ps for strategy. In H. Mintzberg and J.B. Quinn (Eds.), *The strategy process: Concepts, contexts, cases* (2nd ed.) (pp. 12–19). Englewood Cliffs, NJ: Prentice Hall.

Missner, M. (1980). *Ethics of the business system.* Sherman Oaks, CA: Alfred Publishing Company.

Moore, C. (1986). *The mediation process: Practical strategies for resolving conflict.* San Francisco: Jossey-Bass.

Murnighan, K. (1978). Models of coalition behavior: Game theoretic, social psychological and political perspectives. *Psychological Bulletin, 85,* 1130–1153.

Murnighan, K. (1986). Organizational coalitions: Structural contingencies and the formation process. In R.J. Lewicki, B.H. Sheppard, and M.H. Bazerman (Eds.), *Research on Negotiation in Organizations* (Vol. 1, pp. 155–173). Greenwich, CT: JAI Press.

Murnighan, J.K. (1991). *The dynamics of bargaining games.* Englewood Cliffs, NJ: Prentice Hall.

Nash, J.F. (1950). The bargaining problem. *Econometrica, 18,* 155–162.

Neale, M., and Bazerman, M.H. (1985). The effects of framing and negotiator overconfidence on bargaining behaviors and outcomes. *Academy of Management Journal, 28,* 34–49.

Neale, M., and Bazerman, M.H. (1991). *Cognition and rationality in negotiation.* New York: Free Press.

Neale, M., and Bazerman, M.H. (1992a). Negotiating rationally: The power and impact of the negotiator's frame. *Academy of Management Executive, 6* (3), 42–51.

Neale, M.A., and Bazerman, M.H. (1992b). Negotiator cognition and rationality: A behavioral decision theory perspective. *Organizational Behavior and Human Decision Processes, 51,* 157–175.

Neale, M.A., and Northcraft, G.B. (1986). Experts, amateurs, and refrigerators: Comparing expert and amateur negotiators in a novel task. *Organizational Behavior and Human Decision Processes, 38,* 305–317.

Neale, M.A., and Northcraft, G.B. (1991). Behavioral negotiation theory: A framework for conceptualizing dyadic bargaining. In L. Cummings & B. Staw (Eds.), *Research in Organizational Behavior* (Vol. 13, pp. 147–190). Greenwich, CT: JAI Press.

Neslin, S.A., and Greenhalgh, L. (1983). Nash's theory of cooperative games as a predictor of the outcomes of buyer–seller negotiations: An experiment in media purchasing. *Journal of Marketing Research, 20,* 368–379.

Nierenberg, G. (1976). *The complete negotiator.* New York: Nierenberg & Zeif Publishers.

Northrup, H.R. (1964). *Boulwarism.* Ann Arbor, MI: Bureau of Industrial Relations, University of Michigan.

Osgood, C.E. (1962). *An alternative to war or surrender.* Urbana, IL: University of Illinois Press.

Oskamp, S. (1970). Effects of programmed initial strategies in a prisoner's dilemma game. *Psychometrics, 19,* 195–196.

Patterson, J., and Kim, P. (1991). *The day America told the truth.* New York: Prentice Hall.

Pfeffer, J. (1992). *Managing with power.* Boston: Harvard Business School Press.

Pfeffer, J., and Salancik, G.R. (1974). Organizational decision making as a political process: The case of a university budget. *Administrative Science Quarterly, 19,* 135–151.

Pilisuk, N., and Skolnick, P. (1978). Inducing trust: A test of the Osgood proposal. *Journal of Personality and Social Psychology, 8,* 121–133.

Pinkley, R.L. (1992). Dimensions of conflict frame: Relation to disputant perceptions and expectations. *The International Journal of Conflict Management, 3,* 95–113.

Pruitt, D.G. (1981). *Negotiation behavior.* New York: Academic Press.

Pruitt, D.G. (1983). Strategic choice in negotiation. *American Behavioral Scientist, 27,* 167–194.

Pruitt, D.G., and Carnevale, P. J. D. (1993). *Negotiation in social conflict.* Pacific Grove, CA: Brooks-Cole.

Pruitt, D.G., and Lewis, S.A. (1975). Development of integrative solutions in bilateral negotiation. *Journal of Personality and Social Psychology, 31,* 621–633.

Pruitt, D.G., and Rubin, J.Z. (1986). *Social conflict: Escalation, stalemate and settlement.* New York: Random House.

Pruitt, D.G., and Syna, H. (1985). Mismatching the opponent's offers in negotiation. *Journal of Experimental Social Psychology, 21,* 103–113.

Putnam, L., and Holmer, M. (1992). Framing, reframing, and issue development. In L. Putnam & M. Roloff (Eds.), *Communication and negotiation* (pp. 128–155). Newbury Park, CA: Sage.

Putnam, L., and Jones, T.S. (1982). Reciprocity in negotiations: An analysis of bargaining interaction. *Communication Monographs, 49,* 171–191.

Pye, L.W. (1992). *Chinese negotiating style.* New York: Quorum Books.

Quinn, J.B. (1991). Strategies for change. In H. Mintzberg & J.B. Quinn (Eds.), *The strategy process: Concepts, contexts, cases* (2nd ed.) (pp. 4–12). Englewood Cliffs, NJ: Prentice Hall.

Rahim, M.A. (1983a). A measure of styles of handling interpersonal conflict. *Academy of Management Journal, 26,* 368–376.

Raiffa, H. (1982). *The art and science of negotiation.* Cambridge, MA: Belknap Press of Harvard University Press.

Raven, B.H., and Rubin, J.Z. (1973). *Social psychology: People in groups.* New York: John Wiley and Sons.

Richardson, R.C. (1977). *Collective bargaining by objectives.* Englewood Cliffs, NJ: Prentice Hall.

Robinson, S. (1992). *Retreat, voice, silence and destruction: A typology of employees behavioral responses to dissatisfaction.* Unpublished manuscript.

Robinson, R., Lewicki, R.J., and Donahue, E. Extending and testing a five factor model of ethical and unethical bargaining tactics: Introducing the SINS scale. The Ohio State University, Working Paper 96–12.

Rogers, C.R. (1961). *On becoming a person: A therapist's view of psychotherapy.* Boston: Houghton-Mifflin.

Ross, L., Greene, D., and House, P. (1977). The false consensus phenomenon: An attributional bias in self-perception and social-perception processes. *Journal of Experimental Social Psychology, 13,* 279–301.

Roth, A.E., Murnighan, J.K., and Schoumaker, F. (1988). The deadline effect in bargaining: Some empirical evidence. *American Economic Review, 78,* 806–823.

Rubin, J.Z. (1980). Experimental research on third party intervention in conflict: Toward some generalizations. *Psychological Bulletin, 87,* 379–391.

Rubin, J.Z., and Brown, B.R. (1975). *The social psychology of bargaining and negotiation.* New York: Academic Press.

Russo, J.E., and Schoemaker, P.J.H. (1989). *Decision traps: The ten barriers to brilliant decision-making and how to overcome them.* New York: Simon & Schuster.

Salacuse, J.W. (1988). Making deals in strange places: A beginner's guide to international business negotiations. *Negotiation Journal, 4,* 5–13.

Salancik, G.R., and Pfeffer, J. (1977). Who gets power and how they hold on to it: A strategic-contingency model of power. *Organizational Dynamics, 5,* 3–21.

Savage, G.T., Blair, J.D., and Sorenson, R.L. (1989). Consider both relationships and substance when negotiating strategically. *Academy of Management Executive, 3* (1), 37–48.

Schatzski, M. (1981). *Negotiation: The art of getting what you want.* New York: Signet Books.

Schein, E. (1987). *Process consultation: Volume II. Lessons for managers and consultants.* Reading, MA: Addison-Wesley.

Sebenius, J.K. (1983). Negotiation arithmetic: Adding and subtracting issues and parties. *International Organization, 37,* 1–34.

Sebenius, J.K. (1992). Negotiation analysis: A characterization and review. *Management Science, 38,* 18–38.

Selekman, B.M., Fuller, S. H., Kennedy, T., and Baitsel, J.M. (1964). *Problems in labor relations.* New York: McGraw-Hill.

Selekman, B.M., Selekman, S.K., and Fuller, S.H. (1958). *Problems in labor relations.* New York: McGraw-Hill.

Sen, A.K. (1970). *Collective choice and individual values.* San Francisco, CA: Holden-Day.

Sermat V. (1967). The effects of an initial cooperative or competitive treatment on a subject's response to conditional operation. *Behavioral Science, 12,* 301–313.

Sermat, V., and Gregovich, R.P. (1966). The effect of experimental manipulation on cooperative behavior in a checkers game. *Psychometric Science, 4,* 435–436.

Shapiro, D. (1991). The effects of explanations on negative reactions to deceit. *Administrative Science Quarterly, 36,* 614–630.

Shapiro, D.L., Sheppard, B.H., and Cheraskin, L. (1992). Business on a handshake. *Negotiation Journal, 8,* 365–377.

Shea, G.F. (1983). *Creative negotiating.* Boston: CBI Publishing Co.

Sheppard, B.H. (1983). Managers as inquisitors: Some lessons from the law. In M. Bazerman and R.J. Lewicki (Eds.), *Negotiating in organizations* (pp. 193–213). Beverly Hills, CA: Sage Publications.

Sheppard, B.H. (1984). Third party conflict intervention: A procedural framework. In B.M. Staw and L.L. Cummings (Eds.), *Research in Organizational Behavior* (Vol. 6, pp. 141–190). Greenwich, CT: JAI Press.

Sheppard, B.H., Blumenfeld-Jones, K., Minton, J.W., and Hyder, E. (In press). Informal conflict intervention: Advice and dissent. *Employee Rights and Responsibilities Journal.*

Sheppard, B.H., Lewicki, R.J., and Minton, J. (1992). *Organizational justice: The search for fairness in the workplace.* New York: Lexington Books.

Singer, L. (1990). *Settling disputes: Conflict resolution in business, families, and the legal system.* Boulder, CO: Westview Press.

Solomon, L. (1960). The influence of some types of power relationships and game strategies upon the development of interpersonal trust. *Journal of Abnormal and Social Psychology, 61,* 223–230.

Steward, Thomas A. (1989, November 16). New ways to exercise power. *Fortune,* 52–66.

Stewart, J.B. (1992). *Den of thieves.* New York: Touchstone Books.

Stillenger, C., Epelbaum, M., Keltner, D., and Ross, L. (1990). *The "reactive devaluation" barrier to conflict resolution.* Working paper, Stanford University, Palo Alto, CA.

Swinth, R.L. (1967). [Review of A behavioral theory of labor negotiations]. *Contemporary Psychology, 12,* 183–184.

Taetzsch, L., and Benson, E. (1978). *Taking charge on the job: Techniques for assertive manage-ment.* New York: Executive Enterprises Publications.

Thibaut, J., and Kelley, H.H. (1959). *The social psychology of groups.* New York: John Wiley and Sons.

Thomas, K.W. (1992). Conflict and negotiation processes in organizations. In M.D. Dunnette & L. H. Hough, *Handbook of industrial and organizational psychology* (2nd ed.) (Vol. 3, pp. 651–718). Palo Alto, CA: Consulting Psychologists Press.

Thomas, K.W., and Kilmann, R.H. (1974). *Thomas-Kilmann conflict mode survey.* Tuxedo, NY: Xicom.

Thompson, L. (1990a). An examination of naive and experienced negotiators. *Journal of Personality and Social Psychology, 59,* 82–90.

Thompson, L. (1990b). Negotiation behavior and outcomes: Empirical evidence and theoretical issues. *Psychological Bulletin, 108,* 515–532.

Thompson, L. (1991). Information exchange in negotiation. *Journal of Experimental Social Psychology, 27,* 161–179.

Thompson, L., and Hastie, R. (1990a). Social perception in negotiation. *Organizational Behavior and Human Decision Processes, 47,* 98–123.

Thompson, L., and Hastie, R. (1990b). Judgment tasks and biases in negotiation. In B.H. Sheppard, M.H. Bazerman, and R.J. Lewicki (Eds.), *Research on Negotiation in Organizations* (Vol. 1, pp. 31–54). Greenwich, CT: JAI Press.

Thompson, L., and Loewenstein, G. (1992). Egocentric interpretations of fairness and interpersonal conflict. *Organizational Behavior and Human Decision Processes, 51,* 176–197.

Tjosvold, D. (1988). *Getting things done in organizations.* Lexington, MA: Lexington Books.

Trevino, L.K. (1986). Ethical decision making in organizations: A person-situation interactionist model. *Academy of Management Review, 11,* 601–617.

Trevino, L.K., and Youngblood, S. (1990). Bad apples in bad barrels: A causal analysis of ethical decision-making behavior. *Journal of Applied Psychology, 75,* 378–385.

Triandis, H.C. (1982). Culture's consequences: International differences in work values. *Human Organization, 41,* 86–90.

Tsui, A.S. (1983). An analysis of social structure and reputational effectiveness. *Proceedings of the 43rd Meeting of the Academy of Management,* 261–265.

Tsui, A.S. (1984). A role set analysis of managerial reputation. *Organizational Behavior and Human Performance, 34,* 64–96.

Tung, R.L. (1991, Winter). Handshakes across the sea: Cross-cultural negotiating for business success. *Organizational Dynamics, 19,* 30–40.

Tutzauer, F. (1991). Bargaining outcome, bargaining process, and the role of communication. *Progress in Communication Science, 10,* 257–300.

Tutzauer, F. (1992). The communication of offers in dyadic bargaining. In L. Putnam and M. Roloff (Eds.), *Communication and negotiation* (pp. 67–82). Newbury Park, CA: Sage.

Ury, W. (1991). *Getting past no: Negotiating with difficult people.* New York: Bantam Books.

Ury, W.L., Brett, J. M., and Goldberg, S.B. (1988). *Getting disputes resolved.* San Francisco: Jossey-Bass.

Van Zandt, H.F. (1970 November–December). How to negotiate in Japan. *Harvard Business Review, 48* (6), 45–56.

Vitz, P.C., and Kite, W.A.R. (1970). Factors affecting conflict and negotiation within an alliance. *Journal of Experimental Social Psychology, 5,* 233–247.

Vroom, V.H., and Yetton P. (1973). *Leadership and decision making.* Pittsburgh: University of Pittsburgh Press.

Walcott, C., Hopmann, P.T., and King, T.D. (1977). The role of debate in negotiation. In

D. Druckman (Ed.), *Negotiations: Social Psychological Perspectives* (pp. 193–911). Beverly Hills, CA: Sage.

Walton, R. (1987). *Managing conflict: Interpersonal dialogue and third-party roles* (2nd ed.). Reading, MA: Addison-Wesley.

Walton, R.E., and McKersie, R.B. (1965). *A behavioral theory of labor negotiations: An analysis of a social interaction system.* New York: McGraw-Hill.

Weingart, L.R., Thompson, L.L., Bazerman, M.H., and Carroll, J.S. (1990). Tactical behaviors and negotiation outcomes. The *International Journal of Conflict Management, 1,* 7–31.

Weiss, S.E. (1994a). Negotiating with "Romans": A range of culturally-responsive strategies. *Sloan Management Review, Vol 35,* No. 1, pp. 51–61; No 2, pp. 1–16.

Weiss, S.E., and Stripp, W. (1985). *Negotiating with foreign business persons: An introduction for Americans with propositions on six cultures.* Working Paper, New York University Graduate School of Business Administration, New York, NY.

Werth, L.F., and Flannery, J. (1986). A phenomenological approach to human deception. In R.W. Mitchell and N. S. Thompson (Eds), *Deception: Perspectives on human and nonhuman deceit* (pp. 293–311). Albany, NY: State University of New York Press.

Yankelovich, D. (1982, August). Lying well is the best revenge. *Psychology Today, 71,* 5–6, 71.

Yukl, G. (1974). Effects of the opponent's initial offer, concession magnitude, and concession frequency on bargaining behavior. *Journal of Personality & Social Psychology, 30,* 323–335.

Yukl, G., and Tracey, J.A.B. (1992). Consequences of influence tactics used with subordinates, peers and the boss. *Journal of Applied Psychology, 77,* 525–535.

Zartman, I.W. (1977). Negotiation as a joint decision making process. In I. Zartman (Ed.), *The negotiation process: Theories and applications* (pp. 67–86). Beverly Hills, CA: Sage Publications.

Zartman, W., and Berman, M. (1982). *The practical negotiator.* New Haven: Yale University Press.

Zubek, J., Pruitt, D., Pierce, R., and Iocolano, A. (1989, June). *Mediator and disputant characteristics and behavior as they affect the outcome of community mediation.* Paper presented at the Second Annual Meeting of the International Association for Conflict Management, Athens, GA.

Zucker, E. (1991). *The seven secrets of influence.* New York: McGraw Hill.